ETHICAL SUBJECTS IN CONTEMPORARY CULTURE

For A. L.

It is not I, it is the other that can say *yes*.
(Levinas, *Totality and Infinity*)

ETHICAL SUBJECTS IN CONTEMPORARY CULTURE

Dave Boothroyd

EDINBURGH
University Press

© Dave Boothroyd, 2013

Edinburgh University Press Ltd
22 George Square, Edinburgh EH8 9LF

www.euppublishing.com

Typeset in 10.5/13 Sabon by
Servis Filmsetting Ltd, Stockport, Cheshire, and
printed and bound in Great Britain by
CPI Group (UK) Ltd, Croydon CR0 4YY

A CIP record for this book is available from the British Library

ISBN 978 0 7486 4009 6 (hardback)
ISBN 978 0 7486 8166 2 (webready PDF)
ISBN 978 0 7486 8167 9 (epub)

The right of Dave Boothroyd
to be identified as author of this work
has been asserted in accordance with
the Copyright, Designs and Patents Act 1988.

Contents

Acknowledgements

Many people have contributed directly or indirectly to the ideas this book gives expression to. Their encouragement and support, as well as their incisive comments and criticisms, have been most welcome. It is not possible to mention them all by name, and there are many, no doubt, who will not know that their remarks ultimately had an impact. Some of them were strangers, or were members of the audiences at the various places where I had the opportunity to present work-in-progress. During the time of the book's gestation I have benefitted greatly from such opportunities: at Depaul University Philosophy Department; Stockholm University Department of Cinema Studies; Umeå University Comparative Literature Department; Lisbon New University; Goldsmiths College Radical Media Group; the Cultures of the Digital Economy Research Institute at Anglia Ruskin University, as well as at various conferences. I am grateful for the hospitality shown to me by all of my hosts and for the many conversations that it made possible.

I would also like to thank the Arts and Humanities Research Council for granting me a Research Leave Scheme sabbatical semester, for a project closely related to the work presented in this volume.

Special thanks go to following: Terry Andrews, Phil Carney, Tina Chanter, José Cuhna, Tracy Davis, Gary Hall, Keith Hayward, John Hutnyk, Manzu Islam, Anders Johansson, Aideen Lucey, Trond Lundemo, Martin McQuillan, Vince Miller, Diane Morgan, Markus Öhrn, Larry Ray, Nicholas Royle, Janet Sayers, Sean Sayers, Chris Shilling, Miri Song, Alex Stevens, Steve Tyler, Mick Ward, Joanna Zylinska, and the Brightwell crew.

Elements of several of these chapters have appeared elsewhere in: 'Touch, Time and Technics: Levinas and the Ethics of Haptic Communications', *Theory Culture and Society*, 26:2–3 (2009), 330–45; 'Off the Record: Levinas, Derrida and the Secret of Responsibility', *Theory, Culture and Society*, 28:7–8 (2011), 41–59; 'Beyond Ethics

I Have No Alibi', in J. Stauffer and B. Bergo (eds) (2009), *Nietzsche and Levinas: 'After the Death of a Certain God'*, New York: Columbia University Press, pp. 150–64; 'To Be Hospitable to Madness: Derrida and Foucault *Chez Freud*', *Journal for Cultural Research*, 9:1 (2005), 3–21; 'Skin-nihilism Now', in K. Ansell-Pearson and D. Morgan (eds) (2000), *Nihilism Now!: Monsters of Energy*, Basingstoke: Palgrave Macmillan, pp. 198–215; 'Of Ghostwriting and Possession: translating "my father", or *s'éxpliquer avec la mort*', in J. Morra, M. Robson and M. Smith (eds) (2000) *The Limits of Death*, Manchester: Manchester University Press, pp. 198–220. Where such elements occur they are reproduced with permission of the publishers.

1. The Subject of the Ethical Turn

In the second half of the twentieth century cultural theorists of modernity and practitioners of cultural studies tended to see their intellectual endeavour as being fundamentally political in nature. Marxist and neo-Marxist left criticism of culture and society until relatively recently, has been the traditional mainstay of analysis addressing the 'post-WW2 order', the 'end of empire', the fate of the communist project and the numerous crises of globalisation. Over the last twenty years, however, we have witnessed an 'ethical turn' in the theorising of culture, society and politics, as well as of the arts and creative enterprise, which has coincided with and drawn upon the full diversity of postmodern theory. As the modern notion of universality has lost credibility, the concern with 'the ethical' has proliferated and territorialised both the academic disciplines and popular culture. Rather than ethics being confined as sub-branch of philosophy, viewed as the 'queen of the sciences' whose job it has been to guard and preserve the idea of the universality in the temple of pure theory, it has now leaked back out into the wider world of cultural inquiry in general. Philosophical ethics in its traditional forms can no longer exclusively provide the measure for the ethical evaluation of situations, events, and social and political phenomena making up the content of cultural life in general, and ethicality, however it is to be understood, has come to be read off of the surfaces of culture itself. Philosophy, no more or less than any other intellectual enterprise, it has to be acknowledged, is just one of the surfaces of culture.

It is from within the 'postmodern condition', heralded by the Nietzschean proclamation of 'the death of God' and understood, for example by Lyotard, in relation to the economic production of knowledge, that ethics has resurfaced as a watchword in contemporary critical studies of almost everything: from the phenomena of globalised capitalism to the cultural heterogeneity of national life; from the everyday life of personal and social encounters through to international relations; from the suffering of 'the starving millions' to the science of food production; from planetary ecology to the sciences of life. Such a list is in reality essentially interminable as the light by which cultural inquiry identifies and illuminates its objects of interest and concern has increasingly come to be understood as essentially ethical in nature.

The general 'relativisation of the frame of reference' associated with the demise of the universal under the conditions of postmodernity is often considered to signal the collapse of ethics into an insurmountable ethical relativism in which all ethical discourse is effectively contained within the sphere of normative morality; and what we are left with is just idle ethical talk. This would immediately appear to be contradicted, however, by the proliferation of ethical theory aimed at rethinking the ethical, for example in terms of the 'ethics of alterity', the 'ethics of singularity', and the 'ethics of contingency' and of 'the event'; attempts at rethinking the ethical in terms of the ethical demand experienced in the context of concrete events and situations, which, each in its own way and uniquely, give rise to ethical concern as something objective. Various forms of such ethico-cultural theory are to be found, for example, in the writings those whose names are associated with 'postmodern theory' as it is most commonly identified, and with which this volume is centrally concerned: namely, those of Heidegger, Levinas, Derrida, Foucault, Deleuze, Nancy, Badiou and Irigaray. My contention here is that in the work of such thinkers it becomes clear that the question of the ethical must be thought in conjunction with the question of the Subject, and as the question of the Subject cannot be approached independently of the cultural context in which it is embedded, thinking the ethical must be referred to culture in the widest sense of the term. If ethical subjectivity is real then it is only to be identified, or encountered in conjunction with the 'bits' of culture through which it finds expression.

In the course of this book, through a series of critical engagements with the work of these theorists, and with reference to a subset of all the possible bits of 'cultural life' to which it would be possible to turn in order to identify and theorise ethical subjectivity, I aim to show how the ethical might be claimed to underpin cultural theorising; and that the illustration, or the 'proof' of such a thesis can only be sought on the basis of such thematic examples. My own examples here of ethical subjects to be reflected upon from the perspective just outlined, are sexual difference, vulnerability, new media communications, secrecy, censorship, friendship, suffering and death. At this point, in advance of any demonstration, I can only say that this approach is intended to be consistent with the signalling of 'singularity' as a key to thinking the ethical. As Derrida observes: 'the example itself, as such, overflows its singularity as much as its identity. This is why there are no examples while at the same time there are only examples.'[1]

THE ETHICAL TURN AND THE ETHICISATION OF EVERYTHING

One does not have to look far to find examples of the way in which aspects of the ethical turn are reflected in the academic disciplines which, in one way or another, have an investment in culture as their object inquiry. Right across the critical humanities and social studies there is general acknowledgement that ethical thinking figures in the identification of disciplinary subject matters, and is also an element of its reflexive self-understanding of its own activities; and that these both inherently call for ethical scrutiny, awareness, sensibility as well as justification. Who, in any case, would declare ethical disinterestedness in what they devote their working lives to? This does not make practitioners of critical inquiry ethicists; but arguably it is what makes them human.

The observation 'ethics is back' made by Garber et al., editors of a collection of essays published a dozen years ago, entitled *The Turn to Ethics*, would appear to have been on the money, at least in so far as it draws attention to a 'new' level of reflection on the ethical. They said:

> Ethics is back in literary studies, as it is in philosophy and political theory, and indeed the very critiques of universal man and the autonomous human subject that had initially produced resistance to ethics have now generated a crossover among these various disciplines that sees and does ethics 'otherwise.'[2]

Cultural studies during this period, for example, has increasingly come to understand itself as an *ethico*-political project; it has embraced, in some quarters at least, its own 'ethicisation', and it has done so largely on the basis of its appropriations of an assortment of theoretical elements and concepts drawn, especially, from the French postmodern theory of the previous decades. It has been moved along in that direction, for instance, by Joanna Zylinska's *The Ethics of Cultural Studies* (2005). She argues, however, that the touted turn to the ethical in her field is neither simply a novel turn nor in fact a return, as 'an ethical sense of duty or responsibility has *always* constituted an inherent part of the cultural studies project', and that this might not always have been so explicitly stated because, when declaring the field's overt political commitment, cultural studies' theorists have frequently avoided addressing ethical questions directly, as the problem of ethics, with rare exceptions, has been seen as being more the domain of disciplines such as philosophy, political theory or deconstruction-oriented literary theory.[3]

Across the studies her book comprises, of various cultural forms and phenomena undertaken on the basis of what she presents as a predominantly deconstructive and Levinasian perspective, she contextually shows how cultural studies might go about recentring itself, in theory and in practice, around making 'the alterity of the Other' its proper concern.

It may well be true that a turn to ethics is evident across the academy, and that this diversification of ethical concern is partly the result of a sort of interdisciplinary melee of philosophy, theory, the critical humanities and cultural studies broadly defined, and borne in part of the contingencies of institutional organisation and reorganisation, but it remains the case also, as the philosopher Peter Dews wryly notes, that 'it is not easy doing ethics "otherwise"'.[4] This is not so much because ethics is best left to philosophy as such, but because the meta-narratives of universality and the autonomous human Subject have fallen into decline and lost credibility. The problem of how to 'do ethics' under the cultural and epistemic circumstances of the 'postmodern condition' cannot be resolved by way of an essentially normative and critically ungrounded decision simply to adopt a discourse replete with an ethical-inflected terminology. And in this book I shall attempt to show that the problem for the ethicisation of critical thinking and discourse *tout court* is that of developing a sufficiently rigorous concept of *the Subject as ethical*. I shall argue that this calls for more than a discursive emphasis and recentring of cultural critique on alterity and the embrace of the cuddly 'otherness of the Other' *as an idea*; that any rethinking of the ethical in terms of alterity must pass through the question of the ethical Subject *as the substantive ground for the ethical relation to the Other*. As soon as we begin to do that we are confronted with the 'less attractive' proposition of thinking the economy of violence, as Derrida understands this; the necessary or 'arche-violence' of the concept and of 'articulation' that always surrounds the multiple forms of empirical encounter between the Same and the Other.[5] I shall attempt to show that this violence is, moreover, essentially down to the *visceral* materiality of the contact with the Other – the one who in Levinas's *Totality and Infinity*, we are reminded, may come to me in my vulnerability with murderous intent. As Simon Critchley notes, for Levinas 'ethics is lived in the sensibility of the *corporeal* obligation to the other' – and it involves suffering.[6] (See Chapter 8.)

Levinas's ethical philosophy figures prominently as a touchstone throughout the studies comprising this volume. In the last twenty years it has been increasingly widely read and variously applied in the contexts of cultural analysis undertaken across a range of disciplines – such as literary studies, political theory, sociology and cultural studies – alongside its more established locations, such as religious studies and philosophy. The vast majority of such appropriations beyond the confines of philosophy itself, unsurprisingly, focus on Levinas as the thinker of 'transcendence' who insists on the absolute alterity of the Other; one key figure of which is the Platonic 'Good beyond being', which is said to be encountered concretely in the world in the face of the other human being for whom, it is claimed, 'I' am 'infinitely responsible'. The approach adopted in this book, which brings Levinas's thought to the border between philosophy and cultural theory, in various ways and in relation to its specific themes, seeks to recall that this ethical philosophy of 'absolute alterity' begins with an account of how the relation to the Other in Levinas is grounded in his philosophy of *the Same* and that the ethical Subject is 'subject to the conditions of its existence'.[7] In ways that will receive clarification across these chapters (and will be directly addressed in detail in Chapter 2), I want to show how Levinas's philosophy of existence, materiality and finitude is a vital component of his thinking and decisive for how his philosophy overall might be brought to the concerns of interdisciplinary cultural theorising.

The Levinasian thinking of *the Same* is rarely a focus, if it has been made so at all, when his thinking is appropriated and 'applied' to 'real world situations' in the context of ethically oriented cultural critique. There is a correlated tendency to forget the role of the sensate life of the existent, which he holds to be the pre-personal, or rather impersonal, condition of the ethical relation to the Other – a kind of proto-Subject, which is quite happy in its element until it is 'forced' to become an ethical Subject. For Levinas the existent essentially becomes ethical because it suffers the trauma of ethical demand, and, in a redoubled suffering, suffers the other's suffering 'for nothing' (I expand on this in Chapter 8); in other words, as a consequence of the disturbance of its otherwise self-sufficiency and its being quite happily at home with itself (*chez soi*). It is easy to forget that the Levinasian ethical Subject is not 'naturally' given to being good! The significance of this, I just note at this point, is that the Levinasian account of ethical subjectivity does not merely displace the traditional preoccupation with, and 'of', the autonomous, self-centred, rational Subject in favour of the Other, as if the task of ethical theorising was to persuade a pre-existent Subject of the efficacy of such an ethical reorientation of itself and to adopt a more ethical attitude towards 'others'. Levinas's Subject *becomes* ethical on the basis of an affective disturbance of its 'sojourn' in the 'elemental': as an awakening, of sorts, but a rude, uninvited one. In this, as far as the ethical as a substantive event is concerned, ethical philosophy comes 'after the fact', and his account of ethics should be read as a sort of materialist phenomenology of ethicality understood *as* the event of Subject becoming ethical. The Levinasian claim for ethics as 'first philosophy', I will argue in several places, has to be referred to his thinking of the primacy of ethical Subject as an event.[8] (See Chapter 2.)

If that claim is to stand up to critical scrutiny, then there is an obvious sense in which talk of a 'turn' to the ethical – other than as purely cultural phenomenon or intellectual fashion – is a misnomer , as theorising would be in reality, and by its very nature, *already* a manifestation of the ethical relation to the Other. There is indeed a sense in which, as Derrida puts it, 'all value is first constituted by a theoretical subject',[9] but value is always an empirical matter, too, in so far as it is lived. The next chapter will deal directly with Levinas's radical empiricism of the ethical Subject partly in order to assess whether it makes any sense to postulate that the ethical turn itself can be ethically grounded in both its theoretical and empirical dimensions. The chapters thereafter will aim to illustrate the senses in which it can perhaps be claimed to be so. This approach acknowledges both the general description Derrida gives of Levinas's project as the 'ethics of ethics'[10] and the true importance of the question as to whether ethics is ethical. It is implicitly raised, in any case, in the opening sentence of *Totality and Infinity*: 'Everyone will readily agree that it is of the highest importance to know *whether or not we are duped* by morality.'[11] As far as *normative moralities* are concerned, I suspect the answer to the question is: not necessarily; not always and probably rarely, the corollary of which, I suggest, is that 'everyone' (at least anyone inclined to scepticism or critical reflection at all) needs to rethink the theoretico-empirical origin of the ethical.

Despite the multifaceted 'intellectual wing' of the cultural turn gaining ground across various disciplines, it has to be noted that the jury remains out on whether the feted 'ethical turn' represents a fateful turn away from the political, or indeed is indicative, rather, in the extent to which it *abandons* the axiomatic modern commitment to universality, nothing less than a travesty of the ethical itself. This is a view expressed by Jacques Rancière, for instance:

> In order to truly understand what is at stake in the ethical turn that affects aesthetics and politics today, we must first precisely define the meaning of the word 'ethics'. Ethics is indeed a fashionable word. But it is often taken

as a simple, more euphonious translation of the old word 'morals'. Ethics is viewed as a general instance of normativity that enables one to judge the validity of practices and discourses operating in the particular spheres of judgement and action. Understood in this way, the ethical turn would mean that politics or art are increasingly subjected today to moral judgements about the validity of their principles and the consequences of their practices. There are those who loudly rejoice about such a return to ethical values. I do not believe that there is so much to rejoice about, because I do not believe that this is actually what is happening today. The reign of ethics is not the reign of moral judgements over the operations of art or of political action. On the contrary, it signifies the constitution of an indistinct sphere where not only is the specificity of political and artistic practices dissolved, but also what was actually the core of the old term morals: the distinction between fact and law, what is and what ought to be.[12]

If the ethical turn is viewed in terms of its manifestation across the landscape of culture *and* as reflected by a multiplicity of cultural discourses, then alongside those of aesthetics, politics and philosophy more widely, there are also those of everyday life, such as ethical consumerism, ethical audit, ethical tourism, ethical investment, ethical banking and so forth. Rancière is surely right (along with Alain Badiou; see below) to recognise in this kind of populist, catch-all 'ethicisation of everything', the dissolution of the 'proper' in ethical thinking – which is summed up by him here in terms of the conventionally formulated concern for the gap between 'is' and 'ought' and an ontologically grounded ethical Subject. He is right also, in my view, to decry the identification of the ethical with the internal machinations of normative moralising, and to see in this 'subjection' of culture, in both the dimension of aesthetic creativity and in the more socio-anthropologically defined dimension of everyday life, its reduction to critically unexamined, merely normative values. The 'ethicisation of everything' does indeed need to be exposed to an ongoing aesthetic-political critique as rigorous as that traditionally applied to the spheres of art and political life. But the question of *which* art and *which* manifestations of everyday life might prove worthy of such analysis and critique, is surely not decidable in advance. Any bit of culture, surely, offers a potential critical opening for the cultural theorist who thinks of critical thought itself as being a genuinely political form of culture.

Trash TV as much as classical literature, can become the material of a critical political thinking and other forms of intervention. Reality TV celebrity Jade Goody's petulant racist outburst directed at the Indian actor Shilpa Shetty on 'Big Brother' a few years ago,[13] and especially its representation in other popular media, such as news press, magazines and the Internet, is just as fertile cultural ground as 'serious' literature and art, or say a swathe of leaked secret government documents might be, for understanding how racism, or some other form of prejudice or exploitation, is embedded in culture and society by way of the overt and covert activities of its cultural institutions. Uncritical and rhetorical as many contemporary popular ethical discourses may be, and no matter how ethically misguided or ultimately unfounded ethical decision making is as a consequence of their deployment, the appeal of the ethical betrayed by the quotidian compunction to do, and especially today, to say, 'the right thing', to 'distinguish right from wrong', or generally to 'live ethically', ought not to be reduced a priori to a case of false consciousness. To say this is not to deny there is a pressing need to draw out the political implications of the experience of ethical demand which determines the consciousness of the gap between the 'way things are' and 'the way things ought to be', for either individuals or for groups or political bodies of one sort or another. It is rather to acknowledge that ethical subjectivity is not simply an abstraction awaiting the clarification of philosophy. It has to be acknowledged that it is always culturally expressed in some form or other, however inadequately. Ethics, therefore, has to be read off, and, arguably, can only be read off of the surfaces of culture. Culture is, so to speak, the given medium within which ethical demand is experienced as real. A beggar may knock at my door, sick child in her arms asking for food, or a celebrity dressed up in a one-eyed teddy bear suit may front a TV charity appeal, claiming to be able to alleviate the suffering of someone on the other side of the planet if I Ping cash to him now. In either of these situations, of opening my door to a stranger or watching my TV set, I may or I may not experience 'ethical demand'. Consequently I may give or not be generous as a result of this or indeed despite this, but both situations are equally culturally framed and defined in the most general sense, as are the responses they might solicit. A culture of charitable giving does not in itself serve as a measure of 'ethicality' in the deeper, philosophical sense of the ethical. It may just be fashionable to give, it may just be a tax-dodge strategy, and so forth.

Theorising ethicality from a socio-anthropological perspective will not enable us to think the ethical qua ethical. It is no doubt true that if we were to uncritically understand the 'ethical turn' *purely* on the basis of culture and cultural practices, then we could not entertain the prospect, and would not hold the ambition, of understanding ethical demand 'properly' at all. But neither could we attain a properly philosophical thinking of the relation between ethics and politics, or of ethical subjectivity, independently of the cultural situations through which the ethical is experienced and finds its expression. Any ethical theory must work through the materiality of ethical situatedness.

A major premise of this book is that the ethical turn is a phenomenon that is both cultural and theoretical at the same time. It could be described as a phenomenon of 'theoretical culture': theory is just as 'cultural' as any other form of culture through which the ethical turn is manifested; and it has multiple cultural locations. It is of course encountered 'here' (in the tradition and genre within which I am writing and) in this work in particular, in the context of postmodern theory, and especially the French post-structuralist philosophy, which, over the last almost half century, has had a very wide impact right across the critical humanities and social studies. The writings of such thinkers as Lyotard, Derrida, Foucault, Deleuze and Guattari, Nancy, Irigaray and Badiou, for example, have collectively contributed to new kinds of thinking about the ethical, yet, it should be noted, without any of these figures being in any straightforward way, or strictly speaking, ethical theorists or (even less so) moral philosophers as such. Emmanuel Levinas, whose thinking of the ethical figures most prominently throughout these chapters, is alone when placed alongside this list of his younger contemporaries in that almost his entire *oeuvre* is dedicated to the articulation of an ethical philosophy as such, or as he calls it, ethical metaphysics. He stands alone also in this context in his retention of the term 'humanism' (albeit under the rubric of the 'humanism of the other man') as a name for his philosophical project – nominally, at least, against the tide of a certain anti-humanism in European thought.[14] Indeed, all of the above are renowned for their singular and highly original, culturally far-reaching, bodies of work. Yet one must be wary of suggesting that they in any deep sense are collectively responsible for the ethical turn understood as an intellectual project – let alone the cultural phenomenon. The ethical turn does not belong to the specifically French intellectual tradition as opposed to some other nationally or linguistically identified tradition. It is true to say, nonetheless, that they are all inheritors of a tradition of sorts, or, a philosophical legacy, one which is key to their individual contributions to rethinking the ethical and which figures prominently in what all of these thinkers share across their differences (and despite Levinas's apparent commitment to a new concept of 'humanism'). This is the tradition or legacy of a certain anti-humanism.

In his seminal essay of 1968 'The Ends of Man', Derrida addresses the then particular cultural and historical context of an apparently 'French' concern with the question of 'man':

Where is France, as concerns man?
The question of 'man' is being asked in a very current fashion in

France. Along highly significant lines, and in an original historic-philosoph-ical structure. What I will call 'France', on the basis of several indices . . . will be the non-empirical site of a movement, a structure and an articulation of the question 'of man'. Following this it would be possible, and doubt-less necessary – but then only rigorously to relate this site with every other instance defining something like 'France'.[15]

Given that the anti-humanist tradition that Derrida goes on to further contextualise in relation to certain events of 1968 – notably not only those in France, but including the assassination of Martin Luther King and the opening of the Vietnam peace talks – is most directly inherited through Nietzsche and Heidegger, he clearly wishes to make clear that there is nothing exclusively or particularly French, in the empirical sense, in the then contemporary questioning of 'man'. I consider the important implication of this to be that philosophical questioning in general, not only of 'man' or in any particular instance, and not just in 1968, always demands cognisance of the cultural context, or situat-edness, of critical thinking itself. One aspect of the task or project of cultural theorising in an ethical mode, therefore, is to think the nature of the materiality and situatedness of the ethical Subject in so far as this is determinative of its becoming ethical in the first place.

THE ETHICAL SUBJECT IN THEORY AND IN PRACTICE

I recall this moment in Derrida's essay at this point partly in order to establish at the outset a series of protocols for reading this book. Firstly, the term 'Subject', wherever it is written with a capital letter, is used, in a now rather conventional sense, to name that which performs a kind of 'place-holding' for what can be thought of as coming after the Subject understood as 'man' in the modern humanist tradition – which, across the texts of those thinkers whose names I have highlighted, has been subjected to a multi-faceted deconstruction, critique, refutation, displacement, *Destruktion*, *Abbau* or *Überwindung* – or some other notion of critical surpassing.[16] Secondly, and in relation to this, there is no *assumed* ultimate (or primordial) equivalence between the Subject as such, here, and the individual human person: just what an ethical Subject is or might be or become is exactly what this book is 'open to' and in general seeks to interrogate on the basis of its readings of various authors' texts in relation to its themes. Thirdly, the term 'ethical subjects' (lower case 's') pertains to the kind of 'ethical subject matters' the individual chapters identify and engage with, such as sexual differ-ence, the body, touch, communicative contact, control, pain, censorship, embodiment, violence, technology, suffering, death, and so on. This book aims to demonstrate how ethical subject matters on the one hand and ethical Subjects, both theoretically defined and as culturally experienced, on the other hand, are thinkable only in, or indeed as the conjunction of the one with the other.

Both within and beyond the boundaries of the academy, there is a trend within modern culture and society towards explaining and understanding social behaviour and attitudes in terms of individual moralities – *individual* integrity, or the lack of it, the moral strengths and weaknesses of *individuals*, measured in relation to cultural factors widely understood. There is also a tendency to focus on how responsibility can be apportioned or assumed on the basis of a calculation which takes the human being as the natural 'ethical unit'. It is precisely this kind of reductionism of the ethical Subject at a sociological level, which Rancière would see as the root of depoliticisation and the degradation of ethics itself. Certainly, it should be noted, therein lies a real danger: it generates a lot of the idle talk about ethics and the ethical I mentioned at the outset, which tends to hide the fact that there is little 'proper' ethical thinking going on. But a danger stems too from the neglect of the ethical Subject (however this is finally to be understood) as a singular individual (or 'dividual', to borrow a term from Deleuze)[17] as the true bearer of responsibility, or who, as Levinas attempts to show, is the one who stands 'accused' or 'is indebted before any loan'.[18] In neither of these formulations is the Subject assumed to be a 'self' defined as an autonomous entity, present to itself and possessed of its own interiority. And whilst the socio-political phenomenon of individualism may be argued to be a depoliticising force, or the result of a strategic alienation of a more primordial social subjectivity perpetrated by capitalism and capitalist ideology, for instance, it would, conversely, be dangerous to neglect developing a theoretical understanding of the everyday cultural origins of ethical values. It is easy to forget that theory *itself* is not independent of the sphere of the cultural; it always takes place within it: it is driven (and arguably perverted) often, by such things as career aspiration, funding opportunities and the culture of 'academic success' – and hence it too is part of ordinary life. Ultimately, theory enjoys no privileged, extra-cultural access to the Subject of which it speaks, even less so does doing theory make any of us good in a properly ethical sense. Simon Critchley, in the course of his fascinating attempt to bind ethics to the politics of resistance, says this:

> The central philosophical task in my approach to ethics is developing a theory of ethical subjectivity. A subject is the name for the way in which a self binds itself to some conception of the good and shapes its subjectivity in

relation to that good. *To be clear, I am not making the questionable claim that it is the job of philosophers to manufacture moral selves. They exist already as living breathing products of education and socialization.*[19]

His emphasis on the theorisation of ethical subjectivity (or the ethical Subject – he uses these two terms interchangeably) resonates with the aims of this volume – and I certainly subscribe to his caveat here that theory and theorists are not in the priestly business of manufacturing 'moral selves'. However, my approach differs somewhat in that, firstly, I do not aim here to produce a new theory of ethical subjectivity (or of the ethical Subject per se). More modestly perhaps, I aim to uncover the place of the ethical Subject in the context of the ethical thinking of a number of thinkers by way of series of critical, textual encounters which are contextualised in relation to a limited set of examples of ethical subject matters (listed above). Secondly, as I have already indicated and as the following chapters will reveal more fully, the complexity of the question of who or what the ethical Subject 'is' – as this is posed both within and in the wake of the general deconstruction of the Subject as metaphysical – would suggest the naturalising discourse of 'the self' should be avoided at all costs. The ethical Subject may prove to be unthinkable as the human individual conceived in this way, or in any case not limited to it. It might be better thought of as a collective, a multiplicity or an assemblage, for instance – it may not be of woman born! What in any case is 'the self'? If it names something which pre-exists Critchley's 'binding to the Good', how exactly is that to be understood? Why invoke the self at all? Is this binding with the Good, a binding which 'binds itself'? And, what is the power by which it could shape *its own* subjectivity? Of course, when Critchley speaks in this way, he does not bind himself either, as far as his theory of ethical subjectivity is concerned, according to the strictures of the subject–predicate structure of ordinary language – and I approve of his commitment to the use of plain English. Indeed, I shall endeavour to do the same my*self*. However, that said, it is also the case that 'French postmodern theory' is by and large, as is the relevant German philosophy, too, for that matter, characterised by, and stylistically invested in, countering, reflexively, the 'prison house' of conceptual constraints imposed by conventional linguistic expression. And the ethical turn in its theoretical cultural form is not after all unrelated to the Continental European wing of the earlier 'linguistic turn'. As I tell my students, this rethinking of the Subject in postmodern French theory is sometimes difficult to understand, but for understandable reasons. The main reason is not the problem of translation from one natural language to another with respect to the French and German texts in question (although that is not insignificant either), but rather the transition from one epoch of thinking to another. As Jean-Luc Nancy notes in his short introduction to a highly influential edited collection on the subject of the Subject, and which includes texts by Derrida, Deleuze, Rancière, Irigaray, Lyotard, Levinas and Badiou, and is titled *Who Comes After the Subject?*, he says of the contributors collectively:

> All are thinkers of an age of rupture. Which means also: they take responsibility for this age, because the questions they are discussing . . . obviously engage all the ethical and political challenges of our time (as well as the debates *about* what 'ethics' and 'politics' mean today).[20]

He goes on to explain that the end of the Subject as metaphysical in that tradition, and by virtue of a certain end to it brought about partly in their writings, and in whose wake these thinkers work (the tradition of Hegel, Marx, Freud, Nietzsche and Heidegger) is not tantamount to a 'liquidation' of the Subject:

> That which obliterates is nihilism – itself an implicit form of the metaphysics of the subject (self-presence of that which knows itself as the dissolution of its own difference). There is nothing nihilistic in recognizing that the subject – the property of the *self* – is the thought that reabsorbs or exhausts all possibility of *being-in-the-world* (all possibility of existence, all existence as being delivered to the possible), and that this same thought, never simple, never closed upon itself without remainder, designates and delivers an entirely different thought: that of the *one* and that of the some *one*, of the singular existent that the subject announces, promises, and at the same time conceals . . . Not only are we not relieved of thinking this *some* one – this *some* one that the subject has perhaps always pointed towards or looked for, and that brings us back to the same figures: the individual, a people, the state, history, production, style, man, woman, as well as 'myself', 'ourselves' . . . – but it is precisely something like this thought that henceforth comes toward us and calls us forth.[21]

This calling forth, vis-à-vis the subject of the Subject and its philosophical investigation, should be referred, for reasons already stated, to the wider understanding of the ethical turn – albeit with all the cautionary provisos noted so far, including those of Rancière (and Badiou – to which I shall turn shortly). In saying that we are brought 'back to the same figures' of the Subject – 'the individual, a people, the state, history, production, style, man, woman, as well as "myself", "ourselves"'– Nancy gives an indication of the possible familiar names of the Subject, which, after the deconstruction of the Subject as metaphysical, might be theorised otherwise than on the basis of that *traditional* critical undertaking. If a philosophical demonstration of the thesis that the Subject is prima facie an *ethical* Subject is possible, then it is on this basis that any or all of these figures of the Subject (and why not a myriad of others, too?) might come to be understood ethically, or as manifestations of ethicality.

If this were to prove possible, it would, I suggest, provide the basis for a new kind of ethical overcoming of the difference between theory and praxis – a kind of ethical resolution of the theory/praxis dichotomy. Whilst critical theory has its origin in such an ambition, but thinks the task purely in terms of the political scope of theory understood *as* praxis, the ethical turn, however shallowly manifested it may be in some spheres of culture, gives rise in others to the thought at least, of the possibility of a specifically ethical overcoming of the same divide. The question 'who or what comes after the Subject?' would call forth not merely intellectual activity as thinking, conferences, books and new university courses, but would also harbour the ambition that the becoming-ethical of the Subject would play out at the level of precisely such figures of the Subject as those listed by Nancy, and hence throughout culture and society. In other words, it expresses the possibility of a new and radical *ethico-politics* of unlimited reach. And it is on such a hypothetical basis, rather than on the basis of vapid, fashionable populisms of ethicisation, that a 'proper ethicality' would come to figure, too, as a 'proper-ty' of the Subject. This would potentially be transformative of any of its numerous cultural manifestations, amongst which should be counted the fields of cultural studies and theory, the critical humanities, themselves, along with the culture of the academy more widely.

In the wake of the ethical turn, especially to the extent to which decades of effort and creative imagination have been invested in addressing the question of the Subject, it is perhaps with some right, rather than as a consequence of succumbing to the latest fashion, that at least some forms of cultural theorising, philosophising, cultural studies and critical art practice, and so forth, might thus, at least to a degree, be judged to have gained from their various investments in this thing called the ethical turn. This may be the case even as another manifestation of the contemporary academy is busily wasting its time carrying out more than its institutional fair share of 'ethical audits' and sitting in ethics committees whilst at the same time selling itself (out) to prospective 'clients' partly on the basis of its own self-proclaimed bill of ethical good health. It is indeed important to discriminate between ethical claptrap and 'ethics proper', even if what is understood by the latter is at critical variance with Rancière's formulation of this idea, as cited above. There is, I believe, a debate to be had and an argument to be made concerning the ethicality of critical inquiry itself, and the thinking of the ethical Subject is key to it.

The strategy of this book is to make that argument in the form of a series of critical discussions of ethical subjects (in both senses) and thereby to reveal how the ethical in a 'proper' sense must be understood on the basis of rethinking the Subject *as* the ethical Subject as it substantively emerges in its cultural context or situation. What this involves is not simply doing cultural theory making use of concepts borrowed from ethical philosophy; it requires rather, embarking on a project of cultural critique which aims to account for the specific formations of modern subjectivity in fundamentally ethical terms. In other words, it involves showing how ethicality is not an add-on to the life of the Subject but an essential, always contextualised, feature of its formation under the circumstances of everyday life and the various kinds of encounters that characterise it.

THE THEORY/PRAXIS DICHOTOMY AND THE DECONSTRUCTION OF THE CULTURAL EVERYDAY

When considering how the theory/praxis dichotomy might be sublated in relation to the 'properly ethical' rather than the 'properly political', it is important to be wary of the, perhaps unavoidable, appeal to, or retention of, the notion of *propriety* itself. The very idea of any such sublation begs the question of the truth of an experience; an actual instance of ethical demand or responsibility, and whether either of these could justifiably be considered something objective rather than something merely subjective. Any appeal to the proper will find its counterpoint in the invocation of this 'merely' – and it is precisely this haunting of the 'proper' (conventionally associated with the 'real' as objective) by the 'merely' (conventionally associated with the subjective) that the sublation of the theory/praxis dichotomy is aimed at overcoming. This is so because it is *logically* impossible for theory in general to say anything about everyday life without by the same stroke annihilating it, effectively killing off everyday life as a proper philosophical subject. This is an early and decisive critical observation Levinas makes, for example, in relation to Husserl's theory of intuition and the 'primacy of theory' in Husserlian phenomenology:

> Philosophy begins with the reduction. This is an act in which we consider life in all its concreteness, but no longer live it . . . by virtue of the primacy of theory, Husserl does not wonder how this 'neutralization' of our life, which nevertheless is still an act of our life, has its foundation in life . . . Husserl gives himself the freedom of theory just as he gives himself theory.[22]

On the one hand, critical suspicion falls on any theory which neglects to reflexively acknowledge this contradiction as the condition of theorising; on the other hand, any splitting of *the lived* and its *representation* all too quickly falls foul of the charge of its being overly theoretical and neglectful of actual experience or, conversely, paying scant attention to the conditions of ordinary life and failure to divest itself of normative contamination. Rethinking the ethical Subject must similarly begin with and yet divest itself of its 'origin'.

Yet again, no sooner do we embark upon theoretical thinking than we experience precipitative 'returns' to the everyday. The computer I am writing on crashes, the neighbours are too noisy, as I write – I pass repeatedly in and out of the space where these words come from as I write, and so forth. This symbolically illustrates, perhaps reports (this depends on how it is read too), an actual transformation of some aspect of real life in the interruptive interplay of life and thought, or, more accurately, life *as* thought. Does theory bring about practical effects which flow, so automatically, in the other direction? And, if so, are there limits to its scope? Am I being more 'properly ethical' when I perform a simple good deed, such as doing my elderly neighbours' shopping for them, or when I wrack my brains trying to contribute to the body of critical writing on the ethical? Am I only ever doing good when a beneficent result can be identified as following from it? Can theory be used to intervene concretely, to make an alteration to a particular instance of the everyday life of an individual, a class or a population, for example? Such questions as these arrive and (even when unanswered) confirm at least the conjunction of everyday life and ethical concern, at least in the form of *thinking*. Thinking is doing something even if from the outside it looks like doing nothing. 'Doing nothing' is in any case a distinctive way of living in the moment of the everyday (being bored, hanging about on street corners, in arcades or coffee bars, and so forth). All of these are examples of forms of everyday life that have been deemed worthy of critical reflection and serious analysis in several forms of cultural study (by writers as diverse as Freud, Kracauer, Benjamin, Hoggart and Williams) and have been found to reveal deeper structures and hidden forces shaping the everyday social reality from within which we both think and act. In this sense, conversely, frivolous forms of doing nothing have brought about theorising. Theory and everyday life are in various ways conterminal with one another, and there is no ground on which to prioritise one over the other. They are *the Same* (NB not 'the same thing'). The significance of this observation for a theory of the ethical Subject is that both the theory and the Subject can only ever be thought in conjunction with an account of the materiality of their expressions *as* life. The ethical Subject does not belong to philosophy *before* it belongs to the world. We have to think it from within the materialities of its everyday life and on the basis of the spatio-temporality of the world which opens with it. Heidegger was the first to think the Subject explicitly on such a basis (as *Dasein* – a concept which de-subjectifies the traditional notion of 'the subject as metaphysical'): *Being and Time* sets out 'from' the ontic 'toward' the properly ontological and thinks from within the 'ontological difference' of these two. Levinas's thinking of the Subject as the ethical Subject within his ethics of alterity, thinks it on the basis of a radically new concept of time as 'diachrony' which 'opens up' across the difference between the ethical Subject and the 'absolute Other' (*Autrui*); across what he calls the ethical relation. Ethical time for Levinas is thought of as 'interruption': my time is interrupted by the ethical demand of the Other for whom I am responsible: '[T]ime is not the achievement of an isolated and lone subject, but is the very relationship of the subject with the Other.'[23] (I shall discuss this in later chapters on new media communications technologies and on death.) The 'deconstruction of time' which we find in Derrida's writings, for instance around his thinking of *différance* and *gramme*,[24] accounts for how a particular concept of time has come to dominate the way we think about time 'ordinarily', and hence it bears on the everyday appropriation of time as something which dictates and organises action in the world, for example from industrial shift systems to waiting for buses, to rushing or just idling along, being early, late or punctual. All ostensibly theoretical accounts of time, as, for example, 'deferral' or 'interruption' (Derrida); as 'ecstasis' and projection (Heidegger); as the 'eternal recurrence of the same' (Nietzsche) or 'diachrony' (Levinas), are in their own ways connected with any number of simple everyday experiences of temporality – for instance, taking 'time out', 'putting off', 'taking a break', 'giving someone your time' or repetitions of one sort or another such as 'going around in circles', déjà vu, and so forth. The only point I really wish to make at this stage, is that abstract theoretical discussions of time and its relation to the Subject are not formulated independently of what is lived in everyday situations. If theory could be said to take shape *in the withdrawal from the everyday*, then this withdrawal (however we come to understand such a movement) is always a withdrawal from the some*thing* or some*one* Nancy (cited above) speaks of.

ETHICAL PHILOSOPHY INTO CULTURAL STUDIES AND THE CRITICAL HUMANITIES

Of course, the question of the conjunction (and/or disjunction) of theory/praxis begs the issue of the self-understanding of critical cultural inquiry itself. To the extent to which an interest in and concern with everyday life as the object of inquiry is foregrounded, for instance in the cultural critique of authors such as Simmel, Benjamin, Kracauer, Freud, Debord, de Certeau, Lefebvre, Barthes, Bourdieu, Foucault, as well as many others in the anglophone tradition of cultural studies, including Hoggart, Williams, Hall, Hebdige, McRobbie, Gilroy and Grossberg, then it is perhaps possible to identify much of their work as belonging to something which could be called 'everyday life studies' – the distinction of this broad field being evident in its making the everyday world of cultural practices and material objects the focus of inquiry. All of the above writers, for example, have made contributions to cultural theory or cultural studies which are articulated more or less explicitly in relation to the material practices and objects of everyday life. In apparent contrast to such *oeuvres*, for the 'more philosophical', postmodern French theory highlighted above, and which I have cited as the source of the contemporary questioning of the Subject qua Subject, the most obvious field of cultural reference is that of texts and writerly exchanges and textual interactions. Because of this, such 'highly theoretical' work, has often been considered to be quite removed from the *empirical realities* of the socio-cultural sphere, and to be remote from (if not indifferent to) the anthropological, ethnographic and sociological frames of reference applied within much cultural studies writing. Such a critical observation might well be made with regard to texts I engage with in this book (and this book itself): namely, that the literal day-to-day is marginal or largely absent. However, it is my view that the very notion of the literal day-to-day and its identification with 'the empirical' or the 'real' is already problematic – not least because the identification of the literal day-to-day is an example of the epistemological naturalism forgotten as the identification itself is made. Theory is a withdrawal from everyday life, but it never really leaves it: it could be said, rather, to be special kind of distortion of the surfaces of the culture from which it originates. My aim throughout this book is to articulate how the thinking of the ethical Subject, ethical subjectivity and ethicality figure in the works of various thinkers and how their thinking moves between the conceptual and the empirical, in the course of developing notions of the Subject's ethical modalities. The stakes in theorising ethical subjectivity in general are not merely to be measured in the currency of abstract ideas, but in terms of the symbiosis of such ideas and everyday life itself.

The issue of the relationship of theory to practice is thus to be posed and reposed at the points at which intellectual life comes to concern itself with its use-value and its place in the world at large. A concern for the bearing of theory on everyday life may be read as a sign of a certain bad conscience of any intellectual project which would like to see 'results'; results which would take the form of visible transformations, for instance in social and political structures and in the daily lives of Subjects who (or which) understand themselves as social and political actors and members of communities (or *as* communities, for that matter) and so forth. Even worse than failure in this 'practical' respect of showing how it 'makes a difference' *right here and now where things happen* – which in any case will be dependent on any number of other contingent factors – is that the *return* of theory to everyday life seems, *from* an everyday point of view, to be *a turning away from* the goal of intervention *in* the everyday. Engaging in 'theory for theory's sake' would have exactly the opposite of the desired effect sought by the project of returning theory to everyday life: it would help cement the system of domination, which operates at the level of everyday life through its neglect of the everyday as actuality.

The question of the everyday is important for theory, then, not least because it reminds us of the dangers inherent in the institutionalisation of such activities as cultural studies, theory and philosophy and, potentially, the productive alliances which may be made between them. On the one hand, critical thinking and research aims to counteract the processes of cultural totalisation; on the other, it is drawn into forms of everyday 'institutionalisation', for instance under pressure to comply with, alongside those 'ethical audits' mentioned earlier, the requirements of professionalisation, such as the provision of degree courses and certifications; to operate within disciplinary divisions and publication agendas, research audits, and so on, all of which threaten the recuperation of its most radical gestures. Whatever the relation of critical thinking to the everyday, it is at least in part complicated by the fact that it is threatened *by* everyday life, even *its own*.

In 'The Right to Philosophy from a Cosmopolitan Point of View', Derrida speaks of the consequences of such everyday 'imperatives' as 'budgetary balances that give priority to research and training for research that is, often correctly, labelled useful, profitable, and urgent, to so-called end-oriented sciences, and to techno-economic, indeed scientific military, imperatives'. He acknowledges that whilst these may sometimes increase the 'chances' of the philosophical, they also, equally, represent a threat to it, moreover, precisely in their 'looking toward a "pragmatism" or a "realism"'.[25] So the use-value of theory vis-à-vis practice, or the demand that it be relevant, is cast in terms of a demand that comes from within what could be called 'the everyday life of the institution'. In this text and elsewhere, Derrida's defence of the 'right to philosophy' is a defence of the right to a highly qualified 'use-lessness', or open-ended intellectual activity. I subscribe to that defence, and my entire discussion here about the relationship of theory to the everyday and how this might be thought in conjunction with the issue of the sublation of theory/praxis (from either a political or an ethical perspective) is emphatically not to be read as a concern with how 'phil-osophical ethics' can be *applied* to contemporary 'ethical problems'. What I am interested in theorising is the emergence or manifestation of the ethical Subject as a phenomenon of the material, cultural situation which constitutes, to borrow an expression from Levinas, its 'foothold in being'. The institutionalisation of intellectual practice Derrida speaks of, can just as well be viewed as the result of the institutional self-organ-isation of academic disciplines themselves as it can be deemed to result from the policies flowing from within government ministries. In other words, the demand of measuring up to 'use-criteria' in general, which *disciplines* the disciplines themselves, or causes the disciplines to impose self-discipline and censorious self-regulation, can come from 'within' disciplinary borders as much as from 'outside' them. (Censorship and institutional control is discussed further in Chapter 7.)

Against the various demands to adopt 'positions', the philosophical theorists I engage with in this book, I read as theorists of the middle ground between these two accusations of being overly theoretical (or overly textual, or overly literary) on the one hand, and insufficiently empirical on the other. And I concur with Derrida's own observation when he says: 'what a victory for dogmatisms everywhere if anyone who tries to ask new questions, to upset good consciences . . . stands immedi-ately accused of complicity with the adversary'.[26] To avoid uncritically repeating one or the other of these unfounded accusations directed at deconstruction, or other postmodern theorisations of the Subject qua Subject and their restagings of the question of the Subject, we must rise to the challenge of thinking the non-difference between theory/praxis as the non-difference between the philosophico-ethical *and* the empiri-cal manifestations of ethical subjectivity. Having said that, one has to concede that when Derrida writes 'real life may always be absent',[27] then a provocation of sorts is clearly being made. (In Chapter 9 I discuss how precisely such a provocation can cut into and through the personal/intellectual divide in the context of the friendship between Derrida and

Foucault.) I understand and respond to this provocation in this book as a whole, in terms of the challenge to think the ethical Subject as an empirico-theoretical reality. And I take my lead in this from Levinas's account of the ethical as the 'common source of activity and theory':[28] the absolute alterity of the Other can only be approached from within the interpersonal and 'is only possible starting from *me*'.[29]

LEVINAS, BADIOU AND THE CULTURAL SITUATEDNESS OF THE SUBJECT

As already indicated, the ethical philosophy of Levinas is a guiding thread throughout the following chapters, and in the final section of this one I want to set out some of the key parameters of my appropriation of his thought.

As already noted, Levinas is most often read and represented as the foremost thinker of the 'absolute alterity' of the Other and transcendence. Whilst there are clear (though not overwhelming) grounds for doing this, it is almost always by way of neglecting his philosophy of *the Same* and his account of the immanence of the 'existent' (Levinas's early 'place-holding' name for the Subject) within 'existence' as the existential condition of the becoming of ethical Subject. This tends to give rise to the general identification of his thinking with the theological rather than the 'properly philosophical'. My own reading of him here, and as I carry it through into my discussion of various ethical subjects in Chapters 3 to 10, seeks to highlight the significance of Levinas as a thinker of 'transcendence within immanence' (the fuller account of which is presented in the next chapter). My reading of Levinas is very much focused on Levinas's account of how the 'source' of the ethical (the Infinite, the Good beyond being) in the world is only ever encountered in the world.

In the course of this book I aim to rethink and redefine the interrelatedness of ethical subjects/ethical subjectivities, in terms of their being located in dynamic 'ethical materialities' – fluid, contingent, aggregated patterns discernible within the greater cultural whole. And in the course of my discussion of ethical subjects I shall attempt to illustrate how ethical subjectivity exists in a kind of parallelism with them in a conjunction that should be understood as being constituted by *constellated cultural elements*; for instance, in the mediated practices of communication and secrecy, in the form of institutionalised censorious practices, in encounters across sexual difference, or in attending to the death of the loved one, in the myriad forms of *contact* with others, and in experiences of pain, suffering and violence. For the Subject, these are all forms and instances of its being-*in-situ*. Any or all of them may become constitutive of both 'events' (sometimes large-scale, public and in some sense shared) *and* at the same time happening-moments of 'a life' (or localised, private and individualised micro-events.) My aim is to explore the connections between the theoretical description of ethical subjectivity as always located in such phenomena to a quasi-empirical notion of its cultural substrate and to its existence as a moment of the 'here and now'. And though I just spoke of the happening-moment of 'a life', as already noted, there is no attempt on my part to limit the notion of such an existent to a moment of consciousness of particular individuals. It is in the context of such liquid 'cultural formations' (to borrow an old term of Raymond Williams) that we must seek to discover 'ethical subjectivity' as it crystallises, and finds its contingent expression.

What all of this is aimed at uncovering is how such relationally defined and materially expressed 'cultural formations', expressive instantiations of the kind of the ethical subject matters discussed (or indeed any others), are associated with (what we are conventionally inclined to call *subjective*) 'ethical sensibilities'; and, conversely, how such 'ethical sensibilities', which are a function of (what we are conventionally inclined to call *objective*) zones of 'affect', are onto-genetically coextensive. In particular I am interested in the ways such 'formations of culture', or 'cultural situations', can be viewed as 'processes' immanent to what Levinas refers to as *the Same* – which, however else it might be read, I suggest can be considered as a name for the *totality of culture*.

The concept of a 'cultural situation' is used here to express the imbrication of exterior affects, forces or impulses and the constituted subjective interiorities 'who or which', so to speak, inhabit or populate it. I thus consider the ethical Subject so conceived not as a fixed identity, but rather as something *identifiable* across a set of fluid and contingent relations that is at once expressed by and expressive of, a particular constellation of such affects and forces. And, I ask what it would be for such an embedded Subject, or (in)dividual, to act (or to exist) ethically, given that action (which is always action-in-context) cannot on this model be correctly described as being either free or determined *by* a situation, or context, because *such a subjectivity exists in the mode of a parallelism with the immanent, processual unfolding of the situation itself.* Just to be clear, this is not to suggest that abstract thinking must always be juggled with the cultural everyday, as if that were what is called for in order to avert theory's tendency to become 'remote from life' (as discussed in the previous section). It is to focus, rather, on how culture as ideas and culture as material practices are cultural spheres themselves separated only through *processes of differentiation internal to culture*.

My understanding of the ethical turn then, is as a cultural 'event' or 'process' which is coextensive with the materiality of thought. Can 'thought', viewed as a modality of existence, be already 'ethical' in the form of (its) being-*for-the-other*, as Levinas holds? Is the being of thought thus already an affective response to the Other who initiates it as its first mover? If so, in what sense, if at all, can this be properly described as an empirical claim as well as being a matter of 'textuality' (language, interpretation and theory)? My questioning along these lines here is in pursuit of such an experience (or quasi-experience) of ethicality; above all, it concerns to whom or to what it can be *properly* ascribed. The overall aim, theoretically speaking, is thus broadly twofold: firstly, to develop a theoretical model for describing ethical experience in terms of the ethicality of a 'situation' as a feature of its materiality and its contingency, rather than in terms of a unique responsibility which is considered to be owned by an (autonomous) individual, and to be so of necessity – in other words, it needs to be ontologically grounded. Secondly, I nonetheless want to discover if there is a way of retaining the Levinasian notion of the irrecusable character of responsibility as a necessary dimension of what I have just been referring to as a 'situation', and thereby move towards an account of the parallelism between 'ethical subjects' as *both* 'cultural situations' and as 'ethical subjectivity'.

There is a clear resonance between this emphasis on the 'ethical situatedness' of the Subject and the account of the ethical given by Alain Badiou, who proposes an axiomatic thesis of his ethical philosophy in the following terms: 'All humanity has its root in the identification in thought of singular situations. There is no ethics in general. There are only – eventually – processes by which we treat the possibilities of a situation.'[30] In this, at least at the level of the 'situation', on the ground as it were, we hear an echo of Levinasian infinite responsibility: this is a unique moment 'in the life' of a singular ethical Subject who is not free to refuse it. (Ethics is 'necessary' in the philosophical sense of the term.) Yet there is also every reason to be extremely cautious in suggesting any equivalence at all between Badiou's account of ethics and Levinas's, not least because Badiou associates a certain 'Levinasianism' – if not, in the final analysis, the philosophy of Levinas in its entirety – with the most objectionable aspects of what we have all along here been calling the ethical turn. Not least either because Badiou's ethical thought is ostensibly partly articulated by a polemical countering of Levinas's philosophy. As Robert Hughes writes:

Badiou's own thinking of ethics arrives at the moment when the conceptual-ization of ethics in the academy has been brought decisively under Levinas's name, first through the sponsorship of Jacques Derrida, Luce Irigaray and Jean-François Lyotard, and then [he glosses] through its appropriation by the rhetoric of multiculturalist politics.[31]

The gloss is important because as well as referring to exactly what it names, 'multicultural politics', it should also be read as a shorthand for broader uses made of the Levinasian 'ethics of alterity' that are rightly identified by Badiou as being, in part, constitutive of what he judges to be the profoundly *unethical* ethical turn in the academy.

In the opening pages of his *Ethics* Badiou pours scorn on the 'fuzzy' 'return to ethics' and decries the ways in which

ethics designates today a principle that governs how we relate to 'what is going on', a vague way of regulating our commentary on historical situations (the ethics of human rights), techno-scientific situations (medical ethics, bio-ethics), 'social' situations (the ethics of being-together), media situations (the ethics of communication), and so on.[32]

A few pages later he expands, moreover in a very Nietzschean tone:

[Man] this 'living being' is in reality contemptible, *and he will be held in contempt*. Who can fail to see that in our humanitarian expeditions, inter-ventions, embarkations of charitable *légionnaires*, the Subject presumed to be universal is split? On the side of the victims, the haggard animal exposed on television screens. On the side of the benefactors, conscience and the imperative to intervene . . . Who cannot see that this ethics which rests on the misery of the world hides, behind its victim-Man, the good-Man, the white-Man? . . . Every intervention in the name of a civilization requires an initial contempt for the situation as a whole including its victims.[33]

Badiou's rejection of Levinas's ethics rests on two key objections. The first of them pertains more to the uses made of Levinas, in par-ticular in cultural studies and the critical humanities; and which are based on crass appropriations of the ethics of alterity derived from his thought, rather than on what he finds equally objectionable in Levinas's supposedly theological premises. In the first instance, these are the oversimplifying appropriations of the ethics of alterity which are then deployed in relation to the kinds of 'ethical concerns' he lists in the first citation above, to which could be added the preoccupation with identity politics, 'the respect agenda', and so forth in the contexts of multiculturalism, feminism, postcolonialism and other discourses of emancipation. With regard to this first 'objection', I consider Badiou to be entirely correct in his analysis. But at the same time I reject abso-lutely the suggestion that this kind of 'multicultural politics' (and so forth) can in fact be grounded convincingly in the texts of Levinas, as they fly in the face of the letter of Levinas's own rejection *tout court* of the 'politics of recognition' (this will be demonstrated in the following chapter). Such politics are always based on a notion of *recognisable difference* – precisely the kind of *reciprocity* Levinas systematically rejects in his account of the asymmetry of the ethical relation, one name for which is the 'I-Other' conjuncture.[34] Such a weak reading of Levinas's thinking of alterity is therefore as disappointing for sympathetic readers of Levinas as it is for Badiou himself. It is disappointing not merely from a theoretical point of view, but, more importantly, because the potential of Levinas's account of radical alterity to radicalise such politics, by exposing the limitations and contradictions inherent to normative 'identity politics', would thus be neutralised, moreover at the very point at which it is apparently being affirmed. It is particularly unfortunate because it suggests Levinas's thinking of ethical subjectivity *as* infinite responsibility is profoundly *anti-political* in nature, as it is represents a figure of absolute practical impossibility. It is interesting to observe – though that is all – how Terry Eagleton commits such a misreading even as he attempts to piggy-back Badiou's objections to 'a certain Levinas' and to argue Levinas's 'ethical metaphysics' is indeed an appropriate name for his entire philosophy, as it amounts to nothing more than 'a reflection on the conditions of possibility of the ethical itself'.[35] As such it remains, he says, simply, even determinedly and hopelessly, remote from practical 'empirical conduct'.[36] Eagleton in fact confuses the 'Levinasianism' Badiou describes so well, with the 'real' Levinas Badiou himself distinguishes it from.

Now, finally, for Badiou's second objection to Levinas – this one directed towards what he takes to be the 'real' Levinas – and which, from his perspective, is equally serious. It goes like this:

> the [claim for the] ethical primacy of the Other over the Same requires the experience of alterity to be ontologically 'guaranteed' as the experience of a distance, or an essential non-identity, the traversal of which is the ethical experience itself. But nothing in the simple phenomenon of the other contains such a guarantee. And this is simply because the finitude of the other's appearing certainly *can* be conceived as resemblance, or as imitation, and thus lead(s) back to the logic of the Same. The other always resembles me too much for the hypothesis of an original exposure to his alterity to be necessarily true.[37]

As I have already indicated, I do not take issue with this, or any other, properly philosophical demand that the Other's 'absolute alterity' must be 'ontologically guaranteed', and the burden of my argument in the next chapter will be to show that it can be viewed as being so in Levinas and his account of it does indeed meet this philosophical demand, moreover in a very radical fashion, precisely, in his philosophy of the *Same* and his ethical empiricism.[38] In the course of doing this across the book as a whole, I will also effectively be defending aspects of ethical turn in cultural theorising which are, in part, indebted to Levinas's thinking (as well as several others working in the same tradition, especially Derrida) and which I believe can be shown to both meet the demand for philosophical propriety and maintain a commitment to thinking the relationship between ethics and politics.

NOTES

1. Derrida, 'Passions: "An Oblique Offering"', p. 15.
2. Garber et al., *Turn to Ethics*, p. vii.
3. Zylinska, *Ethics of Cultural Studies*, p. ix.
4. Dews, 'States of Grace', p. 108.
5. See Derrida, *Writing and Difference*, pp. 147–8.
6. Critchley and Dews, *Deconstructive Subjectivities*, p. 30 (emphasis added).
7. Ibid. p. 30.
8. Levinas, *Totality and Infinity*, p. 304.
9. Derrida, *Writing and Difference*, p. 27.
10. Ibid. p. 111.
11. Levinas, *Totality and Infinity*, p. 21.
12. Rancière, 'Ethical Turn', pp. 1–2.
13. For more details, see Boyle, 'When Does Ignorance Become Racism?'. Relevant TV clips can be found on YouTube.
14. See Levinas, *Humanism of the Other*. For a commentary on this expression, see Llewelyn, *Emmanuel Levinas*, p. 132.
15. Derrida, 'The Ends of Man' in *Margins of Philosophy*, p. 114.
16. The capital 'S' will, however not be carried through into quotations unless it is already in use.
17. See Deleuze, 'Postscript on the Societies of Control', p. 5.
18. Levinas, *Otherwise than Being, or, Beyond Essence*, p. 111.
19. Critchley, *Infinitely Demanding*, p. 10 (original emphasis).
20. Nancy, *Who Comes After the Subject?*, p. 4.
21. Ibid. p. 4.
22. Levinas, *Theory of Intuition*, pp. 155–7.
23. Levinas, *Time and the Other*, p. 39.
24. See Derrida, 'Difference'; Derrida, 'Ousia and Gramme'.
25. Derrida, 'The Right to Philosophy from a Cosmopolitan Point of View', p. 341.
26. Derrida and Stiegler, *Echographies of Television*, p. 16.
27. Derrida, *Writing and Difference*, p. 32.
28. Levinas, *Totality and Infinity*, p. 27.
29. Ibid. p. 40.

30. Badiou, *Ethics*, p. 16.
31. Hughes, 'Riven'.
32. Badiou, *Ethics*, p. 2.
33. Ibid. pp. 12–13.
34. Levinas, *Totality and Infinity*, p. 215.
35. Eagleton, *Trouble with Strangers*, p. 235.
36. Ibid. pp. 257–8.
37. Badiou, *Ethics*, pp. 22–3.
38. Arguably, Badiou's own rejection of Levinas/Levinasianism is strategic and polemical, and in part not least because of his need to assert his own thinking of 'infinity' against that of Levinas and in the context of the 'success' of Levinas's ethics. It is curious that Badiou and Levinas stand alongside one another in contemporary French thought in their respective 'Platonisms' and their assignment of a key role in their respective philosophies to the notion of infinity: Levinas revives and puts to use the Platonic notion of the 'Good beyond being' as one of those rare instances when philosophy has been interrupted by the thought of something which is unthinkable, and seeks to found ethics as 'first philosophy' upon it; Badiou takes from Plato the idea of the infinite and seeks to understand ontology from a purely mathematical perspective. Badiou expresses a Nietzschean 'contempt' for 'man' whilst Levinas retains the idea of the 'humanism of the other man'. Yet when recalling what Levinas says about love, Badiou takes the trouble to note that 'a Levinas (*un Levinas*), in the guise of the dual talk on the Other and its Face and on Woman' might serve as 'the valet' of his own idea of at least one of his four 'conditions' of what I have spoken of in this chapter in terms of 'philosophical propriety'. (See Badiou, *Manifesto*, p. 67; Hughes, 'Riven'.) In Chapter 7 I will examine in detail the proximity between Nietzsche and Levinas on the ethical significance of love, contempt and suffering.

2. Empiricism, the Ethical Subject and the Ethics of Hospitality

Whilst there is evident potential in Levinas's philosophy for theorising the passage from ethics to politics in the quest to secure an *ethico-political* rather than a purely political sublation of the theory/praxis dichotomy, there are also various stumbling blocks that immediately come to mind. It is problematic in the philosophically technical sense described by Badiou, as noted in the previous chapter. He argues that the ethico-political cannot be deduced from an ethics of alterity at all as 'the other always resembles me too much'. But Levinas's political discourse is problematic (at least for many of his readers) in more straightforward ways: for instance, Simon Critchley[1] and Tina Chanter[2] have both argued that his politics are, overall, worryingly conservative, especially in relation to the family, in relation to gender and sexual difference.[3] And Howard Caygill[4] has presented a sharp critique of the complexity of Levinas's relationship to 'Israel' (that is both sacred Israel, and the militarised state of Israel) thereby highlighting the essential shortcomings of what might be described as the growing body of Levinas criticism which all too simply attempts to appropriate from his philosophy a blithe 'angelicism' vis-à-vis the alterity of the Other. I will return to comment on Caygill's position at the end of this chapter, but before I do, I shall establish the key features of my own reading of Levinas's account of the ethical Subject, as I believe it will offer a new perspective on all of these issues.

In order to show how Levinas's thinking of ethical subjectivity ultimately serves the project of reversing an always violent and conflictual 'politics of recognition' into the 'ethics of hospitality' and 'welcome', I first want to consider the role of Hegel in his philosophy. In principle these are ostensibly scholarly matters open to critical dispute, but at the same time attention is inevitably directed towards the disjuncture, and perhaps irreconcilability, of such theoretical concerns in general with what *immediately* interrupts them, according to Levinas, in the form of a call to responsibility at an empirical, everyday, or non-philosophical, level with respect to suffering in the world. That thought is immediately interrupted by the everyday call or demand of the Other takes us to the heart of the Levinasian idea that ethical theory is already a response of sorts to the urgency of the ethical demand which impresses itself upon us, or, as Levinas would say, on *the Same*.

Of course, the non-philosophical is frequently made a theme for philosophy, but, by definition, it marks the limit of its prerogative: ethics, unlike the science of ontology, is the immediate concern of everyone, at least to the extent to which, as this is said in common parlance, everyone has a conscience, and is aware of the necessary limitations of his or her own knowledge. Ethics is the concern of everyone who has a sense of injustice – in other words, everyone who is troubled 'in' him- or herself and experiences a degree of subjective ethical uncertainty. What may be *represented* in this way as a question of *my knowledge*, Levinas insists, however, must be acknowledged, or recognised, to be a disturbance in or of *oneself*, and thus as having its origin elsewhere, and prior to cognition or knowledge. Ethical demand is something which cuts through and surprises philosophical consciousness: it is 'refractory to our cognitive powers'.[5] For Levinas this is the irreducible sign of my responsibility as something uninvited and not freely chosen by me.

In reality, one could surely argue, political decisions, choices, perspectives concerned with suffering are arrived at or acted upon at the point at which 'time runs out' and the time for any further prevarication as to the meaning of such disturbance passes. But that is not to say that in every moment ethical doubt does not return to disturb such decisions. Does that mean that it is ultimately impossible for ethics and politics to coincide and to be consistent with one another? Or does it imply, perhaps, that the most just politics is always the most rational (and hence the most defensible) politics; which, though falling short of absolute justice and the ethical, is, nonetheless, the best possible in any given circumstance? Is it ever enough to be able to reasonably claim that a politics is *aimed* at justice? And, can we in any case know the answers even to such questions as these, when it is precisely justice which is contested in every instance of politics?

Levinas appears to tell us that *time taken to think* is the moment in which justice passes by – in the specific sense that responsibility is not a matter of calculation and representation (rather than because one prevaricates or freezes, say, out of personal fear in the face of danger). Ethical responsibility in Levinas's sense is always 'mine', moreover, 'mine now'. It is not something subject to ratification by committee or

Party, nor is it in any sense a collective responsibility. It is, therefore, not political *as such*, at least not in these ordinary senses; as far as ethical responsibility is concerned, there is no hiding place for 'me' in the politics of the 'we'. This is the charge that Levinas directs at the Hegelian System.

THE ETHICS AND POLITICS OF RECOGNITION: LEVINAS'S HEGEL

The Hegelian 'we', of the *Phenomenology of Spirit*, which ulti-mately attains 'pure self-recognition in absolute otherness' (*reine Selbstanerkennung im absolutem Anderssein*)[6] according to Levinas, is a recognition which rests on the reduction of the absolute otherness of the Other to the Same. He understands the Hegelian thinking of recog-nition to effectively conceive of the Other as an enemy.[7] The absolute knowing of Hegelian Spirit (or totality) is countered by Levinas with the radically unknowable alterity of the Other (or infinity). Levinasian ethics of hospitality might thus be described as being anti the Hegelian ethico-politics of recognition. As Robert Bernasconi has noted:

> The severity of Levinas's treatment of Hegel is notorious . . . According to Levinas, Hegel is one of the leading representatives of the philosophical tra-dition which has effaced the ethical face of the Other by insisting on the pri-ority of ontology . . . Hegel is cast as a spokesman [he adds, citing *Totality and Infinity*] of the 'ancient privilege of unity', the 'all embracing totality'.[8]

The point I wish to make here does not require the reconstruction of the detail of Bernasconi's argument, which is concerned with establishing, and on Levinasian grounds, a more favourable, a more conciliatory and less antagonistic reading of Hegel. I do wish briefly to recall, however, the *form* of that argument as a prelude to what I shall go on to say about the relationship between recognition and hospitality from the perspective of Levinas's account of ethical subjectivity.

Bernasconi presents a Levinasian reading of Hegel which is at vari-ance with Levinas's own most explicit reading of Hegel, as evidenced in several of his texts. He begins by characterising the Levinasian way of reading the history of philosophy in terms of his 'procedure of showing the infinite within the finite' – as exemplified, for instance, in his readings of Plato and Descartes. He then sets out to demonstrate through a reading of key sections of Hegel's *Phenomenology of Spirit*, how and where the 'interruption' of Hegelian totality by *a form of transcendence which is surplus to it*, occurs within the Hegelian text itself: 'The interruption arises as a *surplus* over what dominates, but the surplus is awoken within what is interrupted rather than brought from the outside. It appears as an ambiguity which cannot be controlled.'[9] Following Derrida's critique of Levinas's Hegel in *Violence and Metaphysics*,[10] Bernasconi endorses and expands upon the observation that there must be more to Levinas's relation to Hegel than simple opposition, for to be opposed to Hegel is to already submit to capture by the Hegelian System. Levinas's refutation in *Totality and Infinity* of the Hegelian 'struggle for recognition' culminating in the reciprocal mutuality of the 'we', on the basis of his account of the Face and the ethical relation, Bernasconi argues, must be retraceable within the Hegelian System itself. And the Levinasian strategy he deploys in order to do this, involves the identification in Hegel's text of what Levinas refers to as the '*surplus always exterior to the totality*'.[11] We can understand this, in the first instance, as what is surplus to Hegel's 'meaning' or 'intention' (in the ordinary sense of what he says without knowing he says it). But it is surplus also, and more importantly, in that it exceeds the totalising force of the System itself. In other words, in order to (possibly) confirm Levinas in his reading of Hegel, one must be prepared to concede that the Levinasian metaphysical premise of the irreducible overflowing of the 'infinite within the finite' (to which we are directed in so many elements of his thought, not only in his readings of Descartes and Plato) is at work in Hegel's System too.

In a rather christianising reading of Levinas (or, perhaps, just as much, a judaicising reading of Hegel), Bernasconi goes on to locate the decisive interruption of totality in Hegel's account of the phenomenon of forgiveness (*Verzeihung*): it is the *saying* of forgiveness which comes through in Hegel's *Phenomenology*; or, in Levinasian terms, forgiveness in Hegel's text is claimed to instantiate a *saying* irreducible to a *said*. Bernasconi goes on to seal his argument with a comparison of Hegel's understanding of forgiveness and Levinas's thinking of 'pardon'. For each of them, forgiveness and pardon are, respectively, associated with the annulment and reversal of time; moreover,

> just as *pardon* is in Levinas an early name for *interruption*, so in Hegel the word *forgiveness* names the time of interruption itself [that is, of the process of recognition]. It is thus a saying which says its own saying.[12]

It is along these lines, and by way of return to Hegel via Levinas, then, that we may come to see that Levinas's 'anti-Hegelianism' needs to be supplemented by a Levinasian rereading of Hegel, such that the eruption of transcendence (here identified with the 'saying of forgiveness *without* a said') within the immanent structure of Hegel's system of thought, is exposed.

What is at stake, then, as Bernasconi shows, is how the difference between Hegel and Levinas is a matter of the difference between the recognition of me *by* the Other and my recognition *of* the Other.[13] If this latter formulation gestures, and clearly so, towards a more Levinasian notion of recognition, and this is to be ethically privileged, then what I want to suggest and emphasise here is that we must also note that the retention and privileging of cognition in the term 're*cognition*' is precisely what maintains the threat of the reduction of the Other to the Same; moreover, at the very point where the difference between these two forms of recognition is understood, or, in other words, is *recognised by me*. As I have indicated, according to Bernasconi, forgiveness interrupts and forestalls the tendency of such a recognition *of* the Other to collapse (back) into the demand of the Same *for* recognition by the Other, and he credits Levinas throughout with a profound 'procedure of thought' which reveals both the ethical significance of that movement and the constant threat, or danger, of such a recuperation to which the ethical is exposed. It is the necessity of this recuperation, I suggest, which equates to the necessity of politics, and yet it also marks the absolute incompatibility (the impossible coincidence) of the political and the ethical.

SEPARATION AND IMMANENCE: LEVINAS'S EMPIRICISM OF THE ETHICAL SUBJECT

There are several reasons why I preface the argument of this chapter with this brief discussion of the complex rather than simply antithetical relationship between Levinas's ethical metaphysics of transcendence and Hegel's ethico-politics of recognition. Firstly, it serves to highlight the limitations of applying conventional critical protocols to Levinas's thought which are aimed at either confirming or denying, say, his notion of transcendence (or infinity) and the absolute alterity of the Other, without acknowledging that these are articulated by him on the basis of their paradoxical manifestation within the finitude of immanential totality. Secondly, it also allows me, whilst recalling the fundamentally Levinasian 'procedure of thought' of showing the infinite within the finite, to propose the exploration another dimension – heavily scare-quoted though I have now explained it must be – of 'Levinas's anti-Hegelianism'.

If, as Derrida has remarked, Levinas 'bequeaths to us an immense treatise on hospitality',[14] one which at its heart demands a rethinking of the relationship between ethics and politics, then I suggest this must be understood in relation to his account of what one might refer to as the *ethical capacity* of the Subject, and the conditionality this ultimately provides for an ethical politics. Ethical subjectivity, as indicated in the previous chapter, is not an add-on to the life of the Subject; it is already the existential condition for the unconditional openness to the Other the Levinasian treatise on hospitality expresses. And it is with regard to his account of the substantivity of the ethical Subject, I propose Levinas's ethics can perhaps best be understood as a form of 'ethical realism', or even, in a way that I shall clarify, 'ethical empiricism'.[15] To explain and justify such a reading I want first to consider his account of the immanence of the ethical Subject, which he discusses in terms of its 'separation' and its 'materiality'. Levinas's account of the existential condition of the ethical relation expressed in terms of the 'separation' of the 'I' and its materiality rarely receives the kind of philosophical scrutiny as do his claims for transcendence. One consequence of this neglect is the conclusion that the appeal to empiricism in his work operates unphilosophically at the level of pathos and sentiment. This belies, I shall now argue, a failure to grasp the significance of the radicalisation of empiricism to be found in his thinking.

LEVINAS AND DELEUZE CONTRA HEGEL

To develop this theme further, I want to explore some affinities between Levinas's thought and that of another famously anti-Hegelian thinker, Gilles Deleuze. I do this, ultimately, in order to explain how what Bernasconi refers to as 'recognition *of* the Other' (as distinguished from the Hegelian struggle for 'recognition *by* the Other') is as rooted in the empirico-existential condition of the ethical Subject as it is in the transcendence, or alterity, of the Other. Separation in Levinas's discourse figures in two registers at once: it both refers to the relation to the absolute Other and serves as the name for the existential condition of this relation; that is, of the Subject's (the existent's) relation to being (existence), such that 'the idea of Infinity requires this separation' in both senses.[16] Separation is both the *condition* for transcendence and the accomplishment (*accomplissement*) of the substantivity of the existent. It is the significance of this latter – and in several senses earlier – moment of separation, which had already been established in *Existence and Existents*[17] that I shall turn to now, and by way of a discussion of some affinities between Levinas and Deleuze and their respective empiricisms.

The conjunction of Levinas and Deleuze may seem an unlikely one to pursue at all, given that the antithesis between transcendence and immanence as fundamental principles of philosophical thought would appear to be the simplest way to characterise the difference between their understandings of the ethical. For Levinas it is only on the basis of the transcendence of the Other that I discover the nature of (and the possibility of acting in accordance with) my infinite responsibility. From a Deleuzian perspective such transcendence – and its attendant humanism – must be viewed, rather, as a figure of ethico-political impotence as a consequence of the essential *im*possibility transcendence implies and such a notion of responsibility requires. For Deleuze ethics *is* ontology, moreover political ontology, whereas Levinas locates ethics 'beyond Being' and, therefore, the scope of any ontology. If one had to choose just two philosophers whose names alone might recall the two divergent trajectories within recent European philosophy in terms of a commitment to a principle of either transcendence or immanence, then these would surely be theirs. It is commonplace to trace the genealogy of Levinas's (along with Derrida's) thought back through Husserl to Kant, and to identify connections between Deleuze's thought and that of Nietzsche and Spinoza. Of course, all three of Levinas, Derrida and Deleuze are thinkers of difference *in some sense*; Deleuze being, perhaps, the thinker of the *processes* of differentiation par excellence, and it is worth recording at this point Deleuze's late characterisation of the 'modern moment' as one in which 'we are no longer satisfied with thinking immanence as immanent to a transcendent; *we want to think transcendence within the immanent, and it is from immanence that a breach is expected.*'[18]

Putting their obvious differences to one side, what I wish to recall and emphasise, is the manner in which for both Levinas and Deleuze the radical separation of the Subject (or 'individuation', in Deleuze's terminology) goes hand in hand with a rejection of Hegelian recognition. Like Levinas, Deleuze sees the fault in Hegel in terms of his account of recognition. I acknowledge that this may seem a rather shaky basis on which to suggest some kind of affinity between his thought and that of Levinas: after all, Deleuze's rejection of Hegel's philosophy of recognition has an entirely different emphasis and tone to it; it is based on his essentially Nietzschean claim that the desire for recognition is inherently servile. He says, for instance: 'What the wills in Hegel want is to have their power recognized . . . This is the slave's conception, it is the image that the man of *ressentiment* has of power.'[19] There is, moreover, a certain *identification* with the power of the master in Deleuze's philosophy: an apparent inversion of what Levinas describes in his various descriptions of the relation to 'the master', for instance in the figure of a *teaching* which comes to me from 'on-high'. However, Levinas, like Deleuze, breaks with dialectic in his understanding of this figure of the relationship to alterity:

> The relation with the other – the absolute other – who has no frontier with the same is not exposed to the allergy that afflicts the same in a totality, upon which Hegelian dialectic rests. The other is not for reason a scandal which launches it into dialectical movement, but the first rational teaching, the condition for all teaching.[20]

For both Deleuze and Levinas, it can be said, Hegelian dialectic reduces what is Other (or different) to the Same; and for both of them the negation of the Other has its counterpart in the imposition of a conventional, codified morality which must be refused absolutely.[21]

RADICAL EMPIRICISM: BETWEEN IMMANENCE AND TRANSCENDENCE

Both Levinas and Deleuze must, nonetheless, each establish the basis for a certain *sovereignty of the Subject*. And I force this seemingly unlikely conjunction between them at this point because it can help us to productively think *the relationship between the formation of the ethical Subject and the contexts of real experience*. (Just what is meant by 'real experience' here, I shall turn to shortly.) The philosophical good reasons for paying attention to their respective ways of thinking difference, *in-between* transcendence and immanence, are to do with the fact that neither Levinas nor Deleuze simply thinks through the antithetical opposition of the two terms; certainly not as this dyad is deployed in much of the history of philosophy. It is certainly not the case either that the differences between these foundational principles of thought, as they are often considered to be, should be subsumed under the wider historically divergent tendencies conventionally gathered under the headings of 'idealism' and 'empiricism'. But in the ways in which both Levinas and Deleuze quite literally *begin to philosophise* and to philosophically address the matter of the relationship of interiority and exteriority as an aspect of their thinking of ethics and the ethical, they might both be usefully described, I contend, as 'radical empiricists'. This is clearly and more explicitly the case with Deleuze, as he adopts the mantle of a certain empiricism from his earliest work onwards (for instance, in *Empiricism and Subjectivity*) – albeit, and I shall come back to this, what he calls *'transcendental* empiricism'. The title of 'radical empiricist' is perhaps less obviously warranted in the case of Levinas – save for the fact that his discourse of the 'infinite within the finite' is articulated around the manifestation, or 'epiphany' of absolute alterity in the face of the other human being.[22]

I stress, I am *not* at all suggesting here that 'Levinas's empiricism' is marked by a slippage towards the 'natural attitude' in the form of a psychologism of interpersonal relations; a naturalism of being moved by the 'outstretched hand', 'the giving of the bread from one's own mouth', and so forth (though, where that kind of reading has been made, and that criticism ensued, one might well concede that Levinas's own prose is at least partly to blame). What I want to do, rather, is to follow through on an often-noted, but not entirely developed comment made by Derrida about Levinas's empiricism:

> By making the origin of language, meaning and difference the relation to the infinitely other, Levinas is resigned to betraying his own intentions in his philosophical discourse. The latter is understood, and instructs, only by first permitting the same and Being to circulate within it . . . [T]he true name of this inclination of thought to the Other, of this resigned acceptance of incoherent coherence inspired by a truth more profound that the 'logic' of philosophical discourse, the true name of this renunciation of the concept, of the *a prioris* and transcendental horizons of language, is *empiricism*.[23]

At the root of *all* empiricisms, Derrida continues, is 'the dream of a purely heterological thought. A *pure* thought of *pure* difference.' It is a dream, he says, because 'it must vanish . . . as soon as language awakens'. One limit of alterity implicit to Levinas's philosophy of the absolute Other, according to Derrida, then, is his empiricism of the 'real experience' of the absolutely Other qua other person: it attempts to lay claim to the impossible; namely, a relation entered into *before language*. Earlier in this essay Derrida already stresses, and with reference to Hegel, that 'empiricism always forgets, at very least, that it employs the words *to be*'; that it is a 'thinking *by* metaphor without thinking the metaphor *as such*'.[24]

With characteristic deconstructive ambivalence, Derrida presents this philosophical gesture of Levinas as both a blindspot with an extensive 'historical precedent' in philosophy and as a signature of Levinas's own radicalism:

> By radicalizing the theme of the infinite exteriority of the other, Levinas thereby assumes the aim which has more or less secretly animated *all* the philosophical gestures which have been called empiricisms in the history of philosophy. He does so with an audacity, a profundity and a resoluteness never before attained. By taking this project to its end, he totally renews empiricism, and inverses it by revealing it to itself as metaphysics.[25]

The empiricism which Levinas is here said to radicalise, is what one might call 'ordinary empiricism'; the empiricism founded by observation and a theory of self-evidence. As Alliez and Bonne define it, this is the empiricism which 'consists in relying on the supposed experience of a sensible truth that can be grasped by a common sense called "representation"'.[26] Such ordinary empiricism is, of course, a feature of what

Deleuze identifies and criticises as the generic and dominant 'image of thought' that philosophy has historically been preoccupied with, and which is marked by the prioritisation of identity over difference.

For Deleuze, 'real' or 'sensible' experience and 'conceptual thought' or 'reflection' are the products of internal differences within being. Whereas Kantian philosophy claimed to identify the transcendental conditions of 'possible experience', Deleuze reverses this gesture making 'real' or 'empirical experience' the condition for (the becoming of) transcendental thought itself. In other words, Deleuze directs us towards a form of thought; an initial *movement* of thought, whose reality is *not* dependent on its ever being identical to itself: *it is not a moment of thought's self-recognition*. Perhaps this is what Deleuze expresses when he says 'only an empiricist could say: concepts are indeed things, but things in their free and wild state, beyond "anthropological predicates"'.[27] To be 'beyond predication' is effectively equivalent to being outside of language. The very suggestion of such a zone of being is, according to Derrida, as he explains with respect to the same gesture found in Levinas, 'the philosophical pretension to non-philosophy'; and it is characterised by 'the inability to justify oneself, to come to one's own aid as speech'.[28]

THE MATERIALITY OF THE ETHICAL SUBJECT

Now, this 'inability to come to one's own aid of speech', I suggest, can be referred to Levinas's radical empiricism, in several ways. Firstly, there is the perspective Derrida himself focuses on: it is the empiricism which audaciously insists on the heterological alterity of Other (or infinity) which is outside or beyond language. But whereas Derrida's questioning of this gesture in Levinas is framed by the observation that it appears *despite* the Husserlian and Heideggerian stages of his thought, what this detracts from is Levinas's equally significant indebtedness to and critical distancing from Bergson; especially his use of Bergson contra Husserl and Heidegger in his early work, particularly *Existence and Existents*. In that text, the discussions of effort, fatigue, work, indolence, sleep and insomnia, together serve to articulate the notion of an *event* said to be prior to any intelligibility and constitutive, moreover, of the 'refusal' of thought per se.[29] He speaks there of existence as an *event* which 'is not a cognition'. And of his method, he says: 'a philosopher has to put himself in the instant of fatigue and discover the way it comes about. Not its significance with respect to a system of references.'[30] This is not the place to restage the demonstration this text as a whole presents with regard to the relationship between the existent and existence, but it should be noted that this quite clearly challenges Heidegger's thinking of the ontological difference, and it does so whilst borrowing from Heidegger in order to articulate the need for a radical break with eidetic phenomenology's understanding of intentionality altogether. Levinas embarks on a kind of reverse-engineering of the phenomenology of intentionality. And whilst this unfolds, as it logically must, by way of a certain metaphoricity and language within which, as Derrida says, 'being already circulates', Levinas's quasi-phenomenological studies of various moments in the material life of the Subject, I suggest more positively, grapple with the processual dynamic of differentiation internal to being, as did Bergson before him and as Deleuze has since.

When Levinas speaks of the material life of the existent and its relation to existence he explicitly makes it clear that this 'is a notion of materiality which no longer has anything in common with matter as opposed to thought and mind' – the kind which 'fed classical materialism'.[31] Instead of viewing this appeal to materiality negatively as the 'philosophical pretension to non-philosophy', we must look instead beyond that classical distinction itself and to what it points to, namely, the materiality from which philosophy itself *lives*. We should focus on *how* Levinas's discourse in *Existence and Existents* (and since) theoretically engages with a principle of immanence. His image, in that text, of the philosopher 'placing himself in the instant', is, to be sure, a transcendent image of thought thus represented, but it is also (and 'before' that) a *practical experiment*, one which Deleuze could recognise, moreover, as essential and necessary. As John Marks comments on Deleuze's empiricism: 'The true empiricist experiments rather than interpreting, and is concerned with signs, which are not objects of recognition, and can only be sensed or felt.'[32] For Levinas the existent does not *undergo* modification, it *is* a modification of existence; it is lived in the duality of the existent's trajectory of 'upsurge and fatigue'[33] – a 'folding back'[34] of existence; a differential movement immanent to being which 'is in a certain sense a substance'.[35] Life itself is thus understood by Levinas as a form of *experimentation with existence* rather than made the *object of a methodological decision*. Note the striking proximity between Levinas and Deleuze on this point: far from being objects of recognition, such movements are understood by both of them as the modalities of the Subject's becoming. Or, to put this in the idiom of *Totality and Infinity*: the pure signifyingness (*significance*) of a sign without a signification is not *reduced* to a signification *in me*, but it nonetheless makes an impression in me; it is neither known by me nor is it an object of knowledge for me, rather it moves, it disturbs, or 'awakens' me. This is the movement which is constitutive of ethical subjectivity, for Levinas: it is 'I' who bear the imprint of the Other-in-me. The later discourse of 'absolute passivity' deployed in *Otherwise than Being* clearly aims to give this idea a fuller expression, for instance here in terms of an 'undergoing beyond the capacity to undergo':

> An anarchic liberation, it emerges, without being assumed, without turning into a beginning, in inequality with oneself. It is brought out without being assumed, in the undergoing by sensibility beyond its capacity to undergo. This describes the suffering and vulnerability of the sensible as *the other in me*. The other is in me and in the midst of my very identification.[36]

HOSPITALITY AS THE REVERSAL OF INTENTIONALITY

If the very modality of the Subject is to be thought of as ethicality itself; as the instantiation of 'hospitable receptivity' to such an 'impression' of the Other in the Same, then, as Derrida has argued, this has to be thought of as the Levinasian *revision* of the philosophy of intentionality.[37] This implies that Levinas's empiricism and his de-thematising reversal of intentionality are presented as the obverse and reverse of each other. I shall just recall in outline how this claim works.

Whilst in Husserl, for example, the thetic and non-thetic moments of consciousness are theoretically distinguishable, they are nonetheless considered to be, in reality, ontologically identical. Eidetic phenomenology thus assumes *what* it subjects to analysis, whereas, what Levinas is pointing to here, as he notes, 'eludes descriptive phenomenology' and calls for a method 'such that thought is invited to go beyond intuition'.[38] Both Levinas and Deleuze, I have shown so far in this chapter, aim lower than intuition: they identify what Alliez and Bonne refer to as the 'lowest materialism of sensation' (rather than the immediate experience accessed by phenomenology).[39] The Levinasian existent is discovered as an eruption of sensation and a process of ongoing struggle to attain a state of individuated separateness which it can, however, *neither of itself secure nor abdicate from*: it is a process suspended, as Levinas puts it, between 'the insecurity of the morrow' and 'the horror of the night'; suspended in the 'insomnia' which is an 'anonymous vigilance'.[40] Such sensation, which is not-yet-thought, and, therefore, even less-yet the content of any thought, is, in Levinas, the irreducible or, to use his word, 'irremissible' movement of the 'there is' (*il y a*). This is, in other words, a key empirical discovery of Levinas's materialist phenomenology, and it is the result of a methodology which is comparable (in the manner I have described) to Deleuze's understanding of the empirical as he expresses this; for instance, in *Empiricism and Subjectivity*, when he says: 'the critique is empirical when, having *situated ourselves* in a purely immanent point of view . . . we ask how is the subject constituted in the given'.[41] The difference between Levinas and Deleuze, and the divergence of their respective notions of ethics would, of course, have to be traced beyond this moment of their methodological conjuncture: firstly, in terms of Levinas's understanding of how the thinking of the Subject must go beyond the question of 'how the subject is constituted' to the question of 'what it is to exist',[42] but also, secondly, in terms of how this 'existence/existent' (and this phenomenology) is ultimately conditioned by the alterity of what is beyond being altogether. However, what this conjunction of their two empiricisms makes clear, is the weight that is borne in Levinas's ethical philosophy by the notion of *separation* and the significance of its double reference to the becoming of the Subject and to the ethical relation between the Subject and the absolutely Other. Hence the Levinasian Subject can be 'properly' claimed, at least within his own rigorous philosophical investigation of it, as an existence in the mode of becoming-ethical. Without (its) separation there can be neither transcendence, nor an ethical relation; but without separation there is no immanence of the Subject either. Levinas thus makes the substantive accomplishment of *singular*, or what he calls 'solitudinous', existence the irreducible condition of entry into the ethical relation:

> The breach of the totality that is accomplished by the enjoyment of solitude – or the solitude of enjoyment – is radical. When the critical presence of the Other will call in question this egoism it will not destroy its solitude . . . The solitude of the subject will be recognised also in the goodness in which the apology issues.[43]

The 'of' in the expression 'recognition *of* the Other', it can now be seen, is a double genitive. It expresses, on the one hand, a form of recognition from the point of view of the Same: in recognising the other-in-me, I recognise the Other is for me unknowable, unthinkable qua Other. On the other hand, if I speculate as to the perspective of the Other – something strictly impossible-for-me – then I find myself, to use Levinas's word, 'commanded' by the Other; I experience ethical demand. In reality, that is to say, from my own perspective, these 'two' perspectives are experienced as one: I find myself, to use another Levinasian term, 'elected' to a responsibility I was never free to offer myself for. (It is precisely this moment which escaped Hegel.) Such responsibility does not come *with* freedom, but *before* it. What Bernasconi refers to as 'recognition' in the expression 'recognition *of* the Other' is not the product of a system of reciprocal negation, but the

meaning of the impression of the Other in me. I use the empiricist terminology of 'impression' here not merely to stress the non-negational
character of this event, but precisely to name its radical empiricality.

Perhaps it is better to avoid the trope of visibility altogether and say
I encounter the Other 'affectively' as the impression of the Other-in-me
at an empirico-affective level. As noted in the previous chapter, from his
earliest work onwards Levinas expressly aims to counter what he calls
the 'neutralisation of life' in philosophy and rejects the way in which
the doxic thesis is integral to intentionality as it is understood by eidetic
phenomenology. It may well appear to offer a new beginning and starting point for philosophy, even one which is aimed at the concreteness
of experience of life, but it no longer *lives* it.[44] 'What counts', as Levinas
writes much later in the Preface to *Totality and Infinity*, 'is the idea of
the overflowing of objectifying thought by a forgotten experience from
which it lives',[45] and what I am proposing here is that his *empiricism
of the substantive Subject* (or 'existent') – just as much as his insistence
on transcendence and absolute otherness – has to be referred to this key
notion of overflowing, or 'surplus'.

The rethinking of intentionality in Levinas is a radicalisation of
empiricism which methodologically takes the form of a 'pre-intentional',
quasi-phenomenology of the substantive Subject. It reverses the cog-
nitional, or thematising, intentionality *into* hospitality. Without an
account of the separation of the Subject in terms of the struggle and
effort of the Subject to exist, the separation which is necessary to the
ethical relation would indeed remain essentially mystical in its assertion
– as Badiou (falsely in my view) supposes. My point all along here is
that the role of empiricism in Levinas's project is poorly described if it
is seen only in terms of a 'pretention to non-philosophy' inadequately
cognisant of the 'limit' imposed by language. The Levinasian reversion
of that 'totality' – of signification into signifyingness, of the Said into
Saying, to cite just two of his formulations for this – does not distil the
empirical reality of sensate life of the substantive Subject from its representation in philosophy, as if to arrive at its pure being. It begins with it.
What it reveals, in the final analysis, is a life already contaminated in its
being – and inexplicably so, from the point of view of philosophy – by
the idea of the infinite/beyond being, which 'comes to me' – and to 'me'
alone (or uniquely) in the moment of an empirical encounter with the
Other.

HOSPITALITY AND THE FRAGILITY OF THE ETHICAL

I am going to move to conclude this chapter now by briefly reflecting on the possible consequences of thinking responsibility and hospitality in terms of the thesis of Levinas's radical empiricism of the ethical Subject and by posing the following question: if the ethical relation is to be understood, indeed can only be experienced in the final analysis, as the violent imprimatur of the other-in-me, how does this bode 'in reality' for the prospect of a truly ethical 'politics of response'?

In his *Levinas and the Political* Howard Caygill calls for a reconsideration of Levinas's ethical thought in full view of his 'personal proximity to the fault lines' of the twentieth century's political history and with an eye on Levinas's *explicitly* political writings and his responses to political events.[46] Caygill begins by recalling his *own* reaction (one might say expressing his own sense of the 'ethical urgency' I suggested above we all 'start out from') to something Levinas once said in a radio broadcast in 1982,[47] which took place shortly after the massacres in the Chatila and Sabra camps in Israeli-occupied Lebanon. In his opinion, in the discussion 'Levinas revealed a coolness of political judgement that verged on the chilling and unsentimental understanding of violence and power almost worthy of Machiavelli.'[48] Caygill says he was particularly shocked to hear Levinas say that 'in alterity we can find an enemy'.[49] This leads him to then suggest that Levinas's account of the relation between the ethics and politics of suffering should be read in a new light:

> Reading Levinas's texts within the horizon of political horror requires the reversal of many of the interpretive protocols that are associated with his work. Instead of extending what might be imagined to be a secured understanding of the ethical into the political, *the ethical emerges as a fragile response to political horror*.[50]

That Levinas's (personal) politics with regard to Israel are ambiguous – being tied up as they are with his notion of 'sacred history', and equally with the historical specificity of what it is to be Jewish after the Holocaust – is in many ways, surely, to be anticipated. Not simply because, as we say, 'everyone is human' and has their own unique personal history of pain, suffering and loss, but because any *personal* politics is by its nature a matter of the response to a suffering which is always doubly 'my own'– both a matter of my own pain and the matter of my suffering *for* the suffering of the Other.[51] This doubleness of my suffering (of my own suffering and the suffering of the Other-in-me) I want to suggest, signifies the chiasmus of the ethical and the political *in me*. It causes me to reflect on the question of to what extent I am the other's Other – a thought always accompanied by uncertainty; and by a moment of recognition, which, as discussed above, occurs *within the Same*.

I shall not attempt here to go into the details of the interpretation of particular events and the sufferings of other individuals and peoples in those events (for that would be an entirely new theme). I only wish to reflect finally on whether Levinas's ethics could ever rightly be expected to extend to the realm of politics, or whether it anticipates such an extension as ultimately being impossible, or, at the very least, always prone to failure. One route to an answer to this problematic would be to think through the role of the third party (*le tiers*), especially as this is presented in *Totality and Infinity*: the third party 'who always looks at me in the eyes of the other';[52] that is, by considering Levinas's claims that politics and sociality are already included within the ethical relation. But instead of taking that route here, and against the background of the account of Levinas's radical empiricism provided, I suggest turning instead to the account of the ambiguity of 'my' vulnerability and exposure to the Other articulated in *Otherwise than Being*.

In *Otherwise the Being*, partly in response to the reading that *Totality and Infinity* was given by Derrida, and its questioning of the place of empiricism in his ethical philosophy, Levinas does not step back from empiricism but, rather, deepens and extends its role. This is to be traced especially in the entire discourse of 'the skin', sensation and sensibility in the later work, where the existent is now discussed in terms of its being a 'being-in-a-skin' and the relation to alterity in terms of 'being-in-one's-skin, having-the-other-in-one's-skin'.[53] (This will be contextualised and discussed further in Chapters 3–5.) The skin, it could be claimed, is the very organ of sensation and the empirical. And Levinas reiterates (as if in response to Derrida's critique of his empiricism) that the reference to the skin is not a metaphor.[54] It is rather to be understood as a 'modality of the subjective'.[55] In *Otherwise than Being* sensation is described as the couplet of the sensing and the sensed – which must be subject to a further reduction in order to arrive at 'sensibility'. The point of this insistence on sensibility, says Levinas, is to expose how the possibility of ethics and justice originates with the '*diachrony* of the same and the other *in sensibility*'.[56] The openness of this possibility is dependent upon the 'modification of sensibility into intentionality'.[57] It is this 'modification', characteristic of traditional phenomenology, which Levinas aims to reverse by means of a further reduction, namely, the 'ethical reduction', and it is by way of this that intentionality is rendered into hospitality.[58]

Needless to say, such a philosophical project of ethical metaphysics cannot guarantee such a 'reversal' at the level of the 'empirically real': at the level of political exigency, the volatility and contingency of the passage from ethics to politics cannot be escaped. Despite the traditional identification of Levinasian ethical philosophy with the absolute alterity of the Other/the other person, he or she is, and on Levinas's account, just as much a being-in-a-skin as I am and hence suffers the 'wound' of alterity. Violence, in Levinas's ethical discourse, is an ever present possibility; it is, moreover, the hitherside of my passivity. Pain thus places the sufferer in a situation where 'it could go either way':

> [My] exposure to the other is at one and the same time the surface of all possible 'contact' and the exposedness to injury, wounding and violence – and physical pain itself. As a passivity, in the paining of the pain felt, sensibility is [also] a vulnerability.[59]

And just as I cannot know from the perspective of Other, who I am 'for him' or 'for her' (to what extent I am for him or her 'wholly Other'), so too I do not know how I will react, given my own vulnerability, nor, for the same reason, do I know how he or she will relate to me. It must not be forgotten that Levinasian ethical metaphysics, and on the basis of its own deepest self-understanding, is an articulation of a relationship to the Other necessarily undertaken from within the Same – no matter how forcefully it proposes de-thematisation, openness to alterity, or practises 'infinition', or stylistically performs an 'apophansis'.

In writing against what he sees as the 'growing body of sentimental commentary' on Levinas that is inclined to forget this, Caygill addresses Levinas's political statements relating to Israel and the history of Israel, but these he finds are conflated with the sacred history of Israel, or rather, messianic Israel. On this theme Caygill cites *Difficult Freedom*, including the following:

> [The] suffering [of Israel] is the condition for deliverance ... [R]edemption will follow a suffering that cannot be repented because Israel was the victim of evil. This position ... is here qualified on the grounds that it 'reeks of Christianity' ... it is [rather] through suffering that freedom may be aroused.[60]

and he comments, 'this rehearses the argument of *Totality and Infinity* that the political ontology of war underlies morality and cannot responsibly be avoided. From suffering [it would appear] we are delivered to politics.'[61] If beyond suffering we are 'delivered to politics', then are we not, indeed, caught up in a *tragic* circuit of suffering – in a movement of repetition? Does the fragility of the ethical and the necessity of politics mean that we are, after all, duped by morality – the very question

Totality and Infinity set out to address (and the conclusion it aimed to redress)? Caygill takes Levinas to task over his attempts at squaring his justification of politics (which is necessarily violent and warlike – if not the outbreak of war itself) with his ethics of alterity on the ground that it amounts to a theory of the 'just war'. But the notion of the just war, I suggest, is *the always questionable* provision of an alibi for the unquestionable suffering war unleashes.

My argument in this chapter has served primarily to show that such a 'reversal' of ethics into politics perhaps amounts not to a reversal as such, but rather indicates how the problem of the ethical is that at any given point – in view, as it were, of any particular suffering – a *decision* is, and must be, made. And in this respect, Levinas provides us with a profound sense of the difficulty of our *position* on suffering: the 'decision' always puts us back in the position where it can, ethically speaking, go the wrong way. Levinas's radical empiricism of the ethical Subject does not pretend to underwrite the political: just because ethical obligation can be expressed philosophically, does not mean its political realisation is ever secured. The suffering of the Other-in-me, similarly may well provoke hostility rather than hospitality, and the call to responsibility for the Other so often identified with Levinas's name, he already teaches us may fall on my deaf ears.

If this fragility of the ethical is to be understood as a function of the contingent totality of any given situation, characterised by a multitude of cultural parameters shaping local normativities, then we can begin to see how situatedness is connected to the ethical possibility of the Subject: its responsibility is inescapable, but its 'goodness' is never guaranteed. In the following chapters I shall consider how this general condition of the Subject is approachable only at the scene, so to speak, of the folding of exteriority/interiority in response to the provocation of the Other. I shall do this by tracing this process in a series of contexts which are as much defined by the theorisation of the Subject as they are by the thematic context itself.

NOTES

1. Critchley, 'Five Problems in Levinas's View of Politics'.
2. Chanter, 'Hands that Give and Hands that Take'.
3. See my discussion of Irigaray's engagement with Levinas in the following chapter.
4. Caygill, *Levinas and the Political*.
5. Critchley, *Infinitely Demanding*, p. 57.
6. Hegel, *Phenomenology of Spirit*, Section 26.

7. Levinas, 'Trace of the Other'. In this essay Levinas aligns Hegel with Hobbes in expounding a philosophy which makes of the Other an enemy.

8. Bernasconi, 'Hegel and Levinas', p. 49 (citing Levinas, *Totality and Infinity*, p. 102).

9. Bernasconi, 'Hegel and Levinas', p. 51.

10. See Derrida, 'Violence and Metaphysics'.

11. Levinas, *Totality and Infinity*, p. 22 (original emphasis).

12. Bernasconi, 'Hegel and Levinas', p. 65 (original emphasis).

13. Ibid. p. 55.

14. Derrida, *Adieu to Emmanuel Levinas*, p. 21.

15. The Levinasian discourse on the 'substantivity' of the existent is appealed to here largely on the basis of the theses presented in *Existent and Existents*. The ethical significance of its hypostasis is, of course, a refrain in Levinas's later writings, where the link between the ethical and the empirical is developed further, especially with reference to the existent as a being-in-a-skin. (I discuss Levinas's discourse of the skin in the coming chapters at length.) In *Otherwise than Being, or, Beyond Essence*, Levinas frequently recalls the connection between the empirical and the ethical. For instance: 'It is by this hypostasis that the person, as an identity unjustifiable by itself and in this sense empirical or contingent, emerges substantively', p. 106.

16. Levinas, *Totality and Infinity*, p. 102.

17. See Levinas, *Existence and Existents*, p. 76. It is through 'effort' that the hypostasis, or 'upsurge' of the existent is accomplished.

18. Deleuze and Guattari, *What Is Philosophy?*, p. 47 (original emphasis).

19. Deleuze, *Nietzsche and Philosophy*, p. 10. For a further brief commentary on this, see Williams, *Hegel's Ethics of Recognition*.

20. Levinas, *Totality and Infinity*, p. 203.

21. On this basis, one could say that Badiou's criticisms of the appeal to the 'ethics of alterity' (discussed in the previous chapter) which comes to be played out in the politics of multiculturalism characteristic of the ethical turn, is in reality more Hegelian than it is Levinasian.

22. It is for this prosaic dimension of his discourse, as much as anything, that Levinas's philosophy has sometimes solicited the accusation of 'collapsing' into empiricism. This suspicion generally revolves around the supposition that his ethics of alterity is presented as directly evidenced by the ordinary experience of the face of the other. However, if such a charge is held to signal the collapse of his thinking into a recognisably *traditional* empiricism because it *equates* the absolute Other with the other person, then clearly the *radicalisation* of empiricism that his thinking represents is missed in the confusion such a weak analysis promotes.

23. Derrida, 'Violence and Metaphysics', p. 151.

24. Ibid. p. 139.

25. Ibid. p. 151.

26. Alliez and Bonne, 'Matisse with Dewey and Deleuze', p. 1.

27. Deleuze, *Difference and Repetition*, pp. xx–xxi.

28. Derrida, 'Violence and Metaphysics', p. 152.
29. Levinas, *Existence and Existents*, pp. 22–5.
30. Ibid. p. 30.
31. Ibid. p. 57.
32. Marks, *Gilles Deleuze*, p. 83.
33. Levinas, *Existence and Existents*, p. 31.
34. Ibid. p. 81.
35. Ibid. p. 81.
36. Levinas, *Otherwise than Being, or, Beyond Essence*, pp. 124–5.
37. Derrida, *Adieu to Emmanuel Levinas*, pp. 45ff.
38. Levinas, *Existence and Existents*, p. 66.
39. Alliez and Bonne, 'Matisse with Dewey and Deleuze', p. 3.
40. Levinas, *Existence and Existents*, p. 66.
41. Deleuze, *Empiricism and Subjectivity*, p. 87 (emphasis added).
42. Levinas, *Existence and Existents*, p. 100.
43. Levinas, *Totality and Infinity*, p. 119.
44. Levinas, *Theory of Intuition*, p. 155.
45. Levinas, *Totality and Infinity*, p. 28.
46. Caygill, *Levinas and the Political*, p. 2.
47. The radio broadcast in question took place on 26 September 1982, a few days after the massacre of several hundred people in the Sabra and Chatila refugee camps by Phalangist forces operating with the tacit support of the Israeli Defence Force. Levinas and Alain Finkielkraut were invited by Radio Communauté to discuss the theme of 'Israel and Jewish ethics'. The transcript of the discussion was originally published in *Les Nouveaux Cahiers*, 18:7 (1982–3), 1–8.
48. Caygill, *Levinas and the Political*, p. 1.
49. Ibid. p. 2.
50. Ibid. p. 2 (emphasis added).
51. See Levinas, 'Useless Suffering'. The theme of suffering is returned to in Chapter 9.
52. Levinas, *Totality and Infinity*, p. 188.
53. Levinas, *Otherwise than Being, or, Beyond Essence*, p. 115. The Levinasian discourse of the skin and its role in articulating the idea of ethical sensibility will be discussed further in relation to the themes of touch, vulnerability and mediated communications in Chapters 3, 4 and 5.
54. Levinas, *Otherwise than Being, or, Beyond Essence*, p. 109.
55. Ibid. p. 26.
56. Ibid. p. 71 (emphasis added).
57. Ibid. p. 71.
58. See Derrida, *Adieu to Emmanuel Levinas*, pp. 50ff.
59. Levinas, *Otherwise than Being, or, Beyond Essence*, p. 55.
60. Levinas, *Difficult Freedom*, p. 70, cited in Caygill, *Levinas and the Political*, p. 168.
61. Caygill, *Levinas and the Political*, p. 168.

3. Sexing the Ethical Subject

Chapter 1 argued that the ethical theory is always read off of 'the surfaces of culture' and that the ethical Subject as some*thing* or some*one* emerges out of a specific cultural situation. Chapter 2 showed, with reference to Levinas's and Deleuze's thinking of the Subject as becoming, how in Levinas this becoming is, on the one hand, grounded in the foothold the Subject has in being and, on the other, how it can be said to be an *ethical* Subject in so far as this movement of ex-istence is already an 'awakening' to the 'other-in-me': the Other is already 'in the midst of my very identification'.[1] Another way of putting this would be to say that the ethical demand of the Other as my responsibility precedes *my* existence; it calls 'me' into existence. This may be contrary to the logic by which the Subject must precede the ascription of its predicate, but rather than thinking of responsibility as something which is 'experienced' as such, Levinas proposes that it is a force at work 'before' the precipitation of the Subject qua Subject from existence in general. However, at the end of Chapter 2 I sought to indicate also, with reference to Caygill's reflections on Levinasian politics, how the condition of 'ethics preceding ontology' did not guarantee the passage of the ethical into the political. In this chapter I shall address further the theme of how the ethical is read off of the surfaces of culture and yet there is no guarantee that the ethical will come to pass such that the ethico-political will prevail.

ETHICS AND SEXUAL DIFFERENCE

Why might ethical demand 'fall on deaf ears'? 'Deaf ears' is a figure of speech, of course – though, then again, perhaps not entirely. If these were real ears we were talking about, we would want to be clear whether or not they were unable to hear or just 'not listening'.

And, would it make any difference whose ears they were, for instance whether they were those of a man or a woman?

According to Luce Irigaray, the ethical has to be rethought on the basis of the materiality of sexual difference – those ears, it should not be forgotten, always belong to a sexuate body.[2] Both drawing on and polemicising against Heidegger, Irigaray argues that it is the question of sexual difference rather than the question of Being which has fallen decisively into oblivion in our epoch.[3] Thinking the ethical requires the restitution of the question of sexual difference to avoid the fateful repetition of the same:

> If we keep on speaking the same language together, we're going to reproduce the same history. Begin the same old stories all over again. Don't you think so? Listen: all around us men and women sound just the same. The same discussions, the same arguments, the same scenes. The same attractions and separations. The same difficulties, the same impossibility of making connections. The same . . . Same . . . Always the same.[4]

In this chapter I shall explore how Irigaray recasts the question of the 'post-deconstructive' ethical Subject in terms of sexual difference, paying particular attention to the way in which the surfaces of culture must be understood to be synecdochally interrelated and continuous with the surfaces of the body. One of Irigaray's key strategies for countering the erasure of sexual difference in the tradition of Western thought is to develop a discourse of the body as sexuate, and to focus on those bodily-cultural surfaces which, in her theoretical discourse, serve as the basis for a new discourse of the body-culture relation as sexuate from the first. The encounter with the Other is thought and theorised by her on the basis of the body-culture double.

Irigaray's philosophy, her own corpus, is already, by this logic, therefore, an exemplar of sexuate cultural theorising. She engages in a style of philosophising that forestalls immediate, reductive recuperation by the masculine theoretical framework and forces her reader to engage with this feminine body (of thought) and its 'sexed discourse'. The presumption of conventional theorising to be objective and 'neutral', which, as noted earlier, Levinas also rejects, is not only false, but in fact constitutes an instance of the masculinist neutralisation of the singularity of the feminine. To redress and to resist such phallogocentric theory, Irigaray writes in a way that forces a response which is inescapably related to the materiality of embodiment. Before any account or *representation of the meaning* of her work, the body-against-body (*corps-à-corps*) structure of communication, *morphologically* determines my responsiveness to those parts which touch the reader according to his or her sex.[5] Coming into contact, touched by her corpus, 'I' (the reader) am called to sensuality specific to my sex; and disarmingly denuded of the masculine-neutral conceptuality with which I think.[6] However, (in my own case at least) my sex (*sexe*) – which also means in French, my penis – represents the limit of communication between the sexes because 'all Western discourse presents a certain isomorphism with the masculine sex: the privilege of unity, the form of the self, of the visible and the specularisable, of the erection'[7] and because 'there's been no detumescence ever'.[8] Contrary to the 'unity' and 'visibility' characteristic of the male-sex-centred theorisation of the Subject, Irigaray develops her discourse on the basis of the non-specularisable sense of touch and the de-centred, multiform character of the female sex:

> [W]oman has sex organs more or less everywhere. She finds pleasure almost anywhere ... the geography of her pleasure is far more diversified, more multiple in its differences, more complex, more subtle, than is commonly imagined – in an imaginary rather too narrowly focused on sameness. 'She' is indefinitely other in herself ... Hers are contradictory words, somewhat mad from the standpoint of reason ... For in what she says too, at least when she dares, woman is constantly touching herself ... One would have to listen with another ear ... [9]

Irigaray's distinctive discourse of female sexual 'identity' has to be listened to with 'another ear', but it must also be borne in mind that the ear itself is already sexed; it is formed by a fold of the same fleshy body whose other folds elsewhere define its sexed identity. Irigaray views language as mediated by the body and her writing attempts to occupy the space between the literal and the figurative. For instance, when she deploys the figure of the Lips (*les lèvres*),[10] both speech/speaking and language are invoked in the same moment as the specificity of the female sex organs. Woman is already 'two', defined by an internal difference, hence capable of experiencing her own identification without waiting to be identified by a schema of representation, visibility and unity. This labial feminism, as I shall call it, is thus, ostensibly a feminism of 'women amongst themselves' in which, in her writing against the grain of Western metaphysics, the morphology of the Lips (that is, the female sex) is employed to reconfigure the feminine by displacing the phallus in the symbolic order of language. By incorporating the bodily into her discourse, beginning as it were from the body's irreducibly sexed morphology, Irigaray produces a species of *écriture feminine* which is able to give expression to the process of female identification. Such a withdrawal from conventional masculinist metaphorics is clearly not something every*body* can relate to *equally*, as it demands precisely, a sexed response. In this chapter my engagement with the Irigarayian corpus aims to evaluate it significance for the sexing of the ethical Subject.

The challenge which Irigaray's thought presents to the masculinism she identifies with reason and its style of theorising, calls for the recovery of sexual difference from within the tradition of sexual *in*difference founded on the supposed neutrality of the masculine perspective. Recalling Heidegger's idea of every epoch having just one issue to think through, the thinking of sexual difference, she suggests, could be 'our salvation': 'our only chance today lies in a cultural and political ethics based upon sexual difference'.[11] Thinking sexual difference is the key, she says, to the inauguration of a 'new age of thought, art, poetry and language: the creation of a new poetics'[12] of life, our relation to the earth and technology; it would be the basis for a new epoch in which phallocracy would be disarmed and, as Alice Jardine puts it, the 'masculine libidinal economy of our metaphysical inheritance'[13] could be transformed.

IRIGARAY'S LABIAL FEMINISM

The project of a discourse of the sexed Subject to counter the masculine-neutral, however, does not signal a breaking off of relations with men. By insisting on sexual difference as being borne by the body/language, and that this can only be approached on the basis of a 'poetics' (rather than 'theory' – which is by its nature masculine-neutral), her discourse is able to work at articulating female identity without simply reversing the traditional sexual hierarchy and without asserting a female totality. Such a totality would be one to which would-be feminist men could only respond by attempting to scale the walls into the lesbian camp.[14] On the one hand, it is true, the female homo-erotics of sexual identification are the basis for a hetero-topic articulation of female *sameness*, something from which men are logically excluded; female sameness is, so to speak, (at least) 'two', whereas male sameness is 'one'. The philosophical task is not to 'resolve' sexual difference dialectically, nor is it to simply demand 'recognition' (of the Hegelian kind discussed in the previous chapter). In this respect Irigaray's thinking of woman as already differing within herself – already touching herself – echoes the way in which for Levinas my experience of the Other is always in the form of the 'other-in-me'. (I will discuss her relationship to Levinas later.) On the other hand, it is the *sameness of the female sex* which she attempts to secure as the condition for a peaceful rather than violent encounter between the sexes; a relationship between the sexes which would break with the phallocentric representation of the feminine on the basis of the masculine-neutral.

The ambiguity of women *corps-à-corps* with men in this

dephallocratising enterprise, I suggest, can be located somewhere between these two remarks:

> Men are always plunging deeper and deeper into exploitation and plunder – without understanding very well why . . . I believe that the race of men needs the help of persons whose function would be to promote self-understanding among men and to set limits. *Only women could fill this function.*[15]

> What I am waiting to see is what men will do and say if their sexuality releases its hold on the empire of phallocratism. *But this is not for a woman to anticipate, foresee or prescribe . . .*[16]

Whilst this labial feminism aims to make possible an encounter between men and women which is not determined by phallocratic control, this is neither to be decided by this feminism, nor exclusively by women as a sex. It is not for women alone to accomplish 'cultural detumescence', but for men, too, to discover processes of identification which will lead to the withdrawal of the cultural phallus. This is not to suggest that such male identification must be reactive or imitative of styles of identification which are employed within feminism more broadly in its attempts to think feminine identity today. But it is to say that what is called for is a new kind of *responding* to the Other; a 'listening'. Listening is a trope and form of sensuality that expresses passivity in comparison to traditional ocularcentrism. Any idea of a 'new masculinity', it can be anticipated, therefore, will require a careful dismantling of the patriarchal totality so invested in specular representation and visibility as the basis of its self-understanding. But no matter how feminist men (themselves) might wish to be, their participation in feminism on any level is fraught with complexity and ambiguity. Feminists are wary of male 'entryism' into feminism, and Irigaray reminds us of the structural tendency of the masculine perspective to operate on the basis of a representational logic which, despite any good intentions, will always hide as it reveals and crush as it moves. She says: 'In public, it is true, man only wants to wage war on his own gender: the other war is meant to remain hidden, secret as if it had been resolved in absolute knowledge and spirit. Which is not true.'[17] This remark cautions against open displays of philosophical (self-)criticism of patriarchy and phallocracy by men, as they are likely to be masculinist anti-heroics in a phony war. A phony war amongst men carried on by them with the aim of 'getting back in with women', but which amounts to little more than a new form of seduction.

Of course, this is not only a philosophical or theoretical matter, it is reflected across the landscape of popular culture everywhere one sees certain cultural norms that reflect the achievements of feminism as they are currently institutionalised – for example, in 'equal rights' and 'hate crime' legislation, social and political measures to protect women against domestic violence and sex-trafficking, and so forth – alongside others which are not perceived to contradict them, such as the ongoing normalisation of other elements of the sex industry in which women's (as well as men's) bodies continue to be commodified. The invisibility of the contradiction goes hand in hand with the view that the sovereignty of the Subject (male or female) is ultimately a matter of freely given consent. It seems, therefore, that neither can any putative new masculinism, whatever its form, simply reassert male identity accommodating the cultural advances of feminism, nor can men become women: men are thus left with the alternatives, both of which are reactive, of either 'getting in touch with their feminine side' and becoming 'more like women', or antagonistically reacting against the very suggestion that this is what they need to do. Any discourse of new masculinity, therefore, faces a kind of double-bind: it is bound, as any discourse is, to the patriarchal metaphysics of identity, but unlike feminism cannot utilise, in the same way, the kind of deconstructive and strategic reversal of hierarchies that feminism has, to a degree at least, successfully exploited. It can, therefore, appear both consistent and unproblematic (to women as much as to men) that feminism has won its cultural battles against patriarchy and that the phenomenon of the post-feminist social and political order, now adequately reflects 'what women really want'.

Feminism could be viewed as having had a strategic advantage which is logically denied to any post-feminist masculinism in that it was able to take the critique of patriarchal totality as it starting point, and it has thus been able to pose the question of feminine subjectivity and *the feminine* in terms of a 'recovery' from its conceptual oblivion and against the background of the social and political structures of women's subalternisation associated with that. Because of the history of patriarchal culture and phallogocentrism of language, any new masculinism cannot adopt a comparable strategy for rethinking masculine subjectivity without the risk of repeating the exclusion of the (female) other. In other words, the reversal of conceptual hierarchies which is the characteristic 'first stage' of deconstruction cannot be employed to equal effect in the rethinking of the masculine. So is it, perhaps, now untimely for men to insist on their identity as such at all? This is not to say that we (men, perhaps in particular) cannot nor should not continue to rethink the ethics and politics of masculine identity through a reconsideration of men's identificatory practices, but it is to say that the deconstructive strategy of placing, in this instance, phallogocentrism under erasure (*sous-rature*) is *itself* a sexuate discursive gesture; a crossing out which is also the *signature* of a sexuate being. The 'sex' of who or what does the crossing out is precisely what cannot itself be erased. Another way of putting this would be to say that every text or system of thought, as much as every hand which authors it and signs it, must be acknowledged as sexuate.

THE SUBJECT, THE BODY AND 'MORPHOLOGY'

Body against body (*corps-à-corps*); my reading/her corpus: Irigaray suggests that the morphological specificities of the embodied Subject are materially determinative of every encounter, of any body with any other body. In order to gain a better sense of the role of body morphology in Irigaray's thinking of sexual difference, it helps to consider the indebtedness of her thinking of the body to both Nietzsche and Freud. If Freud provides the foil for her articulation of the female body's morphological specificity, Nietzsche's account of the body could be said to provide the impetus for its dynamics. Nietzsche offers a critique of philosophy's forgetfulness of the body and proposes that all of thought is in fact 'an interpretation of the body and a *misunderstanding of the body*'.[18] He also gives an account of how the body is born, or rather, borne along, by language, in metaphor and is understood as the source or origin of metaphoricity itself. As Eric Blondel comments, for Nietzsche the body is the scene of the non-unifiable plurality of drives, instincts and organs;[19] the body is 'an underworld of serviceable organs', 'a thousand-fold process'.[20] All of reality for humans is a particular movement of instincts, a chaos which becomes a world only through the body and its interpretation. Nietzsche goes so far as to declare that 'Our most sacred convictions, the unchanging elements in our supreme values, are judgments of our muscles.'[21] The body is precipitated out of the will-to-power and acts as the contingent and ever changing principle of the world's unification, which is only ever provisional. Nietzsche's thinking of the body opposes the thinking of identity which is central to modern metaphysics: his 'images of physiology provide not a foundation for materialism, but a metaphysics of the will-to-power as interpretation'. And he adds, quoting Nietzsche, 'we must not ask: "*Who* is interpreting?"'[22]

From Irigaray's perspective, Nietzsche's thinking of the body in terms of plurality may work effectively at undoing the masculinist, or phallocentric, preoccupation with identity on the basis of unity, but in refusing the 'who' entirely it fails to interpret the specificity of the difference between male and female bodies; it neglects the fact that *the who may be a she* – and it cannot consequently lay claim to the very difference out of which the body, male or female, originates, to the organ of origination, namely, the womb. Sexual identity for Nietzsche is configured in the interpretation (of interpretations) and this interminable metaphoricity governing interpretation is irreducible – it cannot be thought on the basis of a *referential* model of language. Despite Nietzsche's overcoming of the metaphysical distinction between thought and the body, or language and materiality, it nonetheless gives rise to an exclusively masculinist concept of the Subject. It does so, principally, because it neglects the relation of instincts and sensations to sexed organ(ic) differences. Consequently, sexual difference escapes it altogether. In Irigaray's terms, the Nietzschean reversal of metaphysics misses the sexuate specificity of the forces in play which can *only* be articulated on the grounds of the morphology of bodily differences. Most importantly, it cannot gain access to the difference by which *the feminine differs within itself* – as Irigaray, for instance, articulates by appealing to the Lips, but also in respect of *maternity*. She effectively thinks the feminine is the process *differing itself*. As such, the feminine is disruptive of masculinist metaphysics. Like Nietzsche, Irigaray gives priority to the body, but unlike Nietzsche she stresses the morphological difference of male and female bodies; the asymmetry of male and female. For example, she considers the significance of the fact that all bodies, male or female, originally come out of female bodies, but that only female bodies can be said to come out of themselves and therefore have a relation to their sameness through the process of internal differentiation – the bifurcation which occurs with the birth of the child. This everyday miracle is both celebrated and interpreted in Irigaray's prose. Childbirth is both phenomenon and metaphor: Irigaray thinks of it as an *event* prior to the metaphysical distinction between language and material reality. Childbirth subverts the metaphysical law of identity and draws a line under the infinite regression of the 'which came first, the mother-chicken or the egg' quest for origins, at the heart of traditional metaphysics.

The (female) body has what could be described as a culturally specific 'narrative identity', but one which is inscribed on what might be described as its 'morphological facticity'. This 'bodymorph' is the unthought, but nonetheless sexuate, condition of the Subject; it is not reducible, as some of her critics have supposed, to a natural (biological) essence.[23] It is not to be equated either with an impersonal Foucauldian 'discursive formation', or the cultural apparatus as a whole (*dispositif*) out of which the Subject is precipitated. However, when Deleuze says that the 'ethical subject' in Foucault is produced by a 'folding' of thought, it is possible to discern proximity between Irigaray and Foucault. Deleuze's commentary is that the fold of thought is a form of 'auto-affection' in which 'the problematical unthought gives way to a thinking being who problematises himself, *as an ethical subject*'.[24] Irigaray's focus is on the problem of the limits imposed on a folding of thought which might produce female subjectivity otherwise than in the form which results from its being violently cast in a masculine mould. The 'problematical unthought', the feminine substance as it were, she insists to the contrary, is already sexuate. And the Deleuzian 'line of flight' which thinks the Subject as 'a singular complexity, one that enacts and actualises a radical ethics of transformation',[25] Irigaray would equally see as a Nietzschean gesture common to both Foucault and Deleuze, and one which further obscures the question of sexual difference. For instance, when Foucault famously states that 'it does not matter who is speaking'[26] and refuses the question of his own identity,[27] then he is, in effect, refusing to acknowledge the necessarily sexuate origin of thought per se.

THE BODY AND LANGUAGE

Irigaray's sexed discourse plays on the contiguity of the body and language: the sexuate body is, ambiguously, both the object of interpretation and the Subject which does the interpreting, and any interpretation of the body emanates from its contours and surfaces. By approaching the body morphologically, in this way, her discourse aims to redress the disembodied universalist perspective, which views men and women as the same and as belonging to the same 'humanity'. And, because the dominant culture springs from the male body's surfaces, the female body will always be viewed and judged on the basis of its fit, or lack of fit, as projected onto the male 'bodymorph'. The male bodymorph is a cultural surface which is incapable of reflecting female specificity truthfully, and the female sex thus serves to limit the traditional masculinist *mimesis* of sexual difference; it disturbs and disrupts this supposed universalism. It is Irigaray's general contention that no discourse which operates in this manner will be able to articulate the nature of woman's sexuate specificity, her body's pleasure (*jouissance*), her suffering and her desire; such things will be forced to find expression within the masculinist symbolic order. This is, incidentally, at the heart of Irigaray's approach to traditional feminisms of equality which she does not so much oppose, as seek to illustrate the limitations of. Her approach to the body *as* discourse, does not allow that its sex can be either willed or constructed without reference to its actual corporeal morphology. The body is neither a passive, neutral receptor of discursive, cultural sex-projections as the rhetoric of socialisation argues, nor is it simply founded on the physiologico-anatomical body of positive science. The body in Irigaray is both lived *and* its materiality is given to it by language: *it is both flesh and word*. Three brief citations from different places in her corpus can be assembled into a short syllogism expressing succinctly her sustained argument concerning Woman, Man, body and language:

> Language [*langage*], however formal it may be, feeds on blood, on flesh, on material elements . . .[28]

and

> Man, who . . . has a monopoly on the symbolic, has given no thought to his body or his flesh[29]

therefore

> [w]e need to discover a language [*langage*] that is not a substitute for the experience of *corps-à-corps* as paternal language [*langue*] seeks to be, but which accompanies that bodily experience, words which do not erase the body, but which speak the body.[30]

Her attempt to 'speak the body' articulates the body's sexuate being in terms of its 'organs' and the sensuality of the 'forgotten senses' of touch and hearing, all of which, she argues, are overshadowed in the traditional phallo-ocularcentric discourse which denies women the means of a primary metaphorisation of their bodies.[31] Her discourse interprets the anatomical body whilst weaving in phenomenological aspects of the lived body to produce what could be described as a metaphorised lived-anatomy of female sexuality.[32] The poetic style of her discourse, which she describes as a 'double style: a style of loving relationships (and) a style of thought, exegesis and writing',[33] aims at speaking what Lacan termed 'the *jouissance* beyond the phallus', but which he also, in the very same breath, relegated to the mystical and unknowable.[34]

As we have just noted, Freudian psychoanalysis, in interpreting female sexuality exclusively in terms of its deficiency in relation to male sexuality, betrays an inability to break with the masculine-neutral. The presence and visibility of the penis, despite the penis not being the phallus, as Lacan stresses, symbolises unity and the law of identity, and in the symbolic order of discourse this governs, figuratively, the order of things and knowledge. To resist the phallocentric conceptual framework within which traditional representations of the feminine are articulated in terms of absence and lack, Irigaray brings to bear a metaphorics of the female body which refuses phallic representation by way of a discursive reappropriation of various female 'body parts'. These include, for example, the clitoris, the vagina, the neck of the uterus, the mucous membranes, the labia minora/majora, as well as the breasts, womb and female body fluids such as the milk, amniotic fluids and the blood. The female genitalia, apart from being hidden, are also plural rather than unitary. In particular, Irigaray focuses, as has already been noted, on the figuration (and configuration) of the Lips – or rather two sets of Lips: those of both the mouth and the vagina. These are syn-ecdochally and catachrestically related to one another.[35] Both sets are lubricated by the mucous, making them the condition of both love and language. Perhaps most relevant to Irigaray's account of how the Lips figure in female identification is her account of how they are constantly touching one another. The auto-affection which they instantiate sym-bolises the relation of the female body to itself, wholly independently and invisible to the male gaze and its phallomorphic representational schemas:

> woman's auto-eroticism is very different from man's. In order to touch himself, man needs an instrument: his hand, a woman's body, language . . . And this self-caressing requires at least a minimum of activity . . . woman touches herself without any need of mediation, and before there is any way to distinguish activity from passivity. Woman 'touches herself' all the time, and moreover, no one can forbid her to do so, for her genitals are formed of two Lips in continuous contact. Thus, within herself, she is already two – but not divisible into one(s) that caress each other.[36]

A key role of the Lips in Irigaray's account is their figuring of the female sexuate relation to self. That which differs within itself requires no withdrawal from its corporeality in order to establish a relation to itself. It does not need to seek itself outside itself. The Lips reciprocally caress one another and are in contact before reflection distinguishes between the active and the passive. This is not (I am assured) in any literal sense a phenomenological observation: it is, rather, a descrip-tion which refuses any transcendental perspective in favour of the *non-difference of meaning and the body*. This metaphorisation of the female sex in terms of morphological auto-affection is discursively and stylistically presented by way of *poetic insistence*, aimed at the trans-figuration of the female body. And it includes many other female body parts, too, in an assemblage able to resist the masculinist centralisation of the female sex on any one thing. For example, it is the placenta which is 'the first house to surround us', the belly and breasts which give life 'without any reciprocity', and the navel which is the most 'elemental tag of identity'.[37] Elsewhere equal weight is given to the womb, which is, of course, a contested site of interpretation in psychoanalysis, and in the rewriting of psychoanalysis Irigaray's entire *oeuvre* is associated with. The womb is the site of the 'unformed "amorphous" origin of all morphology'[38] in which the morphological bifurcation by which one becomes two in pregnancy takes place. The womb to men, on the other hand, is said to be fantasised as

> a devouring mouth, a sewer in which anal or urethral waste is poured, as a threat to the phallus or, at best, a reproductive organ . . . And the womb is mistaken for all the female sexual organs since no valid representations of female sexuality exist.[39]

Because of Irigaray's style and because of my earlier expressed reservations concerning the violence of representation per se, it would be pointless to attempt to represent something which can only be represented by forcing it to appear as *a system* of parts. Systematic specular theorising might thus be considered, somewhat paralogically, as dismemberment, as a disinterrance of the organs – which is indeed, according to Irigaray, a model for how men see women. The male Subject attempts to understand the whole woman by cutting her up into constituent parts. 'She', on the other hand,

> does not set herself up as one, as a (single) female unit. She is not closed up or around one single truth or essence. The essence of a truth remains foreign to her . . . she does not oppose a feminine truth to a masculine truth . . . Because this would once again amount to playing the – man's – game of castration . . . the female sex takes place by embracing itself, by endlessly sharing and exchanging its Lips, its edges, its borders . . .[40]

Irigaray's 'thesis' of the female Subject is not, however, articulated *polemically*; we find instead a questioning which is a counter-provocation aimed at the withdrawal of the phallus; at driving the phallus to its ruin.[41] After all, Irigaray asks, as if her poetic language were an everyday idiom that enabled one to be matter-of-fact about such things, 'Why is setting oneself up as a solid more worthwhile than flowing as a liquid from between the two Lips?'[42]

This discourse of 'body-writing' which can only be read off the body itself, read off its most intimate surfaces and interiors, makes it impossible for the reader to disregard the morphological specificity of his or her own sex. As Elizabeth Grosz says, in her own analysis of lesbian desire, 'If we are looking at intensities and surfaces rather than latencies and depth . . . [t]heir effects rather than intentions occupy our focus, for what they make and do rather than what they mean and represent.'[43] As the sexed bodymorph is not a neutral surface onto which any-sex-whatever could be projected, the corollary of this is that reading-off-the-body is not characterised as passive reception of a pre-existing semiotic or signifying body. In fact the whole notion of neutrality implicit to theories of socially constructed gender, which appeal to a radical distinction between gender and sex, would ultimately signify, on this model, the determination of sexual difference by the masculine-neutral. This is, according to Irigaray, Freud's greatest error. Her account performatively attempts a reversal: sexual difference *emanates* from the intimate surfaces of the body whose morphological specificities are what they are neither before nor after their expression in discourse. They are, rather, to be traced in the lived narrative of sex and sexuate sensuality. This philosophical corpus thus attempts to heed 'our sexuate relationship with language' itself,[44] and it appeals to the notion of the *sensible transcendental* as a kind of origin of sexuate discourse, in which the opposition between immanence and transcendence is confounded.[45] Irigaray thus conceives of the body on the basis of an inverted Kantianism: it is neither empirical nor ideal, this Kantian distinction itself being an expression of the masculine-neutral. She alternatively thinks the female body beyond its thematisation in terms of what Foucault once called the 'empirical-transcendental doublet'.[46] Rather as for Foucault, according to Irigaray, this doublet signifies a cision in thinking which has given rise to the troubled modernity in which we live. So long as the cision imposes itself on thought, continuing to define the epistemology of our natural attitude (and with it a naturalistic understanding of sexual difference), no thought nor 'any imaginary or symbolic of the flesh' is possible.[47] Rethinking sexuate embodiment thus involves offering discursive opposition to the masculine-neutral and its rocky solidity centring our thinking with a fluid *poiesis* of the 'maternal-feminine' which washes around it, eroding and dissolving its pride of place. The maternal-feminine is given expression through Irigaray's inimitable combination of textual erotics coupled with critical exegesis. It is essentially a style of thinking and philosophising which flattens the hierarchy between language and things. Hence the sexuate 'bodymorph' which supports it is not, as some of her critics who accuse her of essentialism have said, just another name for the objective, anatomical female body, but rather a thinking of the body as a corporeal-discursive 'reality'. As Diane Elam has argued: there is no escape from anatomy for feminism, but this is not because of the irreducibility of the natural but, on the contrary, because our understanding of human anatomical nature is just as constructed as any other discourse and it cannot function as an origin.[48]

IRIGARAY *CORPS-À-CORPS* WITH LEVINAS

Whilst in Irigaray's view Levinas fails to think the relationship between sexual difference and the origin of the ethical, and his philosophy ultimately fails to break with the masculine-neutral, she nonetheless draws directly on his philosophy in order to develop her own account of how sensate life at the level of touch, contact and Eros constitutes the materiality of the ethical relation to the Other. As made clear in the previous section, Irigaray does not specularise the female Subject as 'a whole'; she writes instead a kind of materialist phenomenology of bodily sensations emanating from an array of body parts: organs, membranes fluids and so forth. Consistent with this, her encounter with Levinas's thinking is selective in terms of the specific points of contact it makes with his corpus.

What might be described as her most 'intimate' engagement with Levinas, takes place, principally, in two essays, 'The Fecundity of the Caress'[49] and the later 'Questions to Emmanuel Levinas: On the Divinity of Love'.[50] The first essay is a commentary on the 'Phenomenology of Eros' chapter of Levinas's *Totality and Infinity*, in which she considers the significance of touch within Eros for the articulation of an ethical relation to alterity; a relation in which neither the one nor the other is subjected, across (their) difference, to subalternisation. She is concerned to describe how the ethical emerges out of the threshold (*seuil*) of contact between one and the other, and how the experience and thought of each is immanently related to the specificity of their sexuate incarnation. She adopts a critical tactic which allows her to articulate the contactual possibilities of a 'flesh' whose becoming-word (in being thematised) reverts at every instant back into the unthought sensuality out of which it emerges. 'Touching' can be properly attributed to such a 'textual contact' in so far as this is a touching in which the distinction between word and thing, or language and experience, has not yet been made. This might also be described, I suggest, as a 'readerly embrace' as opposed to a critique, which would involve the violence of representation: it is an encounter in which the irreducibility of sexual difference comes to the fore and demands a sexed response.

The point of contact between them is precisely where Levinas's text itself deals with the phenomenological experience of the threshold of erotic contact, in general, as this becomes discernible as such, *in the withdrawal* from the one-on-one, fleshy encounter between two lovers engaged in the erotic caress. In his meditation on the caress, in the chapter in question, Levinas speaks of the 'voluptuosity' of touching skins as a form in which the 'I' is prone to lose itself in the indulgence of the carnal embrace. And it is his insistent characterisation of the withdrawal from Eros as marking the *failure* of ethical transcendence, that Irigaray identifies as a certain sex-blindness, or, better to say, from her perspective, a sex-numbness. This is the point where, according to Irigaray, Levinas's account misses the morphology of sexual difference as this figures in erotic contact, with the result that he neither accounts for this difference within the sexual contact of touching bodies, nor addresses the important matter of how touching differs in the cases of male–female, male–male and female–female contacts. Consequently, Levinas also misses the significance of the 'fact' that women are (within their sex) 'constantly touching themselves' – as noted above with reference to the Lips. The significance of morphological sexual difference for Irigaray is that the 'ethics of sexual difference' is always also a matter of the ethics of Eros (quite literally related to the materiality of sensual contact between the two 'lovers'). Erotic contact figures, therefore, not only in what is ordinarily understood by prediscursive sensual interaction between two (individuals), but also at the level of relations between the sexes in society in general. But, to discuss this synecdochal repetition of themes – of what happens between touching bodies in Eros and what happens in society at large – in terms of either structure and logic, or in, say, the phenomenological terminology of 'levels' of experience, would be misleading. Irigaray's discursive-materialist phenomenology of the body-to-body avoids getting caught up in the philosophical issue of transcendentality altogether by bracketing the problem of how sensation becomes language. And there is, consequently, throughout her work a certain calculated philosophical disregard for how the touch across sexual difference ontogenetically configures, or figures in, societal relations.

To get a conceptual grip on how the ethical might be said to have its origin in the touch in-between, or across, sexual difference, in the separation, or interruption, of the touching of touching skins, it is necessary to slip between Levinas and Irigaray, as it were, in order to get a sense of friction arising from their contact. Both traditional phenomenological and discursive-narrative styles of theorising touch could be said to share this non-philosophical origin of the interstitial bodily encounter – their common move is to make this an 'object of inquiry'. Irigaray's 'poetics' deliberately avoids objectifying it.

THE THRESHOLD OF TOUCH, ASYMMETRY AND RECIPROCITY

Irigaray's indebtedness to Levinas is evident in her attempting to philosophise whilst *not* withdrawing from the pre-phenomenological realm of sensation. The 'critical aspect' of her engagement with his thought in 'The Fecundity of the Caress' specifically seeks to identify the ethical significance of sensual contact with the body of the Other. Her critique of Levinas is thus Levinasian to the extent to which, in this amorous intertextual encounter she stages and retains, on the basis of a reanalysis of sensibility, an ethical understanding of the tactility of contact. But she also aims to identify the ethical limitations of the Levinasian account of Eros, which are, according to her, to be traced in Levinas's linking of sensibility and touch with the 'fecundity' of Eros understood in terms of the birth of the *male* child. This masculinist model of fecundity limits Eros as Levinas sees it, to the reproduction of 'myself as the other'. Against this preoccupation of the masculine philosopher with himself – as she later comes to express this in 'Questions' – Irigaray presents her own account of *maternity* as a noninstrumental model of the body-to-body relation between mother and child in *birthing*; birthing is the model of the *feminine* relation to the Other par excellence. This figure of birthing is not, however, restricted to the phenomenon of sexual reproduction. As Cathryn Vasseleu has written, concerning Irigaray's relationship to Levinas: 'Erotic pleasure is an imaginary beginning, a birth after and before the present which will never have taken place.'[51] Irigaray presents, rather, an account of fecundity between lovers in Eros, which does not depend, as it does for Levinas, on its 'offspring' for its ethical significance. She attempts to develop Levinas's ethical thinking by 'sexing' the Levinasian analysis of the erotic caress[52] by thinking the movement of difference 'reverting to sameness' without the reversion, at the same time, to structural forms of reciprocal subalternisation of the beloved (*l'aimée*) and the lover (*l'amant*), and, by extension, of women in their relations to men.[53]

On the basis of this performative, erotico-exegetical contact with Levinas, Irigaray seeks to recover the ethical significance of Eros by means of her own discursive phenomenology of touch *within* the caress, which she understands to be characterised by *absolute passivity*. Touch, at the level of sensation itself, is thus claimed to be already sexuate. Whereas Levinas, as we saw in the previous chapter, traces the emergence of the existent to a moment of *separation* arising out of the internal differentiation within impersonal being (*il y a*), Irigaray directs us instead to the birth of sexual difference in the *separation* of one from the other in the form of the internal bifurcation of the mother/child. She thus argues that sexual difference is the precondition of *separate singular existence* in general. Without sexual difference there could be no separation; without separation there could be no ethical relation. Whereas for Levinas Eros fails to become an ethical relation because within it separation is destroyed, Irigaray proposes that Eros is the condition *for* separation. Like other thinkers of the masculine-neutral, Levinas neglects to think birthing philosophically. Consequently Eros remains for him purely a figure of the unethical; a symbol of how separation is lost in the lovers' erotic caress. Despite this, Irigaray does borrow from Levinas's thinking of sensate life in order to direct her reader to 'the sensual pleasure of birth into a world where the look itself remains tactile' and from there seeks to examine how 'sensual pleasure can reopen and reverse' the 'construction of world'.[54] From a philosophical point of view, this calls for a withdrawal from the given situation of mastery (specifically of patriarchy); a gesture of undoing directed at the masculinist construction of the Subject which brings with it the political subalternisation of woman.

Irigaray has of course written at length and throughout her *oeuvre* about the need for feminism to think in terms of a 'sexed culture'[55] but the crux of her engagement with Levinas is not so much focused on the highly complex level of symbolic exchange and society in general, as on the most simple contact of touching skins and what happens between them. She is focused on what Levinas calls the *signifyingness* of such contact prior to its (discursive) *signification*, or, prior to the (philosophical) decision of its meaning. And it is this chiasmus of the phenomenological and the discursive which Irigaray brings to bear on the thinking of sexuate incarnation:

> On the horizon of a story is found what was in the beginning: this naive or native sense of touch, *in which the subject does not yet exist.* Submerged in pathos or *aisthesis*: astonishment, wonder and sometimes terror before that which surrounds it.[56]

This appeal to a scene of pure sensuality in which 'the Subject does not yet exist', is a situation in which the relation to the Other permits no distinction between environment and (what reflection later comes to regard as) the other person. In this pure sensuality, which is neither 'consciousness of . . .' nor representation, but rather enjoyment (*jouissance*), self and other are not yet born; it is only *on reflection* that the touch of the caress is attributed the meaning of a co-existence and untouched by mastery. There is an Eden-like innocence in the blind gropings of erotically intertwined bodies; unfinished, undefined flesh, in which the distinction between sensual touch and what can be thought by means of the metaphorical displacement of touch has not yet taken place. As Vasseleu expresses this: 'tactility is generic sensibility which constitutes the opposition of interiority and exteriority'.[57] In this touching, the alterity of the Other is neither known nor encountered as such: this is why, for Levinas, it remains a figure of the *non*-ethical.

It is from within this threshold (*seuil*) of the touching between two lovers – rather than between the lover (*l'amant*) and the beloved (*l'aimée*) – that Irigaray refers us to the communal reciprocity (a reciprocity without negation) of the Eros she seeks to 'ethicise'. Where Levinas finds 'profanation' and failure of ethical contact in Eros,[58] Irigaray argues sexual difference is the sensible, material condition for the ethical and that Eros gives the example of how the interstitial contact with the Other across sexual difference instantiates the ethical. She demonstrates how the questions of sexual difference and ethics cross over one another and cannot, therefore, be dealt with separately from one another.

If 'The Fecundity of the Caress' can be seen as an expression of the intimate proximity of Irigaray and Levinas, and at the same time marks a breaking off from it, then we can turn to her later, 'post-erotic' reading of Levinas in order to get a sense of, so to speak, 'how it was for her'. This later text is notably entitled '*Questions* to Emmanuel Levinas', and in it she claims to expose the unquestioned patriarchal basis of his 'theological philosophy'. She accuses him of not holding true to his own phenomenological insights; and that his viewing of the caress as the threat of profanation, claims that 'the function of the other sex as an alterity irreducible to myself eludes [him]'.[59] The consequence of this, in turn, is that it obliterates woman as a desiring Subject *along with* man as Subject.[60]

In reworking the theme of touch across these two texts she performatively restages that moment of 'sexual separation', showing it to be independent and secondary to the auto-erotic movement of the feminine as self-touching. Irigaray's feminine figure of 'labiality' is part of a discursive strategy aimed at establishing the revolutionary potential of thinking sexual difference: it can potentially alter every cultural form, every cultural structure, every institution and every notion of truth. No matter how extensive (masculinist) cultural totalitarianism may be, no matter the extent of its figurative hold on the imagination, it can nonetheless be perpetually disrupted by the simple touch of the Other.

SEXING THE LEVINASIAN ETHICAL SUBJECT

Irigaray's labial feminism engages with the phallogocentric tradition on its own terms. She puts forward not so much 'labia-*centrism*' (or a 'vulvology'– a term suggested by Jane Gallop)[61] – an alternative *logos* of the other sex – as an auto-presentation of (the female) sex in a form which demands a sexed response. It 'feminises' the Levinasian idea of ethical demand expressed by the accusative phrase *me voici* (here I am).

She effectively resounds this in a feminine form, as 'here I (a woman) am'. It is a phrasing of ethical obligation prior to an ontological understanding of the Same/Other distinction. For Irigaray, before 'I' theorise or postulate 'my' sexual identity as such, sexual difference, or to be more precise, my sex, already configures all contact between me and the other (sex). This is reflected in the everyday fact that with regard to the question of sexual difference, the sexed body is determinative of any response between 'us two': sexual difference is thereby claimed to be irreducible. It is not irreducible because the sexed Subject *is* an essence, but because it is irreducible *to* an essence.

Finally in this chapter, I wish to draw some conclusions with regard to the task of rethinking masculinity which is being undertaken from a number of perspectives today. Firstly, I conclude on the basis of my reading of Irigaray that a future thinking of masculine identity, or masculinism, cannot simply affirm an alternative phallomorphism, indeed I have argued that Irigaray does not simply affirm labia-morphism. The furtherance of a generalised 'cultural detumescence' requires more than the retreat into cultural sex-separatism or 'cultural homosexuality'. Such cultural separatism would not necessarily address the issue of men's relation to their mothers, nor for that matter would it address relations between male and female homosexuals. Any cultural renewal of masculinity in the wake of this feminism ought not blindly to assert its identity without addressing how phallomorphism impacts on the feminine. Whilst on one level it is clear that the Lips figure in a comparable manner in Irigaray's vulvomorphic discourse as does the phallus in phallomorphic discourse, it is important to note that just as the penis is not the same as the phallus, the female sex organs are not the same as the Lips. At this point one might care to emphasise that the Lips are *only* a trope. This 'only', however, it should now be clear, equally emphatically does not suggest the secondarity of language in relation to a reality it might be thought to represent. On the contrary, it suggests, rather, that the active creation of our bodily selves in language is neither fixed nor determined by nature conceived as being outside of language. Indeed, this relationship to language which Irigaray's writing exemplifies, is re-creational; it expresses the sexuate body as something more real than the reality of naturalism. One thing we learn from Irigaray is that such naturalism is the product of the masculine-neutral at work, building, moreover, the metaphysical foundations of patriarchy. All sexes are thus called upon to reconfigure their bodies. Only in this way might phallic power be eroded and the 'cultural detumescence' Irigaray speaks of, achieved. Irigaray's 'labial feminism' could therefore be described as articulating a sexuate ethical imperative, yet without the issuance of a directive. It calls for 'new alliance between male and female genders' based otherwise than on dialectical negation and opposition.[62] Rethinking of sexual difference is the key to a non-nihilistic, non-violent ethical future for both women and men.

NOTES

1. Levinas, *Otherwise than Being, or, Beyond Essence*, pp. 124–5, 160.
2. The word 'sexuate' is a neologism coined by Irigaray's English translators for the French term *sexué* (see Whitford, *Irigaray Reader*, p. 18). It is an adjectival form of the term *sexe* which emphasises the substantiality of sex defined in relation to the morphology of the body – which will be discussed later in this chapter.
3. Irigaray, *Speculum of the Other Woman*. See Chanter, *Ethics of Eros*, p. 295 fn.1.
4. Irigaray, *This Sex Which Is Not One*, p. 205.
5. Gillian C. Gill notes in her translation of Irigaray's essay '*Le Corps-à-corps avec la mère*', in Irigaray, *Sexes and Genealogies*, p. 9, the French term *corps-à-corps* has connotations of a hand-to-hand struggle.
6. The 'masculine-neutral' is Irigaray's shorthand for the traditional conceptuality and the symbolic discourse it supports. It associates the transcendental subject position with objectivity and claims this is unable to give expression to the female imaginary. See Irigaray, 'Any Theory of the "Subject"'.
7. Irigaray, 'Women's Exile', p. 64.
8. Irigaray, *Speculum of the Other Woman*, p. 303.
9. Irigaray, *This Sex Which Is Not One*, p. 205.
10. For example, in Irigaray, 'When Our Lips Speak Together', pp. 205–18.
11. Irigaray, *Sexes and Genealogies*, p. 187.
12. Irigaray, *Speculum of the Other Woman*, p. 5.
13. Jardine, *Gynesis*, p. 263.
14. For an intriguing discussion of the phenomenon 'male lesbianism', see Zita, 'Male Lesbians and the Postmodernist Body'.
15. Irigaray, *Sexes and Genealogies*, pp. 186–7.
16. Irigaray, *This Sex Which Is Not One*, p. 136.
17. Irigaray, *Speculum of the Other Woman*, p. 109.
18. Nietzsche, *Gay Science*, pp. 34–5.
19. Blondel, *Nietzsche, The Body and Culture*, p. 210.
20. Nietzsche, *On the Genealogy of Morality*, p. 38. (See Chapter 8.)
21. Nietzsche, *Will to Power*, p. 173.
22. Blondel, *Nietzsche, The Body and Culture*, p. 219 (citing Nietzsche, *Will to Power*, Section 556).
23. See Chanter, *Ethics of Eros*, ch. 1.
24. Deleuze, *Foucault*, p. 118 (emphasis added).
25. Braidotti, in Parr, *The Deleuze Dictionary*, p. 148.

26. Foucault, 'What Is an Author?', p. 210.
27. Foucault, *Archaeology of Knowledge*, p. 17.
28. Irigaray, *Ethics of Sexual Difference*, p. 127.
29. Irigaray, *Sexes and Genealogies*, p. 177.
30. Irigaray, *Sexes and Genealogies*, p. 179.
31. Whitford, *Luce Irigaray*, p. 85.
32. Gallop, *Thinking Through the Body*, p. 95; Butler, *Bodies that Matter*, p. 38.
33. Irigaray, *Sexes and Genealogies*, p. 177.
34. Elam, *Feminism and Deconstruction*, p. 53.
35. Gallop, *Thinking Through the Body*, p. 97.
36. Irigaray, *This Sex Which Is Not One*, p. 24.
37. Irigaray, *Sexes and Genealogies*, pp. 14–15.
38. Irigaray, *Speculum of the Other Woman*, p. 47.
39. Irigaray, *Sexes and Genealogies*, p. 16.
40. Irigaray, *Marine Lover of Friedrich Nietzsche*, p. 86.
41. Ibid. p. 119.
42. Irigaray, *Elemental Passions*, pp. 15–16.
43. Grosz, *Space, Time and Perversion*, p. 183.
44. Whitford, *Irigaray Reader*, p. 195.
45. Irigaray, *Ethics of Sexual Difference*, p. 33; Chanter, *Ethics of Eros*, p. 180.
46. Foucault, *Order of Things*, p. xx.
47. Irigaray, *Ethics of Sexual Difference*, p. 87.
48. Elam, *Feminism and Deconstruction*, p. 60.
49. Irigaray, 'Fecundity of the Caress'.
50. Irigaray, 'Questions to Emmanuel Levinas'.
51. Vasseleu, *Textures of Light*, p. 113.
52. Chanter, *Ethics of Eros*, p. 221.
53. Irigaray uses the masculine and feminine variants of these terms to reflect the different relations of lovers to the 'objects' of their love: 'In "The Fecundity of the Caress", I used the term "woman lover" (*l'amante*) and not only, as Levinas does, the word "beloved" (*aimée*). I wanted to signify that the woman can be a subject in love (*un sujet amoureux*) and is not reducible to a more or less immediate object of desire', Irigaray, 'Questions to Emmanuel Levinas', p. 185.
54. Irigaray, *Ethics of Sexual Difference*, p. 185.
55. See Irigaray, *Je, Tu, Nous*.
56. Irigaray, *Ethics of Sexual Difference*, p. 185.
57. Vasseleu, *Textures of Light*, p. 115.
58. Levinas, *Totality and Infinity*, p. 257.
59. Irigaray, 'Questions to Emmanuel Levinas', p. 180.
60. Ibid. pp. 185–6.
61. Gallop, *Thinking Through the Body*, p. 60.
62. Irigaray, *I Love to You*, p. 13.

4. *Vulnerability to Violence and Ethical Sensibility*

Irigaray's approach to the body provides a distinctive model for thinking how the sensual body and the textual body, or the phenomenon and language, are conceptual divisions made 'after the fact' of sensate life itself. The term 'sensate life' refers to the experience which does not yet belong to the body-as-a-whole; the body identified, for instance, by a proper name. Irigaray's approach to the sexed body in terms of its 'morphology' and its discrete sites of sensation, enables her to articulate an ethics of sexual difference which is read off the contingent contactual encounters between embodied Subjects. She puts the body to work 'poetically' in the service of a revaluation of cultural values and practices, and presents a radical alternative to traditional forms of critique which stem from the unexamined conditioning of their conceptual frameworks by the privileging of the male sex. In her encounter with Levinas we saw in the previous chapter an illustration of 'doing ethics otherwise'. Despite the fact that she charges Levinas's thinking with missing the ethical significance of sexual difference, there is a clear connection between them in terms of their attempts to philosophise from the perspective of the materiality of the body, and especially with regard to the idea of the body's surface as the limit or boundary between interiority and exteriority; and as the surface of contact between the Same and the Other.

This chapter will examine Levinas's account of the ethical Subject in its exposure, or vulnerability, to violence, drawing centrally on his presentation of the ethical Subject, in *Otherwise than Being*, as a 'being-in-a-skin' – a term introduced at the end of Chapter 2 in connection with the theme of Levinas's empiricism. Adopting this approach will allow me to develop further the themes of 'contact' and 'touch' already introduced as being key to how ethical subjectivity can be shown to be materially (and ontologically) grounded in the sensate life of the Subject. (In the following chapter I will look, further, at how this way of thinking about the ethicality of 'contact' is relevant to contemporary forms of mediated contact by means of communications technologies.)

SENSATE LIFE AND RETHINKING THE SKIN

The skin at once both symbolises and actually constitutes the boundary of the embodied Subject; it is the organ which separates the Same from the Other and is the surface of receptivity and openness to the Other's alterity. But most importantly, at the level of sensate life, it is the very medium of the empirical, being the lived materiality of sensation. The significance of this characterisation of the ethical Subject will become evident in due course, but let us note immediately, most importantly it refers the question of the ethical to *sensate* rather than *cognate* life. In *Totality and Infinity* Levinas offers a critique of the traditional phenomenological understanding of sensation on the ground that it only thinks sensation on the basis of its objectification by thought:

> The idea of intentionality has compromised the idea of sensation by removing the character of being a concrete datum from this allegedly purely qualitative and subjective state, foreign to all objectification . . . This critique of sensation failed to recognise the plane on which the sensible life is lived as enjoyment. This mode of life is not to be interpreted in function of objectification. Enjoyment, by essence satisfied, characterizes all sensations whose representational content dissolves into their affective content.[1]

Enjoyment (*jouissance*) is the word Levinas uses throughout *Totality and Infinity* to name the relationship of the Subject to its world; to everything which it lives from (*vivre de . . .*) and through which it satisfies its needs: enjoyment is not the *result* of the satisfaction of needs, it is, rather, a modality of life. Levinas is quick to remind us, however, that this plane of life is characterised by enjoyment *or* suffering (*souffrance*).[2] Suffering should not be thought of as the anti*thesis* of enjoyment; both enjoyment and suffering are varieties of the 'pure sensation' in which 'one has bathed and lived as in qualities without support'.[3] Life described in terms of sensation is, rather, Subject-less, or not-yet-Subject, and this is a mark of the difference between Levinas's thinking of sensation and the way it is conceptualised in traditional phenomenology. As this Levinasian 'rehabilitation' of sensation is important for this chapter, it is worth citing the following passage at length. (I here add in references to 'suffering' on the ground indicated above, and for reasons that will become clear in a moment.)

> [S]ensation recovers a 'reality' when we see in it not the subjective counter-part of objective qualities, but an enjoyment [or suffering] 'anterior' to the crystallization of consciousness, I and non-I, into subject and object. This crystallization occurs not as the ultimate finality of enjoyment [or suffering] but as a moment of its becoming, to be interpreted in terms of enjoyment [or suffering]. Rather than taking sensations to be contents destined to fill a priori forms of objectivity, a transcendental function *sui generis* must be recognized in them (and for each qualitative specificity in its own mode); a priori formal structures of the non-I are not necessarily structures of objectivity ... The senses have a meaning that is not predetermined as objectification.[4]

This passage begs the question of the 'meaning' of sensation as Levinas identifies it in terms of the pre-Subjective (rather than the pre-objective) life. In *Totality and Infinity* enjoyment represents the accomplishment of the existent as being-home-with-itself (*chez soi*) as the condition of being able to welcome the Other. In the later work, *Otherwise than Being*, however, the emphasis switches from discussing the ethical encounter with the Other whom the 'I' faces across the threshold of its secure 'foothold in being',[5] or its home, to the threshold between the 'I' and the Other across the boundary of the skin. The skin is both the organ of sensation prior to any representation of experience as 'mine'; and it is the surface of absolute passivity within contact. This philosophy of the skin thus acknowledges that skinly contact with the Other is the surface not only of welcome, but at the same time that of vulnerability, allergy and threat. It is not that in the earlier work Levinas was not concerned with the violence inherent to the relationship to the Other, but the emphasis there is entirely on 'my' threat to, even my wish to kill the Other and on the 'ethical resistance' with which this is met, rendering the complete annihilation of the other qua absolute Other, 'impossible':

> The epiphany of the face brings forth the possibility of gauging the infinity of the temptation to murder, not only as the temptation to total destruction, but also as the purely ethical impossibility of this temptation and attempt. If the resistance to murder were not ethical but real, we would have a *perception* of it ... We would remain within the idealism of a *consciousness* of struggle, and not in a relationship with the Other, a relationship that can turn into a struggle, but already overflows the consciousness of struggle.[6]

Of course, murder is an everyday occurrence and only too 'real', but the entire project of *Totality and Infinity* could be described as the patient reiteration of the surplus of the ethical, which as we noted in Chapter 2 in the discussion of Levinas's anti-Hegelianism, cannot be sublated. In *Otherwise then Being*, partly in response to the reading *Totality and Infinity* had been given by Derrida, and in particular concerning the allegedly naive empiricism of the face to face as the principal figure of the ethical relation in that work, Levinas responds by radicalising his empiricism further. Instead of the face to face, welcome and hospitality, all being underwritten, as it were, by the excess of the Good beyond being, the encounter with the Other is characterised instead by 'my' vulnerability, exposure, obligation and 'my' being held hostage to the Other's excessive demand; 'hostage to the point of perse-cution'.[7] This demand is borne, moreover, on what could be described as the organ of empiricality itself, namely, 'the skin'. In other words, there is an acknowledgement now of the fragility of the ethical response as a worldly reality. If *Totality and Infinity* acknowledged the empiri-cal vulnerability of the Other as his or her susceptibility to murder, for example because the 'sword or bullet has touched the ventricles or auricles of his heart',[8] then the invocation of this *viscerality* serves there to distinguish the (sometimes) murderous power over life and death from the force of 'ethical resistance' which opposes it. Still, far from being other-worldly, murder represents the absolute manifestation of ethical nihilism in that it aims at the complete annihilation of the Other: 'Murder alone lays claim to total negation . . . To kill is not to dominate but to annihilate.'[9] But whereas in *Totality and Infinity* we read that 'violence can only aim at a face'[10] and yet the face is said to resist this violence absolutely and unto death (it cannot be negated), in *Otherwise than Being* the emphasis is on the other side of this relation-ship; on how every Subject is a being-in-skin and the ethical relation is, in effect, an uninvited burden. Ethical subjectivity arises in the form of (my) suffering, but this is not the ordinary suffering (for example, in the sense of a deprivation, loss of freedom); it is rather what Levinas calls 'useless suffering'; suffering 'for nothing', or suffering the suffering of the Other. (A detailed discussion of this idea and this distinction is undertaken in Chapter 8.) In this chapter the focus will be on how the ethical resistance to murder undergoes a 'reversal' into the responsibil-ity of the ethical Subject.

BATAILLE, LACERATED EXISTENCE AND THE SUBJECT *IN EXTREMIS*

It is useful at this point to make a short detour through the identifica-tion of this moment of reversal which another thinker, Georges Bataille, similarly associates with thinking the flesh as the intensive site of both pain and ecstasy and of the connection between, for him, the sacred and the profane which is borne *by the flesh*. The comparison with Levinas is relevant for several reasons. Firstly, it is relevant because Bataille, like

Figure 1 The death of Fou-Tchou-Li by Leng-Tch'e (cutting into pieces), from Dumas's *Traité de Psychologie* (1923), reprinted in Bataille's *Tears of Eros* (1961). (Copyright 1989 by City Lights Books. Reprinted by permission of City Lights Books.)

Levinas, recognises that in order to think sensation qua sensation one has to exscribe the concept of the body as the condition of thinking the non-difference between thought and flesh – hence one has to appeal to a notion of experience which is neither the predicate of a Subject nor yet an object of thought. As discussed in Chapter 2, this is precisely what Derrida reminds Levinas is impossible; as any empiricism of what is held to exist outside of language forgets that being already circulates in language. Secondly, the comparison can be instructive because for both Bataille and Levinas the relationship to alterity (as either religious ecstasy or the infinite, respectively) becomes available to thought on the basis of a 'wounding' of the boundary between interiority and exterior-ity. 'I' am disturbed by 'the Other', but specifically in the form of the traumatic provocation the Other introduces with regard to death. And thirdly, for both of them, this is a matter of *obsession*. Obsession is a theme commented on in Bataille's comments in *Tears of Eros*.

In *Tears of Eros* Bataille shows us this image of a man being tortured (Figure 1).

This man he tells us is Fou-Tchou-Li, who was subject to execution in 1905 by a method called Leng-Tch'e (cutting into pieces). Bataille, writing in 1961, says he had owned this photo, since 1925, and that it has had a 'decisive role' in his life:

> I have never stopped being obsessed by this image of pain at once ecstatic and intolerable ... I discerned, in the violence of this image, an infinite capacity for reversal. Through this violence – even today I cannot imagine a more insane, a more shocking form – I was so stunned that I reached the point of ecstasy ... What I suddenly saw, and what imprisoned me in anguish – but which at the same time delivered me from it – was the destiny of these perfect contraries, divine ecstasy and its opposite, extreme horror.[11]

One can only speculate as to precisely what Bataille means when he says this image had a decisive role in his *life*. What he says in this text is that it enabled him to 'see' 'a fundamental connection between the most unspeakable and the most elevated', and that 'religion in its entirety was founded upon sacrifice'.[12] That divine ecstasy accompanies the most extreme sensation of pain (at least as Bataille himself imagines it in this man's drawn-out dying moments) and that this is evident in the expression on the face of the tortured man ('there is of course something undeniable in his expression'[13]), we have to acknowledge, is as much a 'literary' or an interpretative matter as it is a spiritual or a visceral one. Bataille notes, in any case, that this is one of the most anguishing images 'caught on film' – and his analysis is in fact of the image as such. We do not have the suffering man's testimony, for instance; Bataille was not present at the execution. And when Bataille says the photograph had a decisive influence upon his life, we too can only seek to discern that influence, principally at least, in his own writings. For example, we can perhaps see traces of its impact on his thinking when writing, in 1936, of the religious condition of life as 'the scream of lacerated existence':

> In the course of the ecstatic vision, at the limit of death on the cross and of the blindly lived *lamma sabachtani*, the object is finally unveiled as *catastrophe* in a chaos of light and shadow, neither as God nor as nothingness, but as the object that love, incapable of liberating itself except as outside itself, demands in order to let out the scream of lacerated existence.[14]

Perhaps he is haunted by it, too, in 1947, when he writes: 'To be silent, to die slowly, in the conditions of a complete *déchirure* [laceration/dismemberment]. From there slipping into the depths of silence and with an infinite perspective, you will know from what infamy the world is made.'[15] Both of these quotations are indicative elements of Bataille's attempts to think 'through the body' and to think the body's relationship to death, from the perspective of the body. If we were simply to take his own comment about the impact of this photograph on his life/thought at face value, we might speculate that this aspect of his philosophical *oeuvre* begins with its impact on him. The photograph,

I suggest, has lost none of its affective power to disturb, perhaps not least because if anything, in the age of ubiquitous image-making and transmission, we are all only too familiar with what torture and cruel punishment 'look like', and we know that such agonies are always happening *to someone* right now. Death by violent, murderous *déchirure* in one form or another is a part of our world. The disturbance of this image is neither simply viscerally affective nor simply intellectually provocative. Before this distinction is theorised it already *obsesses* Bataille.

Such obsession, I suggest, stems not from any truth this or any other 'image' might be supposed to represent – say, for example, the amphibology of the extreme pain/religious ecstasy it is claimed make graphically available – but rather from its undecidability. 'Obsession' is Bataille's word for the affective response the image provokes *before* it becomes the object for his several direct and indirect reflections on it, in the above-cited works and elsewhere. It is 'real' before any particular meaning is attributed to it; real before it is represented thematically in, say, anthropological, sociological, political or psychological analyses of it, including in this image of the tortured Fou-Tchou-Li itself. The lacerated Subject, so to speak, catches a glimpse of itself in the obsession this image provokes in the body – but this 'obsessed body' is no more Fou-Tchou-Li's than it is Bataille's than it is yours or mine. Jean-Luc Nancy provides a clue for understanding the Bataillean notion of obsession when he says that Bataille's writing aims at 'emptying experience of thought, through thought'.[16]

It could be argued of course that there are only really matters of literary and media culture and their philosophical interpretation in play here: the various texts, images, inter-textual engagements – those of Bataille, Levinas, Nancy, an old photograph, other images daily brought to mind simply by reading the newspaper report of the 'latest atrocity'. The expressions of inner experience they provide are not, after all, descriptions of particular private experiences or moments of a consciousness. Is not Bataille's picture itself, after all, *just* a photograph of an original 'event' of a torture and a suffering which is merely doubled-up again in its literary repetition in *Tears of Eros*, and elsewhere in his writing? How close, if anywhere near at all, can such 'literary re-enactment' bring us to thinking *déchirure* as a philosophically revealing concept of the ethical Subject as connected to either the phenomena or the thematics of violence, vulnerability and torture?

For the viewer, I want to suggest, the image could be ethically instructive to the extent to which it produces in them (and in you perhaps?) a bodily experience of ambiguity; an equivocation in the body between being *both* a witness to *and* a victim of violence.[17] For

Bataille, for example, this disturbing sensation is read as the impossibility of a solipsistic death coupled with the forestalling, or to use a more Levinasian term, an interruption, of the moment of annihilation. Polemicising against Hegel, Bataille says:

> The privileged manifestation of Negativity is death, but death in fact reveals nothing . . . for a man ultimately to reveal himself to himself, he would have to die, but he would have to do it while living – by watching himself cease to be.[18]

Negativity as the nihilistic will to nothing is not completable by any *one*: it is an incompletable 'end' for the solitary Subject due to the impossibility of coincidence between the singular personal death and (impersonal) death itself.[19] As Maurice Blanchot says, every death is, in this technical sense, 'voluntary': 'in voluntary death it is still *extreme passivity* that we perceive – the fact that action here is only the mask of a fascinated dispossession'.[20]

The irreducibility of the difference, or the 'non-difference', between the voluntary and the passive, belongs to a series which gives us 'literary' access to death, or, the deconstruction of its 'truth'. The *mise en abîme* is, for the willing which falls into it, redoubled at a level on which, for example, we too, as viewers of this image (though it is no longer certain what is ultimately 'on view' in all of this) are implicated in the paradoxes of this reflexivity. I am, at once, disturbed by the instability of my identification with the victim and my ambivalence with respect to my witnessing of this scene. I am, of course, outside its spatio-temporal frame, its historical and cultural context: I view the 'scene' as a whole (for example, in this text, now). But, in my look, I also border on it – I slip in and out of the crowd at the execution. I am 'happy', as it were, to be able to know of the horror and the suffering; to have the taste of life *in extremis*, and any insight it may provide me with, though to access whatever this is, I have to withdraw and to 'think' it. The daily experience of television news, with its constant warnings of 'some viewers may find some of the images in this report disturbing'; not to mention on-line access to less filtered imagery of cruelties, or dramatic simulations of cruelty of all kinds consumed as entertainment – these are all instances of being on 'the edges' of murderous violence and death. As Blanchot says: 'whoever wants to die can only want the borders of death, the utilitarian death which is in the world and which one reaches through the precision of the workman's tools'.[21] Those tools may be those of the executioner, the journalist or the cinematographer – or the philosopher tooled-up with concepts.

So, what happens to 'me' on this edge? I may find myself identifying with the machine-wielding torturer, and being drawn, vertiginously, into a contemplative teetering on the brink of the 'ethical abyss'.[22] Indeed, this is the point at which the witness/victim doubling makes one's skin crawl. It is as if one were, precisely, imagining doing this to oneself. This schizoid imagination experiences difficulty in its manipulation of the simulacra in play at such an edge, as it attempts to maintain the distinction between witness and victim by mapping it onto the I-victim/I-perpetrator distinction (I witness witnessing, and so on, as well as being the witness). This phenomenon is, perhaps, not dissimilar to the experience of nightmares, in which the disturbance experienced is multiplied by the waking realisation that the horror and perversity I am 'exposed to', is in reality, *all of my own making.*

The decisive role that this image had in Bataille's life, then, could be said to be related to the way in which the relationship between his life and his writing (which aims to exscribe thought, as Nancy puts it) cross over into one another. The image of mutilation mutilates the very system of its own representation. The lacerated body for Bataille is neither simply corporeal nor outside of thought; it is rather *abyssal* with regard to such a conceptual distinction itself. The image does not cause thought to fall down a rabbit hole of reflected reflections into a literary play without end; rather, it precipitates a 'me' back into the world of 'real' violent encounters between human beings and of the murderous violent mutilation which is happening in the everyday.

Whilst Bataille's various meditations on the ambiguity of the body *in extremis* reveal the moment of the impossibility of dying as definitive of the Subject, the reversal, or suspension, of annihilation they are ultimately concerned with is invariably 'my own'. I will now turn to how Levinas's account of the Subject as a being-in-a-skin ethicises the ambiguous zone of contact between the 'I' and the 'Other'.

FROM SENSIBILITY TO ETHICS: ON BEING SKINNED

In *Otherwise than Being* Levinas's thinking of the skin is central to his account of vulnerability to wounding as the 'condition' for the ethical relation to the Other. In the Itinerary of that work, Levinas declares his intention to 'disengage the subjectivity of the subject from reflections on truth, time and being . . . and to present the subject . . . *as sensibility from the first* animated by responsibilities'.[23] Two obvious considerations warrant discussing sensibility in relation to the skin and the skin in relation to ethics: locating the skin, so to speak, between sensibility and the material capacity for ethical response. Firstly, there is the fact that the skin is, in every sense, the organ of sensibility: it is not the sense of touch alone that is *of* the skin. The retina of the eye, the tympanum of the ear, and the mucous membranes of the nose and mouth are all skinly sites of carnate sensational intensity and contact with the Other. Secondly, the skin is literally (or, as Levinas says, 'without metaphor') the boundary between the me and the non-me, and it gives me the sense of my being an interiority exposed to exteriority.

I shall now consider the role that the skin plays in Levinas's account of ethical subjectivity as originating in 'unthinking' sensate life rather than with the intellectual concerns of the transcendental Subject. And I shall address the question as to how such an account may serve an 'ethico-pathological' understanding of violence as ethical nihilism (in its ultimately being aimed at the murderous annihilation of the Other) in relation to which the *déchirure* of the skin, as both wound and discursive opening, points the way. Additionally, the theme of sacrifice is central to this analysis in so far as it is a form of sacrificial mutilation which links, as does vulnerability in Levinas's account, sensibility to the possibility of giving. Just to indicate how: for Levinas it is only because I am a being which has tasted bread in my mouth that I am able to sacrifice my own sustenance and make of it a gift to the Other. This is a recurrent figure in *Otherwise than Being*: 'a subject is of flesh and blood, a man that is hungry and eats, [is] entrails in a skin, and thus capable of giving the bread out of the mouth, or *giving his skin*'.[24] Expressions such as this, which abound in Levinas's revaluation of sensibility, beg the question of the relationship between the literal and the figural in Levinas's writing; and empiricism and the representation of the empirically real are at issue throughout. As already noted, the skin is, on the one hand, the substantive, material site of sensation and in this sense the organ of the empirical. It can also literally be given, for example in the form of living and post-mortem organ and tissue donation in a medical context. These are examples of how 'giving one's skin' can be a non-figural form of generosity. This is perhaps a strange understanding of empirical and an unusual form of generosity. The point of referring to them here is to highlight the way in which Levinas's account of the ethical Subject starting from sensate life, repeatedly returns us directly back to 'real life'; to the 'here and now' of the sensual and to life as 'flesh and blood'. In a certain unapologetically, unphilosophical kind of way, one might say that when Levinas talks about the skin he is talking about the actual skin, the skin which can be wounded, which itches, twitches, bleeds, touches, and so forth. But this 'actuality' never comes to rest in the empiricist naturalism of the physical skin as the signified (as it is conceptualised, for instance, within human anatomy), nor does it refer to any idea of the skin in terms of *what it is* at all. His discourse works at refiguring the skin otherwise than in ontological language and without its being represented in a theme or being made an object of thought. The skin, Levinas insists, is 'signifyingness' itself and that 'sensibility' is the 'subjectivity of the subject'.[25] Rethinking the sensibility of the skin in this way is his key to a non-essentialising notion of ethical subjectivity.

In traditional metaphysics, aesthesiological sensuality is relegated to a subservient role in comparison to the sentience which lays its claim to knowledge – including knowledge of 'the skin'. Empirically speaking, on the one hand, the skin is considered to be the unthought materiality of carnate sensation. But, on the other, from the perspective of theoretical reflection, the skin constitutes the limit of my subjective being and the boundary of the Subject enclosed within it. This is attested to in so far as the skin and its diverse sensory surfaces are made an object of various dermato-*logies*. Against this dehiscence of the skin perpetrated by the privileging of theoretical representation, however, it can be argued that the skin is in-between the empirical, substantive materiality of the boundedness of the Subject (which reflection conceptualises as sensation) and the transcendental object of the thought which posits it as such. It is both lived and reflected in thought; it is at once the limit of immanent egological life and also the surface on which the exteriority of everything which is not-me, impresses itself on me. Levinas's philosophy deconstructs the metaphysical 'dermatologics' of the skinned Subject by effectively appealing to the skin's undecidability. His deconstructive rewriting of the skin in terms of its ethicality, works away at the traditional and dominant determinations of its meaning, favouring 'sensibility'; and by approaching the question of Subject *beginning with the skin* and with a view to countering its epistemic objectification: 'the immediacy on the surface of the skin characteristic of sensibility, its vulnerability, is found as it were anaesthetized in the process of knowing'.[26] Any attempt to rethink skinly sensation in relation to sentience (in terms of sensible intuition or a non-thetic *Sinngebung*, as in Husserl), however, must avoid repeating the empiricist sensualism of ontological metaphysics, which solves the problem of the sensing/sensed dichotomy by collapsing reflection onto its object in the coincidence of thought and feeling.

In view of this, it is worth recalling at least the spirit of Levinas's own appropriation of the great leap forward the Husserlian *epoché* represents over traditional metaphysics. The *epoché* addresses both the naive empiricism which supposes sensation to be unmediated closeness to the real, as well as the reflection which takes itself to be true knowledge as distinct from pure sensation. It rejects the thought/ sense distinction central to the empiricist notion of experience and the subject–object epistemology that goes with it, whilst retaining the project of making philosophy a 'rigorous science', based on a 'return to things themselves'. But if the *epoché* avoids the trap of sensualism, it does so by ultimately retaining and (re)privileging theoretical intentionality. Despite this, Levinas acknowledges the importance of Husserl's critique of knowledge as his reduction opens the way for the questioning of the representation of objects of thought in themes. It achieves an 'awakening' of thought to its own 'effects' upon its supposed objects of intuition; an awakening as novel and startling as that which Kant's critical thinking represents in relation to the 'dogmatic slumber' of the naive empiricism, as he saw it, in his own day. Despite these significant advantages, however, Levinas's assessment of Husserlian phenomenology is that it is ultimately 'motivated only by the naive considerations emerging in understanding' and the need to expose 'the arbitrariness of speculative constructions'.[27] The motivation of his own thinking, it should now be clear, is otherwise than philosophical in this sense on every level, and it seeks to trigger another kind of alarm: the alarming experience of being called to responsibility by the Other in the empirical event of obligation.[28]

When Derrida challenges Levinas's empiricism for its appeal to the face of the Other as the sign of absolute alterity, he emphasises that it is inevitably wholly dependent on that which it seeks to renounce, namely, the ontology of the Same. Levinas eventually comes to counter this criticism in *Otherwise than Being* by setting out to demonstrate how 'obligation' is indeed effectively non-philosophical, pre-originary, unthematised signifyingness (or literally non-sense). But by way of his empirico-materialist thesis of the skinned Subject, he brings his ethics of alterity 'down to earth'. Whereas *Totality and Infinity* had spoken of the I–Other conjuncture *as if* this had been articulated from within the 'face to face', and thus as if beyond being, in *Otherwise than Being* sensibility and the ethical are, from the perspective of reflection, claimed to be conterminal: 'Signifyingness, the one-for-the-other, is exposedness of self to another. It is the immediacy of a skin and a face, a skin which is always a modification of a face, a face that is weighted down with a skin.'[29] From the perspective of a being-in-a-skin, the skin does not appear as such at all; rather than phenomenal it is pure sensuality. But let us be clear, to describe the skin in terms of its being the 'condition' for sensory perception, moreover, the empirical condition for this, would be a misnomer. It is a misnomer, however, that originates with thematic reflection as it claims the sensible as the object of its intuition.

Such a privileging of the exterior perspective is, precisely, what gives rise to the body represented, for example, in the natural sciences. Of this 'seen' body, Merleau-Ponty once said: it is 'only a shadow stuffed with organs'.[30]

The term 'sensibility' in Levinas names, rather, neither a capacity of a Subject nor a concept of reflection; it is in-between what empiricist sensualism, on the one hand, considers to be unthought 'pure sensation' and what phenomenology, on the other, regards as the object of consciousness.[31] He expresses this in the following:

> A thermal, gustative or olfactory sensation is not primarily a cognition of pain, a savor, or an odour. No doubt it can take on this signification of being a discovery [but only] by losing its own sense [*sens propre*], becoming an experience *of* . . . , a consciousness *of* . . . , 'placing itself' before the being exposed in its theme.[32]

The expression 'losing its own sense' here plays on the double connotation of *sens* as 'meaning' and as 'direction': sensibility loses its own meaning by becoming the noematic correlate of a *noesis*, instead of maintaining its sense as a pure *noema*: sensibility is, in this Levinasian use of this classic Husserlian terminology, a *noema* without a *noesis*.[33] Levinas here targets the Husserlian axiom that 'all consciousness is consciousness of . . . something' on the ground that it is founded by attributing to sensibility a misdirected intentionality. The point being that both Husserl's phenomenology (explicitly) and Merleau-Ponty's phenomenology (in a less obvious way) remain committed to the 'parallelism' of 'qualities and theses',[34] or, the obverse–reverse structure of sensibility (the Merleau-Pontean 'sensible-sentient').[35] Against this, Levinas declares his renunciation of the intentionality which acts 'as a guiding thread toward the *eidos* of the psyche which would command the *eidos* of sensibility', adding that his analyses 'will follow sensibility in its prenatural signification'.[36] In other words, it will address the signifying of sensibility *before* it is represented in a theme.

The significance *of the reversal of intentionality* proposed here, then, is that only on the basis of *the individuation of the Subject in sensibility* can such a Subject enter into a relation with an Other which is neither reducible to, nor accountable for, in relation to the movements of the Same. The model of intentionality rejected, is rejected because it makes of the Other another for-me – and all 'for-me's are but a function of my project. After all, as already noted, from the perspective of aesthesiological experience, the skin is not experienced as such, no more than the eye observes the retina. The skin is that within which my separate existence is maintained: the 'I' is sensibility and sensibility is enjoyment (*jouissance*), without, in this moment of enjoyment, the skin appearing as such. This 'pre-natural' skinly sensibility is thus already vulnerability in (its) exposedness to exteriority: 'subjectivity is vulnerability, is sensibility'.[37]

The theorisation of separation as the condition for entry into the ethical relation in *Totality and Infinity* (discussed in Chapter 2) reappears in *Otherwise than Being*, expressed in terms of the 'superindividuation of the ego [which] consists in being in itself, in its skin'.[38] The separation (or, now, 'superindividuation') of the Subject – which was described earlier in terms of the sensible existence of bathing in the elemental 'there is', and as prior to any act of negation – is later made the condition for the reversed intentionality which is held to account for its 'obligation'. Because 'superindividuation' occurs at the level of sensibility, obligation is not a matter of the Subject's decision. This Levinasian model of sensibility as a non-negational relation of the individual existent to existence, precisely the 'pure' sensibility which remains inaccessible to the Husserlian *epoché*, lays claim to an event of individuation in which 'I' am in my world without, in the same moment and thereby, exercising mastery over the world of the Other; without violating the place of the Other. Each *one* takes up its place prior to the appearance of any *one's* will.

REFIGURING THE SKIN AND REDIRECTING ETHICS

The ethical significance of the skin derives from the fact that it is, from the perspective of sensible existence, the limit-surface upon which the drama of individual existence as sensibility is played out, for example in enjoyment or in suffering. From an exterior perspective, the skin is what secures my uniqueness, enclosed within a discernible limit. It is then, doubly, the 'condition' for the approach of the Other to me (personally). I am, emphatically, uniquely obliged by the ethical demand of the Other: even before I know myself; before I 'witness' myself; represent myself to myself in a concept and *think of myself* as a unity enclosed within a skin. And, I am, by that very same 'fact', exposed to the possibility of wounding and murder: 'exposedness to wounds and outrage characterises [the skinned Subject's] passivity'.[39]

The general ethical structure outlined in *Otherwise than Being* would confine Merleau-Ponty's analyses entirely to the realm of the Same and its relation to its world. In this respect Merleau-Ponty would be right, in Levinas's view, to question the attempt to identify the boundary between the body and the world at all, because, as Merleau-Ponty himself says, 'the world [itself] is [already] flesh'.[40] And Levinas effectively describes a similar dissolution of this boundary as it is represented in ontology. The existent emerges from the 'there is' (*il y a*) but remains in a closed circuit of need and satiation with respect to it. The 'solitary' Subject is lost in its sensuality and has no representation of itself; it has no idea that there are, as Merleau-Ponty's says, 'landscapes other than its own'. But from the perspective of thematising thought, my skin is not the event of sensible enjoyment or suffering, it is the boundary of my vulnerability. I am for myself a being which is pure surface, a being which, in being-in-my-skin, is every square inch vulnerable. Vulnerability and sensibility are thus the inseparable obverse and reverse of one another. From the perspective of sensible existence this vulnerability amounts to 'uncertainty of the morrow' – for example, encountered in my hunger, thirst, fatigue and pain.[41] And, as I represent my skin-boundedness to myself in thought, I perceive my situation to be one of the essential vulnerability which is identical with my openness to the Other. What may be described as the pure indulgence of the Subject in sensual existence, becomes self-concern only on reflection. Levinas reminds us that this moment of reflection is not constitutive of the ethical relation as such; it is not 'properly' ethical. It is only the moment of concern with moral propriety, and it remains 'internal' to the Same. An integrated thesis in Levinas, then, might be expressed as follows: the consciousness which comes to itself in theoretical or calculative reflection is concerned only to save its own skin.[42]

THE SKIN AS ETHICAL PASSIVITY

To close this chapter I shall briefly propose a reading of the ethical significance of Bataille's obsession with his photograph of the execution of Fou-Tchou-Li on the basis of Levinas's thinking of the ethical passivity of the skin.

I have explained how Levinas's thinking of the ethical subjectivity 'begins with the skin' rather than an interpretation of it. Prior to the formulation of the question about my existence as such, that is, in so far as this concerns *me*: as a being-in-a-skin I am already exposed to the Other as absolute passivity. This is the precondition of exposure to the Other, prior to any determination of the Other's meaning. When Levinas 'theorises' sensibility he often expresses it in the hyperbolic language of absolute passivity:

> a passivity more passive still than any passivity that is antithetical to an act, a nudity more naked than all 'academic' nudity—It is a passivity that is not reducible to exposure to another's gaze. It is a vulnerability and a paining

exhausting themselves like a haemorrhage, denuding even the aspect that its nudity takes on, exposing its very exposedness.[43]

Bataille appears to glimpse such a beguiling passivity in what he finds 'undeniable' and 'most anguishing' in the facial/epidermal expression of the torture victim in his disturbing photograph. Of such an anguished vulnerability, Levinas would perhaps say that what it signifies 'is not the existential "being-for-death" but the constriction of an "entry inwards". It is not a flight into the void but a movement into fullness, the anguish of contraction and breakup.'[44] And he puts his reader in mind at this very point of an equally gruesome image, adding that this describes the relation in which 'a subject is immolated without fleeing itself'.

Levinasian passivity expresses the idea that the 'meaning' or 'sense' of sensibility is decided elsewhere – passivity is a decision which is not mine, and it reverses my 'being-in-my-skin' into 'being-for-the-other' – it comes to me from the Other. The agony/ecstasy of the dying other (in which death is agonisingly and forever suspended – by the torture/by time being frozen in the photograph) which obsesses Bataille, can be given its proper ethical significance by Levinas's philosophy: it is the time of 'my' responsibility for the Other. With respect to the hypostasis of the existent, Levinas says 'sensibility is enjoyment', but the vulnerability of being 'in one's skin' is also said to (re)turn sensibility into 'exposure to the other' and to wounding. The ethical structure of sensibility repeatedly redirects sensibility, as we have seen, into vulnerability. This leads to the claim that 'I am bound to others before I am bound to my own body . . . The other calls upon that sensibility with a vocation that wounds, calls upon an irrevocable responsibility, and thus the very identity of the subject.'[45]

Lastly, at this point let us recall the remark cited earlier from the 'Itinerary' of *Otherwise than Being*: the presentation of the Subject 'as a sensibility from the first animated by responsibilities'.[46] Sensibility is never purely and simply an indulgence of the existent in sensible being: its 'sojourn' in the sensible is 'from the first' interrupted by the obligation which disturbs it. Prior to any being conscious of anything, including my being conscious of my own individual being-in-my-skin, this obligation disturbs me directly and (re)turns my sensibility into vulnerability by bringing me to the surface of my skin in a conscious reflection on the nature of this essential vulnerability. The disturbance which turns sensibility into self-concern precedes my concept of myself as being-in-my-skin. Vulnerability is therefore found to belie an openness, or exposure, to the Other's alterity 'before' I experience my skin as being-mine. This notion of the skin as the material site of obsession with the Other provides an insight into the 'ethical' nature of Bataille's obsession with the image – even if its ethicality escapes Bataille himself:

> It is in the passivity of obsession, or incarnated passivity, that an identity individuates itself as unique, without recourse to any system of references, in the impossibility of evading the assignation of the other without blame . . . the self is the very fact of being exposed.[47]

This retro-intentionality of passivity seeks to account for the alterity of others as absolute Others for whom my ethical obligation is 'real' in that its manifestation is a part of my everyday experience of a movement directed towards me from the outside. It is also, therefore, non-sentimental, in the technical sense of non-ideational (that is, it is not my idea).

What I have attempted to show in this chapter is that such a thinking of obligation is exactly what Levinas's ethics of vulnerability seeks to reverse into 'sensibility', and that this amounts at the same time to Levinas's response to the philosophical conundrum of 'the real': it involves thinking the 'reality of obligation' as the relation between the here and now and the beyond. We have seen also how the violence which is, ultimately, aimed at the skin and at the annihilation of the Other, can be met with ethical resistance. Levinas's entire thesis, is, so to speak, inscribed on the skin: the meaning (*sens*) of the skin is a direction (*sens*); it is 'a one-way street' down which the Other approaches me and has a unique meaning (*sens unique*) for me.[48] The expression *sens unique* connotes both uniqueness and direction. Levinas's account of the ethical Subject as a being-in-a-skin does not lead to a notion of *general* responsibility for others, but to the Subject's unique responsibility for a singular Other. It attempts to show that the responsibility that can be read-off the skin is not a lottery in which 'it might be me' who is responsible, it is me. This uniqueness is 'felt' as inescapably as a wound to my skin. Bataille's obsession with the moment of ecstasy/pain reversal perhaps senses that intensity has the power to obliterate reflection totally, but it does not know its ethical significance: ethical subjectivity is vulnerability to the vulnerability of the Other.

NOTES

1. Levinas, *Totality and Infinity*, p. 187.
2. Ibid. p. 187.
3. Ibid. p. 187.
4. Ibid. p. 188.
5. Levinas, *Existence and Existents*, p. 15.

6. Levinas, *Totality and Infinity*, p. 199.
7. Levinas, *Otherwise than Being, or, Beyond Essence*, p. 15.
8. Levinas, *Totality and Infinity*, p. 199.
9. Ibid. p. 198.
10. Derrida, 'Violence and Metaphysics', p. 147.
11. Bataille, *Tears of Eros*, pp. 206–7.
12. Ibid. pp. 206–7.
13. Ibid. p. 205.
14. Bataille, *Visions of Excess*, p. 185.
15. Bataille, cited in Wilson, 'Feting the Wound', p. 186.
16. Nancy, *Birth to Presence*, p. 61.
17. L. A. Boldt-Irons discusses the literary aspects of the paradoxes of the witness/victim relation in Bataille, and the limits of integrity of a unitary consciousness divided by 'reflection on reflection'. This abyssal 'principle' manifests itself in the way in which 'one sign mutilates another' in Bataille's writing; 'in which we encounter the case of the slipping word, whose capacity for self-destruction or auto-mutilation had been silenced by the straightjacket of discourse'. See Boldt-Irons, 'Sacrifice and Violence in Bataille's Erotic Fiction', pp. 96–7.
18. Bataille, cited in Boldt-Irons, 'Sacrifice and Violence in Bataille's Erotic Fiction', p. 96.
19. I return to this theme in Chapter 10.
20. Blanchot, *The Space of Literature*, p. 102.
21. Ibid. p. 105.
22. This marks the shift from the 'figural' abyssal of the *mise en abîme* to what might be described as the 'empirical abyssal', the event of ethical disturbance in the Subject. Boldt-Irons refers to the specificity of what she calls the *mise en abîme* in Bataille's writing, as that 'technique' by means of which his reader becomes enmeshed in the processes of the text: it 'entails a structural *mise en abîme* of an experienced and perceived *mise en abîme* . . . that neither sacrifices consciousness nor preserves its integrity', 'Sacrifice and Violence in Bataille's Erotic Fiction', p. 96. The 'teetering on the ethical abyss' I refer to here involves a comparable reversal of the figural always back into what could be termed the 'ethical incarnate', or sensate life. However, whereas Boldt-Irons's purely literary interest remains that of the 'mutilation of signs', I turn to the Levinasian notion of the Subject as a being-in-a-skin in order to locate the zone of affective sensibility within which the theoretical distinction between the figural and the empirical has yet to appear.
23. Levinas, *Otherwise than Being, or, Beyond Essence*, p. 19 (emphasis added).
24. Ibid. p. 77.
25. Ibid. p. 15.
26. Ibid. p. 64.
27. Levinas, 'Philosophy as Awakening', p. 214.

28. See Davies, 'On Resorting to an Ethical Language', p. 103.

29. Levinas, *Otherwise than Being, or, Beyond Essence*, p. 29.

30. Merleau-Ponty, *Phenomenology of Perception*, p. 138.

31. Levinas, *Theory of Intuition*, p. 169.

32. Levinas, *Otherwise than Being, or, Beyond Essence*, p. 65.

33. In the Husserlian theory of intentionality, the object of an intentional consciousness is called the *noema*, the act of consciousness 'itself' the *noesis*. Towards the end of *Totality and Infinity* Levinas says: 'One of the principal theses of this work is that the noesis–noema structure is not the primordial structure of intentionality', p. 294.

34. Levinas, *Otherwise than Being, or, Beyond Essence*, p. 68.

35. See Merleau-Ponty, *Phenomenology of Perception*.

36. Levinas, *Otherwise than Being, or, Beyond Essence*, p. 68.

37. Ibid. p. 54.

38. Ibid. p. 118.

39. Ibid. p. 108.

40. Merleau-Ponty, *Phenomenology of Perception*, p. 138.

41. See Levinas, *Existence and Existents*.

42. See Derrida on 'the economy of saving oneself', in *Gift of Death*, p. 87.

43. Levinas, *Otherwise than Being, or, Beyond Essence*, p. 72.

44. Ibid. p. 108.

45. Ibid. pp. 76–7.

46. Ibid. p. 19.

47. Ibid. pp. 112, 118.

48. See Bernasconi, 'One-way Traffic', p. 95.

5. The Ethical Subject of New Media Communications

The previous chapters have examined how the Levinasian account of ethical subjectivity is derived on the basis of a materialist phenomenology of sensate life and have sought to clarify how his 'ethics of alterity' is ontologically grounded in the materiality of contact, touch and the affective relationship to other experienced on the passive surface of 'the skin'. Levinas's discourse of the skin, the wound, allergy, and so forth, and of the ethical Subject as a being-in-a-skin, it has been shown, is neither simply figural nor metaphorical, nor is it expressive of a literalism or naturalism. It must be referred back, rather, to his thinking of the empiricism of the pre-phenomenological life of the Subject as an existent whose existence is prior to the differentiation between language and lived experience. It is from within this claimed perspective that this notion of the skin could be said to refer to the 'actual skin', but to the actual skin *before* it is conceptually or thematically re-presented. The skin in Levinas's discourse is not an object of knowledge, a some*thing*, nor is the being-in-a-skin a some*one*. The skin is presented in terms of what it *does* rather than what it *is*. This could be summed up in the following way: the being-in-a-skin is being 'in touch' with the Other. To think the skin in this way, as ethical sensibility, does not logically predetermine or delimit what actually constitutes the materiality of the contactual interface with the Other; and 'the skin' is, effectively, the *generic* name Levinas assigns to this. The claim to the *ethical immediacy* of touch and contact is not for that reason contradicted by the reality of what is conventionally understood by *mediated communication*, nor, of course, is the responsibility of the Subject restricted to whoever or whatever is literally within its reach. Generically, the skin in Levinas's discourse is a name for a surface with a particular responsive capacity; a surface of response-ability.

FROM THE FACE TO THE INTERFACE

This account of the ethical encounter with the Other in terms of touch begs the question of the role of technology in the everyday forms of contact with others which are characteristic of contemporary everyday life and which materially structure the many forms of being 'in touch' with others. Whilst on the one hand these might pithily be described as having multiplied in the age of electric and electronic communications media, on the other, *technicity* might equally be said to have always been an aspect of communication. For instance, even in a simple face-to-face situation, language is already a *medium* of communication and *a device* which facilitates contact with others. This chapter will offer an ethical analysis of technics of communications technologies in terms of the transformation of *modalities of contact* they introduce and relate this further to the theorisation of the ethical Subject in terms of sensate life. It will focus in particular on the contemporary prospect of the incorporation of 'haptic media' into the communicative interfaces of everyday digital communications.

Japanese artist Yoichiro Kawaguchi's 'Gemotion' 3-D touch screen, represented in Figures 2 and 3, is an illustrative example of the principle of a haptic, interactive medium. It anticipates, in an abstract form, the possible future development of haptic media and it serves as a model demonstrating the general possibility of the enhancement of digitised communications to fully include the sense of touch. 'Gemotion' is both an artwork as well as a working model of how sensory digital media communications could involve immersive, 'full bodily' contact, achieved in the form of dynamic, responsive, touching surfaces, or 'skins'. In recent years technical research aimed at developing haptic interfaces for managing communications between human beings and machines has made considerable progress towards introducing them into various aspects of contemporary cultural forms ranging from gaming to the performance of remotely controlled surgical procedures. It seems reasonable to anticipate that today's Wii video-gaming, for example, will in the not too distant future seem as crude as the original 1970s Space Invaders now does in comparison with the latest Xbox interactive experience. Such examples as these, and various other forms of haptic communications technologies as they already exist, serve to remind us of how even telecommunicative contact is essentially a bodily, sensory and tactile experience.

In this chapter I shall attempt to make clear why the development of 'haptic media' and the immersive media-communication environments and communicative situations they promise to configure, involving ever

Figure 2 Artist Professor Yoichiro Kawaguchi with his 'Gemotion' 3-D touch screen. (Image courtesy of the artist.)

more intensively the fullness of the sensory apparatus, calls for a reconsideration of the ethical dimension of sensuality itself, and in particular what could be termed in the wake of Levinas's thinking, the ethics of contact, or touch.

For the most part, the cultural theorisation of media-related virtuality (the popular name for which is 'cyberspace') has remained preoccupied with the visual, and has tended to limit its scope in general to the sphere of the politics of representation. Media and cultural studies work, for instance, has predominantly adopted a visual, or rather an ocularcentric, paradigm in its analyses of cultural forms and technologies, as these have become extensively integral to everyday life. And whilst it has been directly argued, by Mark Hansen,[1] for instance, (whose thinking of the haptic I shall discuss below) that such a paradigm is inappropriate for understanding the nature of the relationship between the human being and digital media information, and the kinds of human–machine interactions the digital introduces, just how

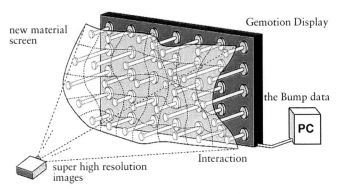

Figure 3 Operational diagram of 'Gemotion' 3-D touch screen. (Image courtesy of the artist.)

immersive sensory media environments bear on the ethical materiality of communications, as discussed in previous chapters, still awaits direct attention.

My concern here is, then, with how 'the haptic' (in its overlapping reference to the sense of touch, technology and 'affectivity' in general) bears on the notion of the ethical by virtue of the part it plays in the formation of ethical subjectivity. The discussion in the first half of this chapter will establish how the body–digital information interface (discussed at length by Hansen) can be viewed as an 'evolution' in the materiality of sensation and the sensory apparatus itself.[2] The second half will argue, building on the discussion of 'the skin' and of the sense of touch in Levinas of previous chapters and on Derrida's analysis of touch in his *On Touching – Jean-Luc Nancy* in particular, that the ethical implications of such an evolution of sensuality (in my view neglected by Hansen) can be approached on the basis of a rethinking of the human–machine interface as a new form of 'the skin'.

KEEPING IN TOUCH WITH HAPTIC MEDIA

Across the range of possible future uses of haptic communications technology, we will surely discern an enhancement of sorts of the experience of what it is to be telecommunicatively 'in touch' with others. The expression 'to keep in touch', for instance, in English as well as in many other languages, recalls a certain priority of the sense of touch in the context of personal relationships; special or intimate relationships with others whom one might literally, when in shared physical space and proximity, normally touch in one way or another – stroke, caress, hand-hold, massage, kiss, palpate, pat, and so forth. Haptic media are clearly in their infancy today. Their future uses are likely to include the enhancement of telecommunications in general, by way of the reconstitution of the richness, fullness and plenitude of sensation. And in the future, it also not unreasonable to assume that by virtue of their familiarity, their impact on our lives will be as transparent to us as that of television today.

However, to view such a technological development of telecommunications as facilitating the reconstitution of an 'original' pre-existent sensible reality is hardly the correct way to think of what each new media technology introduces to the 'total media environment' – to borrow a famous phrase of Marshall McLuhan – which we already inhabit. Reality, in many different senses, it has been widely argued, is transformed by processes of technological incorporation, as these produce new technical objects in relation to which new possibilities arise; new ways, that is, of living the everyday; new ways for forming relationships with others, new forms of social and political interaction, new ways of creating knowledge and expressing and circulating ideas. From sociological, political and cultural perspectives, such developments are self-evident in a diverse array of new phenomena and the broad cultural dynamics which emerge in the context of changing media-communications environments. From the invention of writing to the latest manifestations of 'social media', communications technologies have historically given rise to new ways of being in the world and a new experience of the worldliness of the world itself. In the context of an accelerated rate of transformation of communications in the digital age, the impact of new media on the experience of everyday life has become central to much of 'cybercultural studies' and its sociological commentary and cultural theorising of the social impact of information technologies and computer-mediated communications in general. Even more fundamentally, it has been widely argued, technology in general and digital technologies in particular are key to the rethinking of the Subject in relation to the 'post-human'.

The increasingly ubiquitous nature of digital technologies as they already exist has placed them at the centre of contemporary attempts to philosophically rethink the body and embodiment in terms of 'technicity.' The notion of technicity appealed to here is broadly that of Gilbert Simondon[3] (developed by Bernard Stiegler[4] and latterly Mark Hansen): technicity is what is fundamental to both technological machines and the human body with respect to the ensembles of conjoinment they give rise to in the processes of their interfacing. By 'interfacing' I refer to that in-between zone of prosthetic-hybridisation of body and machine, which is at the centre of the wider extensional connectivity interfacing generally accomplishes in relation to progressively more distant elements of the extended cultural ensemble. Mark Hansen's work on the digital visual arts in both his *New Philosophy for New Media* and *Bodies in Code*, though not in any way centrally concerned with the ethical as such, presents powerful arguments concerning how the human body and digital information need to be thought in conjunction with one another, and indeed, one might say, quite literally *as* a conjunction: a labile, processual and contingent entity. This involves, for instance, bearing in mind his particular focus on visual arts, thinking of the visual in terms of haptics and affectivity. Hansen argues that 'digital imaging', for instance, should be regarded as a process incorporating the impression of the visual information (as a materiality) on the human organism, such that the material body is processually modified by it; modified, that is, with respect to space and time, or to be more precise, motion and duration. Drawing on the philosophy of Bergson, he proposes thinking of the body as an enframing 'centre of indetermination' within the continuum of the total media environment.[5] And, as everything is ultimately a question of the body's 'continuity' with its environment, the body's 'modifications' ripple outward, across all of the registers of its affective being – the biological as much as the political, the emotional as well as the intellectual. What Hansen says of the 'visual', though, on his own model is to be taken as applicable to the senses and sensation in general: we are invited to think of *all* of the senses in terms of hapticity. His bigger philosophical thesis concerning the human body here is that it is proactively and proprioceptively reflexive. Such an 'affective body' does not need to wait for the judgement of a 'consciousness' or the decision of the meaning of an experience of, say, an idea or a work of art (or, for that matter, as I shall consider below, an encounter with another person). It is, rather, to be thought of as being subject to a transformation resulting directly from its *contact* with them. As such an indeterminate centre of affective processes, the body is not defined by simply being passively acted upon by externalities of one kind or another – for there is no essential distinction which fixes the difference between the internal and the external – but by virtue of its *inclusion within* the information processing ensemble per se. It must, in brief, be considered as a function, to use a Bergsonian idiom, of an 'aggregated' ecotechnical 'whole'.[6]

It is not surprising that such haptological thinking, in its reference to sensation in general, identifies as a primary focus (for philosophising itself as much as ordinary life activities and experience) the connectivity of the body to its total environment. Alongside Simondon, McLuhan, I suggest, ought perhaps to be credited as being one of the first to draw attention to how modern media must be viewed in the context of the entire history of the relation between the human and technology in general. For McLuhan realised that any discussion about content, or information, carried by media, would remain arbitrary if it were not grounded in each case in an understanding of the transformative capacity of the 'total media environment' as such for the human. It was for him, accordingly, the transformation of the 'total media environment' that each new medium introduces (writing, print, radio, TV, digital, and so forth) that places the greatest demand on the reconceptualisation of that environment. The 'totality' of that media environment, one could say, was the name McLuhan gave to what we are inclined to refer to today, in the wake of various new media technologies including haptic media, as its *immersive* character. (A *fully* immersive medium could be defined, then, as including forms of virtual reality in which the sense of touch is made part of the sensory-motor system enabling the manipulation of virtual objects by means of the transmission, and eventual 'reconstitution' at the surface of the human skin, of 'haptic information', for example concerning density, resistance, weight and texture.)

HAPTICS, HAPTOLOGY, HAPTOCENTRISM

The haptically codified media environment which this technology gives rise to is one which will allow human beings to *touch one another* in new ways. This makes the question concerning how our thinking of the ethical is related to sensation seem all the more concrete and urgent. How does the digitisation of sensory information and its communication (by way of data, inputs/outputs, feedback) bear upon our understanding of the ethical given that the ethical is also rooted, one way or another, in the communicative practices of *contact*? This question, let us be clear, is no doubt related to, but ought not to be reduced to, that of the 'ethical implications' of the sensory enhancement of the experience of cyberspace which haptic media introduce and materialise. The distinction I am making here is between questions concerned with changes in behaviour and attitude, say, between agents operating in cyberspace, and the question of how a new technology of sensory affect impacts on *the formation of ethical subjectivity itself*. The first set of questions might be concerned with how, when identity is fluid and personal contact is understood as 'mediated' (rather than being immediate, or direct), this changes agents' ideas of privacy, commitment, responsibility, culpability, offence, and any number of other social norms and mores – in short, concerned with matters of cultural normativity and normative morality. The second kind of question, with which the present work is concerned throughout, is essentially philosophical in character and, in this specific context, is directed, rather, at how the formation of ethical subjectivity is related to the conditions of embodiment understood as being a priori technological.

In the context of the ecotechnical whole (without yet addressing the question of whether we must think of this 'whole' in terms of its finitude or infinitude; as a 'totality', and whether it permits of alterity in any sense) being 'in touch' or touching another, surely, has always been a matter, quite literally, of the *materiality* of con-*tact*: of the tactility of bodily technics; of the technics of the 'sensory apparatus'. It was intuitively, rather than with any great philosophical insight, that McLuhan grasped how media were – and always had been, from speech, through writing to print as much as in the electric age – 'extensions of the senses', and how technologies have always been the material modalities of the psyche extended into the world. With a great deal of philosophical rigour, though with little reference to media in the ordinary sense, Derrida provides a highly nuanced and detailed deconstruction of the distinction between mediate and the immediate as this has operated in the history of Western philosophy since Aristotle.[7] And he does this specifically in its relation to the value variously afforded to the sense of touch. What he says is helpful in the context of the argument I wish to make that any analysis of the 'haptic media environment' in the age of digital technology must needs address the question of how that environment *materially transforms the sense of touch* (as we live it/experience it/feel it) and changes the way we conceptualise sensation in general.

The emergent haptic media environment forces us towards a rethinking of sensation in its relation to technics. Derrida himself engages in such a reconceptualisation of this in various ways in *On Touching*, in particular in his reflections on what he calls 'humanualism' – a term he introduces in the course of thinking through the inseparability (or necessary interfacing) of the human (toucher) and (hu)manipulation of the (touched) material environment.[8] Even the fleshy human hand, Derrida illustrates, cannot be considered to be 'natural' as opposed to 'technological'. And as 'manipulation' always involves touch in one form or another, this is just one way in which the primacy of touch comes to the fore. This is just one of several examples Derrida discusses as evidence for how a certain haptocentrism has always been at work beneath the ocularcentrism of Western thinking down the millennia – be this the ocularcentrism of the Platonic Sun, the Cartesian light of reason or of the notion of En*light*enment and the transcendental tradition in general.

In a classical Derridean move, he argues that any revaluation of touch must *avoid* the *re*-invention of 'haptocentrism' – which would, in effect, be no more than another version of the traditional privileging of presence or immediacy. Such haptocentrism, he shows, is evident in every implicit reduction and subordination of touch to (its) re-presentation.

Now, for the most part, the cultural theorisation of the virtual undertaken within the Western tradition – even when such theory is engaged in the critique of that tradition – has been concerned, in one way or another, with questions of representation and misrepresentation: for instance, with the image *as* representation, or with the symbolic representation of events, intentions, identities, social practices, and so forth. I noted above how in cultural studies, for example, the ethics and politics of representation in the 'mediated environment' has long been a key concern. The emergent practical realisation of the digital haptic media environment, however, whether viewed from the perspective of the arts and philosophy, cultural studies or the technological sciences, is in various ways conterminal with the rethinking of the senses in general in terms of *affect*.[9] This development has led to a rethinking of the visual outside of the paradigm of representation, and Hansen's approach to digital art, as I have indicated, is an example of the treatment of vision as a mode of haptic, or affective, sensibility. In terms of affect theory, touch can be viewed as being fundamental to each of the other senses it is traditionally distinguished from: 'all' of the senses are in a sense haptic in that they are dependent on the transmission of movement, and all movement is ultimately registered on the surfaces of 'skins'. As noted in the previous chapter, the retina of the eye, the tympanum of the ear, the mucous membranes of the nose and mouth are all sites and surfaces of affective intensity – they are all equally, as Levinas puts it, 'the edges of the nerves'.[10] In this respect all of the senses (plural) are perhaps just one (singular); they are all, so to speak, *in one sense*. For this reason, according to Derrida, who appeals to Nancy's notion of the singular-plural,[11] the investigation of touch needs to proceed by way of an exploration of, precisely, the interconnection between 'all of the senses' – and, indeed, all the senses of the word 'sense', too – as the very concept touches upon how sense and sentience, or sensuality and thought, are related to each other.[12] It is because intellectual reflection pulls apart the senses and privileges vision that it is so difficult to think this material commonality immanently and without invoking 'visuality'; and it appears, moreover, as if this 'sense of sense' were innocent with respect to this very division of the senses and the privileging of vision. This is a division and privileging which, seemingly naturally, aligns vision and visibility with what is called 'common sense'; with the traditional metaphysical nexus of objectivity, observability and truth as the root of the empirical. It is not that with the arrival of the 'haptic media environment' on the cultural scene, as it were, this ocularcentrism ought now simply to be regarded as deficient or erroneous with respect to haptics, or that 'haptology' should replace it on the grounds that touch is, or somehow must have always been, more originary or fundamental than vision. The issue I am identifying here, rather, is the inadequacy of the thinking of touch based on its supposed *re-presentation*, in this instance, by way of the concept of 'haptics' (the haptical image or indeed *as* the 'haptic data set'). Any thinking which claims to render touch knowable as such, in this way, or which claims a greater truth concerning touch than that of lived sensation itself, by definition, would be inadequate to it. One erroneous response to this difficulty, for instance, would be to suppose that the brain sciences today, by way of their accounts of what the brain is 'doing' but which does not register in, nor is available to consciousness, amounts to positive evidence of 'affective proprioception'. Mark Hansen relies, in my view, too heavily – and ultimately uncritically – on such positivism in his general account of the haptic, and he reproduces precisely the kind of haptocentrism Derrida warns against.[13] Even in the most subtle philosophies of sensuality – such as Merleau-Ponty's, for example – this leads to a certain ambivalence concerning the epistemic and ontological distinctiveness of the sense of touch. Derrida points this out, for instance, when he notes that in the *Phenomenology of Perception* Merleau-Ponty presents such 'ambiguous formulations' as the following: 'Experience does not present [the senses] as equivalent: it seems to me that visual experience is truer than tactile experience'[14] alongside others such as, 'the unity and the diversity of the senses are truths of the same order'.[15]

What this ambiguity indicates, I suggest, and not just with respect to Merleau-Ponty (who, of course, is also known for being 'the' philosopher of ambiguity itself – but I shall leave that to one side) is that the relationship *within* touching between the toucher and the touched always begs the question, as Derrida expresses it, of the 'who' or 'what' – of who or what touches in this thing called 'touching'. All along (and in harmony with Nancy on the theme of touching) Derrida's refrain is that 'touching is (itself) essentially untouchable', that is, *unrepresentable* and ultimately, therefore, unthematisable.

So can touch be thought at all? If not by way of *re*-presentation, then certainly also not as *direct* or *immediate* presentation of one thing/person to one other thing/person, for touch precedes, precisely, the differentiation of the subject and the object. Touching precedes the terms of the contact which happens with 'I touch you'. No wonder then, with a certain lightness of heart perhaps (and the heart, incidentally, is discussed elsewhere in the book in terms of the 'syncope' – the heart which touches itself by feeling itself beat), Derrida says (perhaps to himself) 'I cannot bring myself to believe in it very much – touch, that is.'[16]

The technical challenges faced by haptic media engineers and data algorithmists may well be taken to be those of how best the sense of touch can be represented (in other words, simulated). But, before those come to mind, I am suggesting, the digitisation of 'touch data' substantively amounts to a 'techno-evolution' in the *materiality* of what has hitherto been designated as the *sense* of touch. And, once haptic media become a part of our everyday communicative practices – once this technology is, literally, in-corporated into the communicative interface – the actuality of touching will, I suggest, be in the process of undergoing a transformation by way of acquiring a new form of materiality. In this respect, at least, Hansen's account of the body–digital information interface in terms of a 'section' of a Bergsonian affective continuum is insightful. However, what I would add to this, firstly, is that what haptic media 'do', effectively, is technologically re-engineer the skin (or the 'skin section' of the continuum); and secondly, that 'the skin', after Levinas, can no longer be presumed to have as it primary reference the bio-physiological epidermis (nor, for that matter, some synthetic physical substitute for such a skin – say something like a data-glove or data-body suit). Rather, the skin should be rethought as the inter(sur)face of sensibility; of touching itself – that is, prior to the determination of the distinction between toucher and touched. The term 'skin', nonetheless, could well be allowed to continue to stand as the name of the site wherein *the event* of contact takes place. Contact *(with-)in* this sense (literally, *in* touching) is simply not susceptible to an analysis on the basis of the distinction between the mediate and the immediate, and the skin as a medium, along with all other forms of what we ordinarily call 'media', does not, in fact, mediate between 'two'. This paradox of the 'oneness' of touching only appears to be a paradox for a consciousness which arrives late on the scene and which has already given itself a world of subjects and objects. Touching precedes my sense of my own being-in-a-skin and my subjectivity as a 'oneself', as we saw in previous chapters: the oneself or Subject is the product of a certain *withdrawal* from contact, a movement away from an other. That is why this sensibility associated with 'the skin' (whatever its actual medial materiality), according to Levinas, is the very 'subjectivity of the subject'.[17] And, this is consistent with Derrida's suggestion, quite late in *On Touching*, that 'a thinking of touch must at least go through a theory of skin'.[18]

In *New Philosophy for New Media* Hansen does argue that in the interaction with haptic information the body becomes the 'active source of framing' rather than 'a passive site of technical inscription',[19] but his account of haptics still begs the question of how such a touching body differentiates itself from a touched body – be this an object or another Subject (which may be a person, but could equally be *any body whatever*). But how can a body be a 'centre' of anything without being *designated* or *recognised* as such? In this respect, the focus Hansen places on the dynamism of movement effectively assumes the identity of the body in question on the basis of a certain naturalism, albeit expressed in terms of the phenomenological givenness of the primacy of its non-differentiation, and hence he neglects to address the problem of the boundary between the Same and the Other. In his later *Bodies in Code* he does dedicate several important pages to a discussion of the skin, significantly considering how 'the skin constitutes the locus and support for a primordial materialization of the sensible' and relating this to the 'essential technicity'[20] of the human being, but the discussion there still eschews the question of the *ethics of touch*. When Derrida says that the thinking of touch must at least go through a theory of the skin, the emphasis can be taken to indicate that without this, the prospect of alterity is annihilated. In other words, there is no space, no gap, no opening between the Same and the Other. Hansen's concept of the body as a 'centre of indetermination', in its neglect of the skin in this sense, renders it ultimately egocentric and narcissistic – no matter the stage of its technogenetic evolution, be this measured in terms of its incorporation of clothing, transportation, hybridisation with wider techno-cultural forms, or its inhabitation of digital virtual landscapes, or indeed any other forms of its material extension.

THE ETHICS OF TOUCH AND THE TEMPORALITY OF THE ETHICAL SUBJECT

As explained in earlier chapters, Levinas's materialist phenomenology claims to discover in sensibility the irreducible structure of ethical subjectivity. Ethicality as the possibility of openness to the Other is the possibility of an existent whose ipseity is accomplished by virtue of its being a being-in-a-skin. This perspective can help us to think about the ethical dimensions of the nascent 'haptic media environment', presuming we accept the proposition that 'technological materiality' is that out of which 'reality', or the embodied experience of the real, is forged; versions of such a thesis are to be found in both Bergson and Deleuze, and in Hansen's appropriation of the thinking of these two philosophers. Chapter 2 explained the manner in which Levinas, too, is a thinker of immanence who also draws on Bergson and shares with Deleuze (at least to a degree) a theory of the becoming-Subject which ultimately rests on an account of the process of internal differentiation *within* being. This chapter seeks to relate this process of the becoming of the Subject in Levinas's existential thinking to his ethics of touch.

Cathryn Vasseleu summarises the thrust of Levinas's ethics of touch well when she says that:

> Levinas considers touch as the exposition of an affective involvement with others . . . [it] is a subjection to alterity before it can be posited as the locus of its own manifestation. Proximity is the communication of an anarchic sensibility that occurs before the subject can gather itself into a position in relation to this otherness which cannot be assembled in a representational present.[21]

The proximity of touching, she adds, is thus a 'contaminating communication rather than a communication based on a relationship between subject and object'.[22]

The question I want to return to now, against the background of this image of communication as affective transmission in sensibility, is one that was raised earlier and concerns the sense in which affective sensibility can be said to be 'ethical'; as affective contact with others does not in any obvious way appear to guarantee this. As also I noted earlier, touch, after all, might just as well take the form of violence, the 'murderous blow' as it might hospitality and tenderness. In fact, as was discussed in Chapter 3, in *Totality and Infinity* Levinas's account of the caress (between two) – and which we might consider here as an instance of affective contact – is presented as an example of the *un*ethical. He refers to it, for instance, in terms of its being a 'profanity'.[23] It is said to be unethical, principally, in that it is a *communion* of two and as such lacks by way of being closed to what he calls the 'third party' (*le tiers*) – whose 'involvement' in every I–Other conjuncture, or the ethical relation between two, is the necessary condition of justice. In other words, the ethical is an *im*possibility for sensible being by virtue of its being beyond the power of the sensible existent alone. And yet, the caress and other 'erotic' forms of contact are also held to signify the possibility of the beyond of this impossibility, namely, the possibility of ethics. Now, whilst Levinas's discourse of the 'third party' suggests that transcendence and representation inevitably figure in the possibility of justice and ethics (as if justice and ethics were only ever available to the thematic reflections of consciousness), it is their rootedness in the materiality of sensation that he claims makes them possible at all.

Levinas's exposition of this claim in *Otherwise than Being*, just to recall, is both indebted to and critical of the Husserlian *epoché*. He criticises that aspect of Husserl's method which presents phenomenological descriptions of sensations only as modalities of consciousness. For this Husserl bears the philosophical responsibility for the 'modification of sensibility into intentionality'.[24] Husserl's analyses remain essentially epistemological in nature and fail to penetrate to the sensible fundament of subjectivity. However, it is only on the basis of the Husserlian exposure of such a thematising movement or process intrinsic to thought that Levinas himself will eventually be able to claim its reversal by way of his own 'ethical reduction' of it. It is sensation – understood by Levinas as the couplet of the sensing and sensed – which must be subjected to this further reduction in order to arrive at 'sensibility'. The point of this insistence on sensibility is to reciprocally 'expose' how the possibility of ethics and justice originates with the '*diachrony* of the same and the other *in* sensibility'.[25] Time is literally the essence of the ethical Subject:

> When not reduced, sensibility is the duality of the sensing and the sensed, *a separation, and at once a union, in time, a putting of the instant out of phase,* and already a retention of the separated phase. As reduced, sensibility is animated, a signification of the one-for-the-other, a duality not assemblable of the soul and the body, the body being inverted into a for-the-other by animation, a diachrony other than that of representation.[26]

The Levinasian 'ethical reduction' is thus not a reduction by reflection. It pertains rather to the very 'inversion' of the body into the 'being-for-the-other'.

It is at this point we can see, I suggest, how Levinas provides an 'ethics of temporality' of the very kind Hansen, in one of the very few references to ethics in *New Philosophy for New Media*, appears to identify as precisely what is needed. The reference comes up in relation to his discussion of Varela's 'protentional-retentional matrix of perception', which concerns the constitution of the 'now' and the correlated ability of both the brain and the computer to compute on the microphysical instant.[27] In view of this hypothesised correlation, he says:

> [In] the context of contemporary technologies that do in fact compute on the microphysical instant, it is imperative that we bring out the 'phenomenological difference' or singularity specific to retention – that is, the synthetic interval comprising duration – and that we identify it (in distinction to the microphysical, but also to memory) as the now, the very basis of human experience *qua* living.[28]

It is far from clear on the basis of what is said here, however, whether this neo-positivist account of the facticity of time perception ('Varela's work on the neuro-temporality of perception . . . objectively fixes the

temporal threshold for present-time consciousness at 0.3 of a second'[29])
could be the basis of an 'ethics of temporality' which would be anything
other than the auto-affectivity of a solipsistic ego. How could it ever
amount to more than the retentional recollection of the internal movements of *the Same*, which differs only *from itself* across time? Indeed,
Hansen seems to recognise this when he continues thus:

> Following Bergson, we must allow the now of perception to become con-
> taminated with affectivity: we must identify the now with that threshold
> within which perception of the flux of an object affects itself, and thus
> generates a supplementary perception, a perception of the flux itself,
> time-consciousness.[30]

In other words, on this model, the alterity of the Other would be
nothing more than the dislocated movement of the Same.

Time, specifically time in Levinas's sense of it as 'diachrony'– the
notion of the 'instant' as being out of phase with itself across the distinction between the Same and the Other – is of the essence here. The
'inversion of the body' mentioned above, *back*, as it were, into sensibility, which diachronous time accomplishes, is what allows Levinas to
describe the 'contact' of touching as being *at the same time* the separation of the toucher and the touched. The 'animation' of the Same as
'for-the-other' (as expressed in the above citation), is older than any
act of consciousness switching between protentional and retentional
phases constitutive of the 'now' – which Hansen insists we identify
in the light of the latest cognitive science, and effectively as a sort of
measurable brain-speed. 'Animation' in Levinas's discourse is, rather,
a matter of sensibility; and the temporality of touch is not a matter
of the speed of synaptic processes, but of separation and alterity. The
diachronic trajectory of sensibility, Levinas attempts to show, lacks any
retention and precedes every protention. This is a bit like saying that
when I touch you, this is an event of separation and differentiation:
tactility is the material event of such a dehiscence. In other words, our
technical possibilities for 'touching' – whatever the material actualities
of those available to us – are, precisely, the material possibilities out of
which ethical subjectivity emerges.

THE ETHICAL IS ALWAYS
(UN)MEDIATED CONTACT

In the context of the haptic media environment, touching is, strictly
speaking, no more and no less 'mediated' or 'immediate' than it ever
was in this ethical sense. However, it is the case – and Hansen, as
I understand him, makes an argument to this effect – that the very

'materiality' of touch undergoes a transformation in the context of technological development. *What* it is that undergoes this transformation we can, quite usefully I suggest, (continue to) refer to as 'the skin'. But 'skin' must now be thought of as the 'in-between' of the Subject as a some one or something and the Other. Such a notion of 'the skin' as an 'inter(sur)face' does not restrict what constitutes the skin to any particular technological form, but rather refers it primarily to the *materiality of the process of communication*; the site of affective transmission and exchange of movement. It directs thought, I have argued here, to the ethical dimension of contact as 'touching' – whatever this is or may become; whatever 'touching' means. Touching is, in any case, strictly speaking, 'unknowable'.

Finally in this chapter, I shall try to follow that pointer of Derrida's in *On Touching*, the one cited earlier: namely, that any account of touching must go by way of a 'theory of the skin'. It is rather surprising that in his reading of Levinas in this book, which focuses largely on touch in *Totality and Infinity*, there is no discussion of what Levinas actually says of the skin in his later *Otherwise than Being*. As we have seen, his later account of ethical subjectivity in the later work is expressed – and at length – in terms of the Subject as a 'being-in-a-skin'. The skin, in this text, is a much used and widely deployed figure of liminality: it forms the boundary maintaining the distinction between the me and the not-me; it is the surface of my contact with the other person; it gives me the sense of my own interiority, and at the same time it is the surface of my exposure to exteriority and, hence, to the possibilities of wounding and violence as well as tenderness and welcome. It 'is at one and the same time the surface of *all possible "contact"*'.[31] As such an ethical interface, this notion of the skin, I suggest, can be held to refer to *any* possible form of affective materiality; hence to any existing or future forms of 'haptic media' which may come to serve as the primary site of exposure to alterity. In this sense the thesis is future-proof from the point of view of the actual technics of contact. Derrida's remarks on how there is no discrete sense of touch, are, at least, consistent with this Levinasian view of ethical sensibility as being, quite literally, *the matter* of 'the skin' and that the skin's materiality is neither determined in advance by, nor restricted to, any specific technical form of contact between the Same and the Other.

The corollary of this conclusion is that the ethical subject matters which normative morality identifies as significant will be specific to the manifestations of ethical subjectivity to which the contemporary total media environment gives rise. This is perhaps discernible today in the everyday contexts of digital culture and the 'wired society' in which, in a multitude of ways, the relationship between ethical propriety and transgression on the one hand and new forms of subjectivity on the other takes shape in conjunction with technologies of data production, storage and retrieval. The following chapter will examine the way in which the contemporary digital media environment has given rise to the 'data Subject' and it will further contextualise this in relation to the ethics of secrecy.

NOTES

1. See Hansen, *New Philosophy for New Media* and *Bodies in Code*.
2. I follow Hansen's use of the term 'evolution' here to refer to the technogenetic production of the being of sensation – or of touch, in other words, as the form of what he also calls 'primary tactility'. This, he argues throughout, is always already a matter of the interface of embodiment and technology. (See *Bodies in Code*, especially Part 1.)
3. See Simondon, *Du mode de l'existence des objets techniques*.
4. See Stiegler, *Technics and Time*.
5. Hansen, *New Philosophy for New Media*, pp. 5–8.
6. I have in mind here Bergson's thesis expounded in his *Matter and Memory*, p. 7, that 'matter . . . is an aggregate of "images"', and Deleuze's appropriation of this thesis in his *Cinema 1* (especially in ch. 1).
7. Derrida, *On Touching – Jean-Luc Nancy*.
8. Ibid. pp. 152–7, 185.
9. For an overview of the diverse deployment of affect theory in cultural studies and philosophy, see Gregg and Seigworth, *Affect Theory Reader*.
10. Levinas, *Otherwise than Being, or, Beyond Essence*, p. 15.
11. See Nancy, *Being Singular Plural*.
12. Derrida, *On Touching – Jean-Luc Nancy*, p. 15.
13. Hansen must, nonetheless, be credited with a sophisticated and nuanced understanding of the 'risk' of positivism, something which he identifies and discusses at length in the context of an analysis of Stiegler's relationship to Derrida in his essay 'Realtime Synthesis and the *Différance* of the Body'.
14. Merleau-Ponty, *Phenomenology of Perception*, p. 234 fn.1, cited in Derrida, *On Touching – Jean-Luc Nancy*, p. 206 (original emphasis).
15. Merleau-Ponty, *Phenomenology of Perception*, p. 221, cited in Derrida, *On Touching – Jean-Luc Nancy*, p. 206 (original emphasis).
16. Derrida, *On Touching – Jean-Luc Nancy*, p. 116.
17. Levinas, *Otherwise than Being, or, Beyond Essence*, p. 15.
18. Derrida, *On Touching – Jean-Luc Nancy*, p. 267.
19. See Tim Lenoir's Introduction to Hansen, *New Philosophy for New Media*, p. xxi.
20. Hansen, *Bodies in Code*, pp. 60, 78–9.

21. Vasseleu, *Textures of Light*, p. 98 (emphasis added).
22. Ibid. p. 98.
23. Levinas, *Totality and Infinity*, p. 257. See also Derrida, *On Touching – Jean-Luc Nancy*, p. 90.
24. Levinas, *Otherwise than Being, or, Beyond Essence*, p. 71.
25. Ibid. p. 71 (emphasis added).
26. Ibid. pp. 71–2.
27. Hansen, *New Philosophy for New Media*, p. 259.
28. Ibid. p. 259–60.
29. Ibid. p. 234.
30. Ibid. p. 260.
31. Levinas, *Otherwise than Being, or, Beyond Essence*, p. 55.

6. Secrecy and the Secret of Ethical Subjectivity

Some archives must not remain inaccessible, and the politics of the secret calls for very different kinds of responsibility, according to the situation. Once again, that can be said without relativism but in the name of another responsibility which must each time be singular, exceptional, and thus as the principle of any decision, itself in some way secret.[1]

SECRECY IN A WIRED WORLD

The interplay between secrecy and disclosure has recently crystallised as a defining feature of the contemporary zeitgeist of the 'wired' culture and society. It is intrinsic to the multifarious phenomena of communicative capitalism's diverse trade in data and information, from the details of private lives, consumer habits, tastes and preferences to the production, packaging and distribution of informational products of all kinds within the knowledge economy; and the value of 'secrets' and the price (in several senses) of their disclosure is a matter of great public interest and fascination. The exploits of 'hackers' and 'crackers' are today not only typical items of daily news, but effectively key to the processes of news gathering and production themselves (as the 2011–12 News International phone-hacking scandal illustrates perfectly). These are all characterised by data-network interventions of one kind or another. Tabloid celebrity phone-hacking and serious political data-journalism both exploit this new technical capacity of networks and the data they carry. More than two decades ago Deleuze and Guattari anticipated that 'the more the secret is made into a structuring organizing form, the thinner and more ubiquitous it becomes'.[2] The interplay between secrecy and disclosure is now indeed ubiquitous, and is evident in an extensive multiplicity of concrete contexts structured by the incorporation of digital communications into almost every aspect of daily life and the technocratic management of society. For journalists as much as for academics, for suppliers as much as for consumers of goods and services, for 'friends' as much as for 'enemies', the digitally mediated and stored data archive is both the topic and the resource: something, as Featherstone notes, 'researchers need to make sense of the world, but also the resource, the interface which cuts into and opens up that world'.[3]

In relation to this, it has been widely observed, we witness a generalised loosening and transformation of the boundary between the public and the private which is materially driven by the means of communication individuals have at their disposal and the uses they and other agencies they engage with, make of them.[4] Just as the cradle-to-the-grave notion of the Welfare State as an expression of the collective, public responsibility of each for all is being ushered off the stage in neo-liberal societies, the cradle-to-the-grave recording and publication of individual lives is becoming commonplace. It seems irresistible not to see the decline of the 'public sphere' in Western democracies as the counterpoint to the rise of 'public individualism' expressed through what could be termed communicative self-publicity. 'Public life' as the notion of what some individuals engage in ostensibly 'for the sake of the public', at least to a large degree, is being progressively supplanted by the multiplicity of lives lived in public. This latter phenomenon coincides with what has often been called the democratisation of the means of publicity and is associated with personal lives increasingly volunteered to the public gaze, for instance through media platforms such as Facebook, YouTube, Twitter, Flickr and the blog, whilst other information which is not 'volunteered' is recorded by the likes of CCTV, Google Street View, loyalty cards, phone logs and other forms of transparent surveillance – transparent in the sense that the public is either passively accepting of, or largely indifferent or oblivious to them. The trade in such records and their data signals an extension of commodification to subjective life itself. The inevitability of life lived 'on the record' in the form of the eponymous data trail is almost impossible to avoid, at least in the advanced techno-cultures of the world. Such widespread mechanised and hyper-individualised self-surveillance, coupled with a mixed economy of controlled and uncontrolled data release, combined with the development of meta-techniques of analysis, display and presentation, have given rise to the production of new styles, forms and notions of knowledge and new senses of secret knowledge and secrecy itself. And, as Jodi Dean noted a decade ago, in such a techno-culture for which 'publicity' has become 'the organizing element of [both] democratic politics and the golden ring of [the] infotainment society', 'the public' has a developed a thirst for the disclosure of secrets of all kinds, personal secrets through corporate secrets to state secrets.[5] The culturally predominant notions of the secret and secrecy are consequently now closely allied with information and the control of access to it.

No doubt the specific possibilities that the digital introduces have a bearing on the overall character of how the public/private distinction plays out in contemporary cultural and social contexts and situations, but it is equally clear that the possible breach of this boundary, or conversely, its maintenance and security, has also always been a function of the materiality, or the 'mediality', of communications media themselves.[6] Any simple, would-be private conversation by virtue of its very vocalisation carries with it the possibility of being overheard; any note, any mark or inscription, in wax, clay, ink, print or any other analogue recording already carries with it the possibility of falling into unintended hands. In other words, as soon as there is communicative expression at all, the conterminal issues of its destination, security and secrecy arise as a consequence of the 'record' which is necessarily produced. The potential impact of the digital combined with the miniaturisation of storage was dramatically realised in the year 2010–11 with the WikiLeaks haemorrhage of 'secrets' into the wider public domain in the form of around 400,000 classified documents on the wars in Iraq and Afghanistan and on US diplomacy. One man, allegedly (Bradley Manning, by his own account), with security clearance and a memory stick (and assisted by WikiLeaks, itself further assisted by several of the world's leading newspapers), effectively demonstrated how easily 'switchable' the relationship between secrecy and disclosure is in the age of ubiquitous digital recording. From a conventional security point of view, it could be claimed, these disclosures were an 'accident waiting to happen' – but if so, it was one presaged, I suggest, not so much by old-style infiltration, double-agency and espionage, or by the managerial folly of allowing rather large numbers of personnel to have access to classified databanks as such (it is claimed around three million individuals had access to the 'cablegate' files, for instance) so much as by the banality of the destinerrant[7] private email 'leaked' into the public domain courtesy of the 'reply to all' button; by the inevitability of the 'lap-top left on the train', or the confusion of unlabelled CDs – or other such scenarios. That is not to deny the fact that in this case Bradley Manning knew what he was doing – at least in the sense that he acted intentionally and surreptitiously when he downloaded the information he was later to pass on, via WikiLeaks, to the global public. Such an event of information disclosure was, rather, an implicit technical possibility of the techno-materiality, or mediality, of digitalised recording, information storage and transmissibility.[8]

The 'WikiLeaks phenomenon' has raised the ethical and political stakes of the debate concerning the wider implications of the contemporary dependency of a globalised culture on digital communications and digital 'record keeping'. These stakes are raised in so far as it is not only 'secrets' (in the form of 'classified documents') themselves that have been disclosed, and on an unprecedented scale, but a new measure of the extent of the culture of secrecy at work in supposedly open societies that has been disclosed along with them. And, along with these 'disclosures', as happens with any breach of security, a new sense of the impossibility of absolute security in relation to the medium of their disclosure emerges. The singularity of the WikiLeaks phenomenon as a 'disclosure event', or 'breach of secrecy', is clearly related to the materiality of the medium (or media) through which it became possible as such. And whilst it might be said that it became possible on the basis of a specific mediality, this ought not to be identified in either purely technical terms (of, say, the digital rather than the analogue, or computer code rather than printed pages or taped conversations) or purely in terms of the human 'sources' without whom the circuit of informational disclosure supposedly could not happen. The specific mediality of the medium which made the disclosure event possible as such, is a combination of its various human and technical elements (as we ordinarily think of these things as distinct from one another); but it is more accurately to be identified, I suggest, in terms of an aggregation – of access, organisation, collaboration on the one hand, and data recording, storage, transmission protocols, and so forth on the other. It will be my contention in this chapter that issues surrounding the ethics and politics of secrecy/disclosure in their deepest sense must be addressed on the basis of the 'originary technicity', or 'necessary prostheticity', of the human in so far as it is always already embedded in and expressed (or 'externalised') through a communicative apparatus.[9] And it is against such a background of materially mediated communications that the question of responsibility with respect to secrets and their disclosure must ultimately be posed.

THE ETHICO-POLITICS OF SECRECY AND DISCLOSURE

In contemporary popular discourses the question of the responsibility, or irresponsibility, with regard to the disclosure of 'secrets' is largely framed in terms of 'transparency', the openness and sharing of information, and the coincidence of these with a certain end to censorship and control as these were operative in 'disciplinary societies'.[10] Such an ethos of the 'freedom of information' in its widest sense is often weighed against such things as rights of ownership, intellectual property and privacy. But as well as being matters of general public concern, and beyond such normative representations of 'ethical' and 'political' issues associated with them, the relationship between secrecy and disclosure is also a directly philosophical matter. The critical analysis of the contemporary techno-cultural contexts of secrecy and disclosure, I wish to suggest, must ultimately take into account the manner in which this dyadic distinction in several senses is prefigured even in the emergence of Western philosophy itself and the metaphysics that ensues from it, in so far as the 'first' thought of Being in its relation to truth as presencing (as 'bringing something to light') is pre-eminent within it and essential to it. In other words, the question of secrecy/disclosure must be viewed as essentially philosophical in character, and for this reason one must take care not simply to subscribe to the naturalistic and naturalising discourses of secrecy as *opposed* to disclosure.

In his discussion of the notion of truth as ἀλήθεια (*alethia*) in the Heraclitus Fragment B16, Heidegger shows, for instance, how the 'fundamental trait of presencing itself is determined by remaining concealed and unconcealed' – and that this takes place in Heraclitus's thinking.[11] Moreover, Heidegger's reading of the Fragment, consistent with his general thesis of the 'history of Being' as the history of this double movement, presents us with the challenge to think 'revealing and concealing' not 'merely as two occurrences jammed together, but as one and the Same'.[12] The post-Heideggerian thinkers Levinas and Derrida (whose thinking of the secret is central to my argument here), on the one hand concur with the necessity of thinking secrecy/disclosure as inseparable: there can be no thought of the concealed qua concealed, it can only be figured or expressed on the basis of its withdrawal qua 'unconcealment' – as such a double movement. Yet, on the other hand both of them argue still that the 'absolute' or 'ultimate' secret remains the unthought (and unthinkable) condition which breaches the totality of the Same understood as the non-difference between concealment and unconcealment. Rather than thought falling into the abyss of an epistemological infinite regress (of the *secret* secret) or becoming fixated on the slipping away of Being in every thought or concept (the oblivion of the secret), both Levinas and Derrida speak of thought's encounter with, and its disturbance by, an 'infinite responsibility'. In the context of his wider philosophical contention that 'ethics is first philosophy', Levinas, for instance, refers to this as an 'indebtedness before any loan' and as '*the ultimate secret of the subject's incarnation*'.[13] Polemicising against Heidegger, he says that 'the comprehension of Being is not the most intimate work of thought and does not lead us to the ultimate secret of subjectivity'[14] and that 'the difference between the Infinite and the finite is a non-indifference of the Infinite to the finite' and it is this which is 'the secret of subjectivity'.[15] Derrida, for his part, expresses both his 'taste for the secret' as a defence against 'totalitarianism' (in both the political and the politico-ontological senses)[16] and his general concurrence with the Levinasian notion of infinite responsibility which breaches totality (understood as the thought of the Same):

> I would say, for Levinas and for myself, that if you give up on the infinitude of responsibility, there is no responsibility. It is because we act and live in infinitude that the responsibility with regard to the other (*autrui*) is irreducible. If responsibility were not infinite, if every time that I had to take an ethical or a political decision with regard to the other (*autrui*) this were not infinite, then I would not be able to engage myself in an infinite debt with regard to each singularity.[17]

They both thus think of the secret in essentially ethico-political terms: the secret must be 'kept' or 'preserved' (*entamé*), not because it is 'my' personal prerogative to reveal or hide, tell or not tell something (in any case, I do not know it or possess it as such), but because it is my obligation in the sense given by the paralogical phrase 'indebtedness before any loan'.

This 'Levinasian-Derridean' insistence on infinite responsibility and the ethical moment of the encounter with an absolute alterity which is 'in me' in the form of a secret I am obliged to 'keep', can easily be misread in terms of a privileging of the secret as 'privacy' over the 'publicity' of disclosure. This would amount to a privileging of the ethical *at the cost of* the political, understood as publicity in the sense of openness and communality based on the sharing of secrets, or the disavowal of secrecy in general; because secrecy is by definition socially and politically divisive (the Latin *secretus* originally means 'to set apart'). In his article 'Public Secrets', Jeremy Gilbert seeks to reject this notion of the keeping of a secret which is claimed not merely to be unknown but unknowable, on the ground that if saying I have a secret in me is a meaningful statement at all, it must imply that it is, at least in principle, shareable and communicable, even before I make any decision as to whether to share it or make it 'public' in any way whatever.[18] His critical rejection of the Levinasian-Derridean discourse of the 'absolute secret' centres on the question of what the possible point of a secret which no one knows could be: if no one knows it, it is not really a secret at all, just an 'unknown'. His reasoning is that for me to hold a secret at all, and for this thing to be regarded as a secret in the first place, I must have already shared it with someone, or be able to share it – at the very least with myself. It must be 'on the record', so to speak, and thus recallable, at least by means of my own psychic memory. Gilbert rightly points out, citing a theme in Levinas, which he notes is 'echoed' in Derrida, that the secret 'isolates' the self, and thus cuts it off from entering into political communion with others, despite the unequivocal insistence of Derrida that this isolation or 'separation' that the secret effectuates is not to be equated with 'privacy': 'the secret is not reducible to the private'.[19] Gilbert is thus driven to conclude that a 'partial equation' of the secret and privacy, at least, persists (in his version of the Levinasian-Derridean thinking of the secret) and that its implications for the political are in fact quite clear: namely, it culminates in a certain a-politicism that must be rejected.

I cite Gilbert's critical reconstruction of Levinas's/Derrida's thinking of the secret here because it provides a clear image of what could be described as a political thinking of secrecy/disclosure *at the cost* of the ethical, and of how this arises as a consequence of relegating the ethical to the sphere of the private. However, what Gilbert neglects to recall (and the reason why his critique misses its target) is that for both Levinas and Derrida, in every 'singular' context, situation or event, it is the demand for justice (rather than, for instance, the protection of individual privacy under the law) which marks the refolding of 'all of the others' into the uniqueness, or singularity, of 'my' responsibility. The signature Levinasian formula for this – 'the third party looks at me in the eyes of the Other',[20] for instance – is echoed in Derrida's several workings through of the phrase '*tout autre est tout autre*', or, 'every other is every other other, [and] is altogether other'.[21] In fact, rather than invoking the privacy of the secret, both Levinas and Derrida are at pains to describe how the *res publica* is always present in the demanding look of the eyes of each and every other I encounter.

Now, whilst it is important to acknowledge the connection between the keeping of a secret and the 'separation' or 'isolation' of the one who keeps it, just how this separation is understood is key with regard to whether it implies an a-political subjectivity withdrawn from and closed off from sociality or an *ethico*-political subjectivity of openness towards others. And in this regard, one cannot simply neglect to recall how the hugely important term 'separation' in Levinas's discourse (discussed at length in previous chapters) refers to *both* the absolute (transcendent) difference between the 'I' and the Other (*autrui*) and to the (immanent) process of differentiation between the 'existent' (Levinas's term for the pre-personal 'dividual') and existence in general (*il y a*). Just how separation is related to secrecy is ultimately crucial to the matter at hand: namely, whether the separation of the existent signifies a withdrawal from sociality with others or is, rather, the condition for entry into sociality – and indeed whether these two things are mutually exclusive. Certainly, Levinas appears to argue that the security of the 'I' in its various modes of being-at-home-with-itself (*chez soi*) is to be viewed as the basis for sociality with others in general. It is the very same security (or what could be called the being-in-secret of the 'I') which constitutes the ground for the indivisibility, uniqueness or 'singularity' of its responsibility. 'My' responsibility, for Levinas, it has to remembered, is a pure accusative, an obligation which I did not choose, rather it 'chooses me' – it is incurred by 'me' prior to any idea I have of myself. Whilst this attempt to secure the ethical within the political might not lead to the politics of 'collectivism' (as Gilbert no doubt rightly recognises), it does surely express an idea of the ethico-politics of 'pluralism': for instance, in the section on 'Separation and Discourse' in *Totality and Infinity* we read:

> The real must not only be determined in its historical objectivity, but also from interior intentions, from the secrecy that interrupts the continuity of historical time. Only on the basis of secrecy is the pluralism of society possible. It attests this secrecy.[22]

So, at the very least, it has to be acknowledged that this is not the pluralism of self-centred, *private* individualism (in my view the legitimate target of Gilbert's entire article). It is aimed at establishing, rather, a pluralism of 'unique' or 'singular' responsibilities.

What I am suggesting is that if we are to develop any sense of what might count as responsibility in the context of a normative discourse of the ethics of disclosing secrets – secret records of one kind or another, and of which the WikiLeaks phenomenon serves here as an example – then this difference and this connection between ethics and politics is what we need to be clear about. And my suggestion is that the normative idea of responsibility as *shared* responsibility is only ever understood in terms of 'politics' and the political. It is understood in terms of the political efficacy or effectiveness of disclosure as a political strategy pertaining to a principled, ideological project of openness and transparency. The very notion of striking a blow against 'wrong-doing' (as Julian Assange, for instance, has on occasion put this) through informational disclosure, remains politically grounded rather than ethically grounded. If we continue to think of secrecy/disclosure in terms of a simple opposition, as I suggest every such politics of secrecy/disclosure does, then the question as to whether secrecy is the 'enemy of justice' or whether disclosure is, *at least sometimes also*, the 'enemy of justice', will remain a purely political affair for the manner in which the singularity of any particular situation or context will always be overlooked. Such a politics of disclosure will remain 'unethical' to the extent to which it leaves no room for 'the exception'. And as Derrida has demonstrated at length in several texts concerning the law, justice and the 'mystical foundation of authority', it is allowing for 'the exception' that serves as the ultimate defence against a certain tyranny and totalitarianism.[23] Rather than reiterate his well-known argument here, what I want to draw attention to and emphasise for my own purposes, is the significance of the fact that such a deconstruction of the law/justice is itself a putting on record of the 'secret' of the law – namely, its ultimate illegitimacy for being founded on an originary violent act of self-assertion. It puts on the 'public record' what was already in a sense implicit in the 'record of the law' (kept on 'the rolls', the books of statutes and case law, in the memories of lawyers and judges, and so forth) – irrespectively, historically speaking, of the medium of that record. For the law to be practised, in other words, it has to have been recorded (in some medium or other in the first place) and to be recall-able, reiterable by way of 'memory': *of necessity* the law has to be a 'matter of record'.[24] Derrida's account of the law thus centrally invokes the question of its irreducible mediality. But the ethical Subject, or subjectivity 'for whom' this record matters in any given instance, cannot (itself) be a 'matter of the record': it is not recalled, one might say, but 'called' into existence in the form of an obligation 'in each instance' or 'situation' with regard to the record as the *general* disclosure of law. It is in this sense, then, that this singular 'for whom it matters that justice in any particular case be done' is itself the secret that remains secret.

THE ETHICO-TECHNO-POLITICS OF ARCHIVAL OPENNESS, MEMORY AND RECALL

By critically examining the relationship between ethical subjectivity so conceived, 'the secret' and secrecy in the cultural contexts of 'archival openness' and information disclosure, I shall turn now to how the formation of such ethical subjectivity might be understood in terms of its relation to the techno-politics of secrecy/disclosure, memory and recallability. I shall propose an account of the of the ways in which the current technical transition and 'democratisation' of archival upload/download fundamentally challenges the existing structure of control over such things as censorship, free speech and cultural memory, all of which I shall consider as matters pertaining to the memorialisation of events. (The subject of censorship is expanded upon in the following chapter.) In doing so I aim to demonstrate how Levinas's thinking of the 'ultimate secret of subjectivity' as 'infinite responsibility' (as what is, so to speak, both on and off the record, at once both public and secret) can serve to guide our understanding the ethico-techno-political in the context of digital archive culture in general. This calls, in part, for the thinking of 'infinite responsibility' in relation to the technics of information recall in terms of 'scale'.

The leaking of 'secrets' (in the forms of 'censored' or 'classified information') by WikiLeaks, it is widely noted, was on an unprecedented scale (it involved an estimated half a million documents in total). 'Scale' is a particularly interesting aspect in this context. Talk of the 'unprecedented scale' of the disclosure of information in this case explicitly refers to the number of discrete classified documents that have been placed (or may yet be placed) in the public domain. The contents of these documents, mostly recording the minutiae of 'on the ground' events (acts of violence, destruction, murder and torture, through to the personal opinions of diplomatic actors with respect to exchanges with their various counterparts) forces reflection on the nature of the relationship between the actions of a multiplicity of individual agents (soldiers, 'terrorists', diplomats, heads of state, and so forth) and the sense that the public develops of the reality of the events associated, on a larger scale, with their collective actions within the global context. The 'imagination' required to scale up and consolidate thousands of little memos, details, notes and images – records – into an intelligible panoramic quasi-historical narrative of 'what happened/is happening', in practice takes the form of the imaginative deployment of data visualisation and other techniques of data analysis and presentation. (Whether this imaginative work is that of a psychic or technical mnemonic apparatus is less important than the fact that there is a 'generic capacity' for consolidated recall necessarily at work.) This 'data processing' produces a meta-record; a 're-production' of the war events, diplomacy events and so forth, of which the many individual records were a part originally when access to them was restricted, and becomes enfolded into the 'publicity event' (including the 'WikiLeaks drama' itself) which is consequent upon their public disclosure. What exactly the records re-present, and, as it were, what, in their presentation, they present for the first time, or indeed may come to present or represent through all of the possible and unanticipatable future uses of them, is effectively a matter of their subsequent selective recall and organisation. And, can we in any case separate supposedly primary 'real events' from the secondary technical processes that are constitutive of them (data collation, computation, visualisation, narrativisation, and so forth),[25] or, indeed, from the possible, generic further processing of any set of records with respect to future events in which they may come to have a part? After the avalanche of the WikiLeaked information into the public domain (if there is such a thing distinct from the contingent publication of such 'data sets'), can we say we are any closer to the events to which this information pertains? This question begs another about the general relationship between the event and information: *in what sense, if any, is the event on record and is the event recordable at all?* The same logic can be applied to the relationship between the event and record as it applies to the relationship between justice and the law: 'saying the event' is not possible, or rather, it is both necessary and impossible.

> Saying the event is saying what is, saying things as they present themselves, historical events as they take place, and this is a question of information . . . this saying of the event as a statement of knowledge or information, a sort of cognitive saying of description . . . is always somewhat problematical because the structure of saying is such that it always comes after the event. [Also], because as saying and hence as structure of language, it is bound to a measure of generality, iterability and repeatability, it always misses the singularity of the event. One of the characteristics of the event is that not only does it come about as something unforeseeable, not only does it disrupt the ordinary course of history, but it is absolutely singular.[26]

No amount of disclosure or transparency, one might summarise, renders the event visible, graspable or knowable as such – for 'the event itself' is not on the record; it is not recordable as such. And if we accept this necessary condition of *the absence of the event from the record* generally speaking, then just how are we to think of responsibility in relation to the informational archive which mediates our relationship to it?

Bradley Manning has offered a concept of information that has found resonance amongst a global public: 'Information should be free. It belongs in the public domain.'[27] And for his part in 'freeing the information' he has sacrificed his own freedom. The US government, his master and now jailer, claims to the contrary that democracy and open government are both dependent on the maintenance of secrecy and that only a controlled degree of openness and transparency is consistent with these aims. The current UK government's recent establishment of a Public Sector Transparency Board[28] stands as a further example of how the institutionalisation of data release in the name of transparency goes hand in hand with the delimitation of 'openness' as an ideal or principle. However, because 'the public' as an entity is essentially constituted in relation to media communications, the given set of practices of publicity characterising it at any time (a thesis expounded by Baudrillard in the 1970s, and long before the ubiquitous digital recording described above),[29] it is always ontologically ahead of what are, therefore, necessarily backward-looking concessionary gestures of transparency and openness made by political bodies, power blocs or elites of one kind or another, whose own existence, in reality, is no less owed to the same, overall media communications system constitutive of 'publicity' as such. All Bradley Manning did, one might then argue, was facilitate the transfer of data from one part of the total data system to another. In the age of the 'total digital archive' it is, in the final analysis, surely this archive itself (viewed as the latest mnemo-technical exteriorisation of 'the human') that demonstrates a proclivity to 'leak'. (This makes it all the more perverse to hold him personally responsible, in any sense, for the 'disclosure of secrets'.) And, is not this leakiness a function of what could be described as the information system's material configuration; a function of miniaturisation, distributed files, bit torrent protocols, universal accessibility, multiple entry points, software as well as hardware potentials, and so forth? The Iraq and Afghan 'war logs', the US diplomatic cables records, records detailing the financial dealings of Swiss bankers managing the tax evasion activities of their clients; all of these pertain to secrecy/disclosure events which were always already inherent component 'potentials' of the system, kept and preserved, in a matryoshka doll-like fashion, within the 'WikiLeaks phenomenon' event – an event whose greatest significance lies in its disclosure of *all* of this, including the very disclosive capacity of the greater recording apparatus itself.

Baudrillard, it should be remembered, needed none of this digital recording technology to exist in order to stake his fatalistic claim that the logic of communicative capitalism in the mediated society was driving towards the 'disappearance' of public social reality, which he spoke of in terms of the 'implosion of the social into the media'.[30] The disappearance of social reality *as it had been known, experienced and naturalised* in modernity, he argues, takes down with it the public sphere associated with the Enlightenment. Let us also recall, Baudrillard need only appeal to the illustrative example of the simple opinion poll in order to describe the form of the key cultural process by which, on the one hand, Subjects are radically individualised vis-à-vis information, and, on the other, reality itself collapses into a mediated 'statistical representation' based on the individualised interactivity between the Subject and the system of communication. If one were to update this thesis to the age of ubiquitous digital recording, then one might argue, firstly, that what characterises the present situation in general is the evermore total automaticity of the submission of data of all kinds to the 'global databank'; and secondly, that information overflow *within* the system across the boundary between a 'secret cache' and 'the public cache' is essentially uncontrollable (as neither complete containment nor a clear division between the two is either theoretically or practically sustainable). This situation is popularly identified today with the failure of information elites to contain either the flow of information or the desire of the majority to gain access to information without restriction. Hence the security of so-called 'secrets' is at one and the same time both the priority for, and the Achilles heel of, various power blocs, such as governments, international organisations and global corporations, and a new scene of direct action against them. Further, the restricted access to information, in the popular imagination at least, is consequently understood as the 'new censorship'. Because everyone in principle now has the capacity to upload content to the public domain, old-style censorship which relied heavily on the prevention of informational content production and distribution has given way to regimes based on denial of access to extant information. In this cultural context, 'the secret' becomes the name of what is, supposedly, deliberatively and consciously withheld by means of security informational subsystems designed to keep secrets secret, which, in turn, themselves are only disclosed and become known (and thus matters of the overtly 'public record') on the basis of their own breaches, or technical failures. It is in this way that the dominant concept of the secret for the public remains restricted to the notion that 'they', or someone somewhere, *possesses* a potentially *exposable and shareable secret*.

It is against the background of this idea of the secret that the real-politik of secrecy is played out between power elites concerned to keep secret information and their 'opponents', such as information activists and libertarians, or just 'the curious', who either set themselves the task of campaigning for ever greater freedom of information concessions from those elites, or who take direct action (such as hacking, leaking and whistle blowing) to 'free information' in order to expose alleged crime, corruption, skulduggery, and so forth. What I want to suggest is that the normativity of this politics of secrecy is characterised by a publicly shared notion of the secret as what is 'on the record', and that therefore the 'dispute', consequently, is normatively framed in terms of making the record transparent and public. And yet it is precisely the situation of the technicisation of memory as the recallability of what is on the record (in general, that is either before or after the development of digital technology as such) which exposes the *limitation of such a metaphysics of the secret*. The shared axiom of these overtly opposed positions is that secrets are essentially exposable, can be rendered visible and are knowable, and that this knowability, or epistemic status, is grounded on the fact that *what is secret is necessarily 'on the record'*; and that it can therefore be recalled and remembered.

Yet another way of expressing this shared axiomatic of the secret is that secrets are essentially human and that, generically speaking, 'data processing' is the technical means of access to them. What this axiomatic is forgetful of, though, is that it assumes that the human is itself already a known and in no way a secret to itself. In other words, it assumes the human has access to itself, or is transparent to itself, when in fact there is no self-knowledge of the human which does not involve a detour through the 'record' of its own self-discovery. (And, this is recorded generally, to use an expression of Derrida's cited above, in the 'structures of language', and thus stored in the totality of the archive of 'cultural texts' – or, to give this a more familiar name, 'cultural memory' – of which 'Western philosophy', incidentally, is just one, moreover one which, according to Heidegger, *begins* with the thought of the non-difference of concealing/unconcealing.) It *forgets*, in other words, that there can be no knowledge of the human which is independent of the necessary condition of its technical expression – and hence 'recording' in the generic sense I have given to this here. While this new techno-cultural situation (of data storage, accessibility, and so forth) to the extent to which it can be said to be defined specifically by digital recording, is indeed transformative of the relation between the secret and its disclosure (the precise measure of which it is perhaps impossible to grasp *in the present*), it is not *wholly original* in so far as the materiality (or mediality) of any form of both expression and recollection, as noted earlier, has always been the condition of communication in general. In whatever medium, as soon as there is *expression*, there is an *impression* – a 'mark', an imprimatur of sorts; or, as Derrida argues, there is already a sort of archivisation at work.[31] So, digital recording in this sense introduces mnemo-technical novelty against a background of the necessary technicity of memory as the production of a record and, hence, an archive; and *any* form of technical expression/ impression implies the same failure of *total control* over its destination.

Arguably the most striking aspect of the novelty of digital recording is the exponential growth in quantity and accessibility. With this the capacity for judgement (or judgement by proxy – relying on expert others) has not only become rare, but is losing its ground altogether, and in this environment conspiracy theorising has multiplied.[32] With this development, informational power elites, such as global corporations or state governments which seek to restore or assert authority against a rising wave of popular mistrust – by offering in one form or another 'greater transparency' through the revelation of 'secrets' (be these their own or those of their enemies or opponents) – cannot expect to bring an end to that distrust by doing so. There is always room, from the perspective of the public, for the riposte: 'you only get to hear what they want you to hear'. In other words, in the absence of any absolute authority in which the public trusts, the 'politics of secrecy' takes the form of an information war in which claims and counter-claims concerning the efficacy or transparency of some information in comparison to other information are pitched against one another. In the context of such an information war, 'responsibility' vis-à-vis secrecy and disclosure will tend only ever *to be understood politically* and as a matter of calculation and recalculation in view of 'the latest disclosures'. So, for instance, to return for moment to the WikiLeaks phenomenon: those who counter secrecy with disclosure will only be able to do so on the basis of at least a degree of secrecy of their own. It is because the very idea of full and open disclosure is a logical impossibility that not only will conspiracy theorising dog those who claim to practise such a policy, but, may one not also ask in all seriousness: can anyone ever really know entirely whether or not by disclosing anything at all they have acted as someone else's stooge? For as soon as anything is on the record it is already public and total control by any agency whatever is essentially impossible.

THE UNKNOWABLE SECRET – OF WIKILEAKS, FOR INSTANCE

In drawing this chapter to a close I shall pose the question of who or what is responsible for whom or for what in the light of an informational disclosure event such as the 'WikiLeaks phenomenon' – which I have taken all along to be emblematic of the digital archive culture which constitutes the context ethical subjectivity today.

In an article with a decidedly conspiracist sounding title, 'Who Is Behind Wikileaks?', the Canadian professor of economics, Michel Chossudovsky offers, in journalistic terms, a corrective to the view that the WikiLeaks revelation of secrets is what it appears to be: 'Progressive organisations have praised the Wikileaks endeavour . . . The leaks are heralded as an immeasurable victory against corporate media censorship. But there is more than meets the eye.'[33] What Chossudovsky aims to bring to light in his 'exposé' of WikiLeaks' own secrets (partly drawing on WikiLeaks' leaked emails) is the manner in which the WikiLeaks project is complicit with the very forces of corporate media and government censorship it overtly exists to oppose. This 'complicity' is a function, especially, of its collaboration with the mainstream media whose involvement not only in the further distribution of leaked material but also its selection (and redaction) was, according to his evidence, anticipated 'from the outset'. Chossudovsky's view is that because WikiLeaks 'enlisted the architects of media disinformation to fight media disinformation' (the mainstream press), it is engaged in 'an incongruous and self-defeating procedure'. The evidence supporting this conclusion is largely to be recognised in the manner in which the recuperation of credibility by government agencies and individuals was achieved through the selective release, emphasis and positive spin placed on specific leaked records, whilst at the same time demonising further the WikiLeaks project and searching for grounds for prosecution (for instance, under the Espionage Act). This analysis clearly leaves open the question of whether the use of mainstream media by WikiLeaks is naive, a form of (conscious or unconscious) self-censorship and control, a flawed strategy, or just indicative of a certain normative 'sense of responsibility' with regard to the possible unintended, undesirable consequences of leaking classified information. And I will leave such questions open here.

My own conclusion is this: so long as the freedom of information revolution is understood exclusively in terms of the *politics* of secrecy and disclosure, a certain 'complicity' is absolutely inescapable. In the case of WikiLeaks this is not so much a matter of whether, despite appearances, there is a case to be answered concerning the organisation's proximity to 'the establishment' – as Chossudovsky drives at in his discussion. Nor is it simply that it is impossible to control the destination or use of any record pulled from any archive whatsoever, or that the accuracy of the record of an event is always open to question. It is more a matter of the manner in which WikiLeaks' capacity to continue its project of disclosure, its activities and its organisation in general *are premised on the protection of its own secrecy* and above all that of its 'sources'. This is a practical and technical matter as well as a political necessity in the ordinary sense. We need, however, to think beyond the question of any alleged (politically defined) complicity with what may or may not be known or shared amongst protagonist communities in an 'information war' in order to raise the question of the relationship to the unknowable (rather than the merely unknown) which renders such differences of perspective possible in the first place. Can a democratic community be based on knowledge, or the 'state of knowledge' at a particular time, at all, if, as digital archive culture perhaps allows us to think more clearly than ever before, what all new knowledge amounts is to a series of 'latest disclosures'? Or, alternatively, is not every possible community founded, of necessity, on what is disclosed *and* remains hidden at the same time?

What remains hidden in every instance of information disclosure is 'the secret' of the responsibility which comes with its publication *but which itself necessarily remains 'off the record'*. This is the responsibility which is unique, or singular, to the 'informational event' and the medial condition of its archivisation. It can be regarded, I have sought to demonstrate in this chapter, as a form of what Levinas calls the 'ultimate secret of subjectivity' itself; the secret which, precisely, *separates* the Subject (the 'I' or the 'me' in Levinas's terminology) from Being in general, or the 'disclosed totality of the world'. Perhaps we can consider that 'disclosed world' today under the sign of the 'infosphere', or as the 'global archive' or 'database'. Each and every such a Subject does not *know* how, or for what, it is responsible in the light of the disclosed information (or so-called 'secrets') in relation to which it seeks the meaning of that responsibility. What it learns though, for example, is that heinous crimes were committed in its (or 'my') name, that it (or 'I') stand accused – with each and every new disclosure, prior ignorance of which can never serve as an excuse. This is a notion of responsibility before any possible disclosure, or any 'record', and it corresponds to the disturbance which is experienced with each and every disclosure but which itself remains a secret 'in me'. It is in this sense that 'infinite responsibility' is singular, indivisible, unshareable and the secret I am condemned to keep – and it is also why 'there is no point in searching for the secret of what anyone may have known'.[34]

NOTES

1. Derrida, *Paper Machine*, p. 162
2. Deleuze and Guattari, *A Thousand Plateaus*, p. 299.
3. Featherstone, 'Ubiquitous Media'.
4. See Boyd, 'Facebook's Privacy Trainwreck'; Hogben, 'Security Issues and Recommendations'.
5. Dean, 'Publicity's Secret', *Political Theory*, p. 624.
6. See Agamben, *Means without Ends*, p. 60. I follow his use of the term 'mediality' here: it refers to the connection between the material and technical form of a medium and its capacity to produce material effects.
7. This is a Derridean neologism that is used in various places in his *oeuvre*, and, strictly speaking, its 'meaning' is context specific. It generally names both the capacity and, in a sense, the inevitability, of a communication to go astray and to arrive in unintended places, or to be received differently

than could have been anticipated by the sender. For a fulsome discussion, see Hillis Miller, *For Derrida*, ch. 3.

8. See Brunton, 'WikiLeaks and the Assange Papers'.
9. See Stiegler, *Technics and Time*, p. 18; Beardsworth, *Derrida and the Political*, p. 49; Clark, 'Deconstruction and Technology', p. 240.
10. Deleuze, 'Postscript on the Societies of Control'.
11. Heidegger, *Early Greek Thinking*, pp. 106–7.
12. Ibid. pp. 112–13.
13. Levinas, *Otherwise than Being, or, Beyond Essence*, p. 111 (emphasis added).
14. Levinas, 'Transcendence and Height', p. 21.
15. Levinas, 'God and Philosophy', p. 138 (emphasis added).
16. Derrida and Farraris, *Taste for the Secret*, pp. 56–9.
17. Derrida, 'Remarks on Deconstruction and Pragmatism', p. 86.
18. Gilbert, 'Public Secrets'.
19. Derrida and Farraris, *Taste for the Secret*, p. 75. See Gilbert, 'Public Secrets', p. 29.
20. Levinas, *Totality and Infinity*, p. 213.
21. For example, as discussed by Derrida in *Archive Fever*, pp. 76, 99 and in *Gift of Death*, p. 82, where the French is rendered into English as 'every other one is every (bit) other'.
22. Levinas, *Totality and Infinity*, p. 58.
23. For example, in Derrida, 'Force of Law' and *Resistances of Psychoanalysis*.
24. For a fascinating genealogical account of the relationship between law and the media technologies of its recording, see Vismann, *Files: Law and Media Technology*.
25. See, for example, *The Guardian* newspaper's Data Blog, available at <http://www.guardian.co.uk/news/datablog/2010/oct/23/wikileaks-iraq-data-journalism#-data> (last accessed 12 January 2011).
26. Derrida, 'A Certain Impossible Possibility of Saying the Event', p. 446.
27. Bradley Manning, quoted in *The Guardian*, 29 November 2010, p. 2.
28. See<http://data.gov.uk/blog/new-public-sector-transparency-board-and-public-data-transparency-principles> (last accessed 12 January 2011).
29. See, for example, Baudrillard, 'The Masses'.
30. Ibid.
31. Derrida, *Archive Fever*, p. 28.
32. On this topic, see Birchall, *Knowledge Goes Pop*; Sunstein and Vermeule, 'Conspiracy Theories'; Brunton, 'WikiLeaks and the Assange Papers'.
33. Chossudovsky, 'Who is Behind Wikileaks?'.
34. Derrida, *Archive Fever*, p. 99.

7. Censored Subjects

> There is never any pure censorship or pure lifting of censorship, which makes one doubt the rational purity of this concept.[1]

CENSORSHIP AND THE PRESENT CONJUNCTURE

The year 2011 saw a unique centenary – the centenial disestablishment of the Swedish Board of Film Censorship (Statens Biografbyrå – hereafter SBB). The SBB was established around fifteen years after films had first begun to be screened in public in Sweden. Since the earliest film performances in the last years of the nineteenth century the police authorities had been responsible for the licensing of such screenings, and had granted or refused licences in the context of the prevailing popular concerns about detrimental effects of the new medium on audiences, and, as is the case today, in the context of film classification regimes, with a view to the supposed dangers film images posed to minors. In 1905 in a move which initiated the transition of control of film performances to the state, the Office of the Governor of Stockholm published a declaration that included the following:

> Exhibitions of films shall not include any material that is offensive to public decency or disrespectful to the authorities or private individuals, nor pictures depicting the commission of murders, robberies or other serious crimes, and exhibitions that are open to children shall not include pictures depicting events or situations that are liable to arouse emotions of terror or horror in the audience or for other reasons be considered unsuitable for children to look at. Furthermore, pictures that are liable perversely to excite children's imagination or otherwise to have an adverse effect on their mental development or well-being shall not be passed for exhibition at performances to which children under the age of 15 are admitted.[2]

Not long after this a government bill was introduced which led to the establishment, in 1911, of the SBB. Thereafter the SBB was the legitimate authority whose task was to examine, and if considered necessary, censor, all films to be shown in Sweden, essentially in accordance with the same guiding principles elaborated in the 1905 declaration. Interestingly, the bill was passed only after its provision to censor 'cinematic pictures, the showing of which is liable to give offence for religious or political reasons' had been excluded, on the grounds that it gave too much scope for *subjective* interpretations. Whatever else one might say about the approach adopted at its inception, there was clearly an element of secular liberalism evident in the mission of the SBB. This was quite the opposite of the case with the overall system of cultural censorship in Britain in operation for most of the twentieth century, which drew heavily on the laws pertaining to blasphemy as well as on the Obscene Publications Act. One of the peculiarities of the censorship of film in Sweden from the first to the last day of the existence of the SBB is that, in accordance with the law and what one might call, for sake of brevity, the tradition of Swedish open government and liberal democracy, all of the excised, censored material was archived and awarded the status of a public document. As such it was the duty of the SBB to preserve this material and to make it freely available to be viewed by any member of the public, Swedish or foreign, upon request. The censorship of film under the authority of the SBB, and controlled access to the censored material, was thus consistent with the principle of free expression as enshrined in Swedish law. Rather in the tradition and spirit of Sweden's landmark Freedom of Printing Act 1766, film censorship neither aimed at the prevention of the production of any kind of film material whatever, nor at the absolute refusal of public access to it, but rather at the control of its perceived potentially undesirable effects on the population under the anticipated circumstances of its screening.

At the time of its eventual closure one hundred years later, in 2011, which brought an official end to film censorship in Sweden, the SBB, under the directorship of Gunnel Arrbäck for its final twenty-five years, had not in fact made any cuts at all to a film since 1995. Arrbäck herself had made it clear in several public statements in the last years of the SBB that the mission and purpose of the organisation was, in her view, anachronistic in its assumptions, and, in view of technological developments such as global TV and the Internet, now fundamentally misguided in its belief in its own power to protect audiences from any supposed negative effects of viewing allegedly 'harmful material'. It should be noted in any case at this point that the crudely causal 'effects theory' of media influence, which is often appealed to in this context and often referenced by such a discourse of public harm, is long since

dead in the water as far as most media and communications theorists
are concerned. There has simply never been good evidence produced to
support it. (To acknowledge this is not to deny in any way the need for
adults to take some care and responsibility with regard to what they
allow young children to view or experience, just as they might in other
real-life situations which they judge to call for protective measures of
one sort or another.)

Upon the SBB's official closure, the responsibility for the regulation
of all film to be viewed, effectively in both public or private locations,
passed to the Swedish Media Council (SMC) whose remit is not to
censor at all, but explicitly to *classify* media products, advise and offer
evaluations of research into the impact of media material in all its forms
on minors. A major part of the new Council's activities are broadly
comparable to those of the British Board of Film Classification (BBFC),
which defines its role in terms of maintaining a balance between the
liberal principles of its own classification guidelines and the rigid inflex-
ibilities of certain aspects of the law.[3] The BBFC began life in 1912 as
The British Board of Film Censors and changed its name in 1984 when
it was assigned the new responsibility of classifying video material for
home consumption. Unlike the SBB, the BBFC (in both incarnations
and from its inception) has always been an independent body: it was
originally set up by the film industry itself, partly with aim of heading
off state interference. Cuts made by the BBFC nowadays are likely to be
agreed in consultation with film directors and media companies in relation to their own commercial concerns surrounding the likely impact
of the classification licence awarded on box office returns. They are
also made if there are deemed to be good grounds for supposing that
any material could fall foul of the Obscene Publications Act. A primary
activity of the organisation is to undertake what is, in effect, market
research, aimed at ascertaining what the film (and video) consumer is
likely to find objectionable, unacceptable, unsuitable for children, and
so on, in relation to a range of themes and subjects, on the basis of its
own perception of current norms. To the extent to which the SMC and
the BBFC engage in these kinds of activities, they could be described as
constituting part of the bigger cultural machinery whose purpose is to
match up the media consumer with the media cultural product. They
both directly and indirectly mediate between distributors and, for the
most part, anxious-parent consumers; the former generally wanting
to meet their target audiences' expectations and the latter wanting to
know in advance what they are likely to get in terms of raw imagery.
The transformation of censorship regimes and institutions into classification services in countries such as Sweden and the UK corresponds

to the changing cultural context as a whole: the open market in media products, the development of media technologies and their domestication, and the idiosyncrasies of national and local laws and jurisdictions.

Regimes of censorship and the beliefs surrounding them are, in this way, a feature of historically specific cultural formations. In rational, secular societies, there is a popular expectation that any censorious measures are justifiable on the basis of 'good reasons'; that scientific arguments and evidence are presentable – when, for example, censorship is claimed to be necessary for the protection from harm of certain groups of people, or society at large. And if there is no scientific consensus for, say, psychological damage to children or anyone else (historically a key concern of SBB) resulting from viewing of products of the film industry or the consumption of any other cultural industry products; if there is no evidence, to invoke for a moment the discourse of the British obscenity laws central to the history of censorship in Britain, of 'depravity and corruption' being caused by exposure to film, literature, TV, and so forth, then this situation challenges the legitimacy of censorship on such spurious grounds. In short, it can be acknowledged, as the last director of the SBB appeared to do, that on the balance of the evidence none of the concepts involved in the censorship system practised by the SBB stood up to rational scrutiny.

The anachronism of film censorship, at least in the Swedish case, one might say, then, has at least three dimensions to it. These correspond, firstly, to the medium itself: the consumer of film increasingly watches film, or perhaps better to say nowadays 'moving image media', in a digital format and as often as not elsewhere than in public places; secondly, to the fact that in the age of global television and the Internet, no matter how the state presides over, manages or interacts with independent classificatory bodies, or regulates the media industries and legislates, in many instances it is completely unable to control private access to such images; and, thirdly, to the weak credibility of the theory of (and the supposed evidence for) the harmful effects resulting to a general adult public from exposure to film images.[4] By 2011, if not for quite some time prior to that, film censorship 'as Sweden had known it' had clearly become impracticable, inoperable even before one got to the question of whether or not it was unwarranted. Whilst the suggestion of its being unwarranted will always remain open to dispute in the context of prevailing normative cultural values, one could nonetheless say that the socio-political context of the end of film censorship coincides with the de facto techno-cultural demise of materiality of film as the medium for the circulation and experience of moving images, and that this effectively renders all but irrelevant any debate about the *legitimacy* or otherwise of censorship. So even putting aside all matters of principle, such as being for or against censorship in general, film censorship became, in every sense, redundant. With the closure of the SBB we have an example of how censorship of at least one medium in at least in one country and in a particular institutional form came to an end.

The question that I shall address a little later in this chapter is the following: can such an end to film censorship as this one – ending, that is, in a classification system in which an advisory body aims to mediate between the public, the law and film makers – be regarded as an indicator of a new stage of cultural maturity in our European societies, and a step closer to securing the freedom of expression of the Subject and a new form of post-censorial subjectivity? And once again, I suggest, we can only address that question in view of the role that media themselves play in the transformation of the 'total cultural situation' to which the Subject belongs. Before I do that I want to briefly discuss an 'artistic footnote' to the 'end of film censorship' in Sweden which raises the issue of the relationship between censorship and creativity.

MARKUS ÖHRN'S *MAGIC BULLET* AND CENSORSHIP AS ART

In 2008, three years before the SBB was to be disestablished, the Swedish artist Markus Öhrn exercised his democratic right to file a request to view the contents of its archive of censored film: he simply walked into the institution and asked to view its entire contents – which turned out to be around forty-nine hours of film clips which had been archived between 1911 and 1995. He subsequently was granted permission to digitise the material with a view to using it to create an art installation. His completed work, titled *Magic Bullet*,[5] finally took the form of a chronological compilation of the entire SBB archive of censored film. The installation runs for around forty-nine hours in total, starting in 1911 and ending in 1995. Depending on the year running when the viewer enters the screening, he or she is likely to encounter an apparently random sequence of themes, settings, styles and genres of film: cowboy fisticuffs in Hollywood movies to scenes from an anal fisting 'instructional' film; Jerry flattened by Tom's frying pan; the torture of a partisan by the Gestapo; cartoonish B-movie simulations of brutal violent acts next to gang bangs and rape scenes; and an assortment of pornographic scenes, some involving animals, and real and simulated sexual violence. Such clips run consecutively in the sequence of original archival logging and thus reflect, in a speeded-up mode, the products of the censors' labour in the course of performing their day-to-day working routine.

Magic Bullet was shown at the 2009 Gothenburg Film Festival and has since been shown at the Stockholm Museum of Modern Art and the Völksbuhne Theatre in Berlin, where Öhrn has since (in 2012) been employed as a theatre director. The installation is at once a striking historical document, an artwork 'about' archivisation, and an at times amusing, at times tedious, in fact sometimes almost unwatchable exhibit that provokes laughter and slight embarrassment – amongst many other responses. The experience of watching it feels oddly contemporary: it is a bit like watching TV when someone else is using the remote to constantly channel-surf, and every programme on every channel is simultaneously at a point of contextless intensity. Beyond the immediate audio-visual onslaught of sequences, Öhrn's installation is particularly effective in provoking reflection on the relationship between censorious practice as physical 'cutting-out', which is evident in the almost subliminal glimpses one gets of damaged and scratched end frames and archival labelling marks, as these passed through the projector during digitisation. The viewer cannot forget that *Magic Bullet* is not 'a film' but an installation made of archival 'raw material'; work produced in the context of an institutionalised regime of censorship whose mission was at one and the same time to preserve, index and catalogue this material 'stuff' with a view to both keeping it and keeping it from its intended cultural context of being seen. By presenting the viewer with a collation of censored film clips – clips, ranging from a few frames to a few minutes of continuous film, which were excised at a particular historical moment from their original contexts – *Magic Bullet* foregrounds how the technical processes at work, such as cutting, editing and archiving, are enmeshed with the wider socio-technological management of society as a whole. In order to create the work, Öhrn had to do something on a practical level rather similar to what the jobbing censor would do – handle the material, work with machines and, of course, view the images. And, by thus further 'recontextualising' this archived material, the installation itself reiterates a singular idea of the 'end of censorship' as itself being of a specific time and place, a form of work, and an institutional setting. *Magic Bullet* redirects us, in this way, to the particular situation in which we find ourselves today, and to how the understanding of censorship must be reformulated in the context of new techno-cultural processes shaping contemporary society.

So, to summarise three points to be taken forward from the discussion so far: firstly, both the normative concept of censorship and censorious regimes and practices always belong to particular times and places; they are not a-historical and we can only conceptualise censorship on the basis of material practices by which it is carried out. Secondly, moving out from this particular example of *Magic Bullet*, I want to propose that 'censorship in general' (in a given situation) is actually the condition for the production of any work of art, or any act of creativity in the first place. Without both censorship *and* transgression – which are unthinkable in isolation from one another – creativity as art, knowledge production, politics, 'revolution', and so forth, would never take shape; there would be uninterrupted sameness, or totality. Thirdly, in particular I want to suggest that censorship is always also a matter of the archive and of *archivisation* – and herein lies, perhaps, *Magic Bullet*'s own most singular provocation as a critical and conceptual work: it problematises what it substantively (re)presents; namely, a *system* of censorship comprising a specific mediality. The medial elements of this system include the following: the archival storage of film as material, the institution of censorious authority under the law (the SBB) and the constrained form of publicity it allows; the 'scene' of the public space of the material's screening (the SBB viewing booth, the film theatre, the museum, and so forth). It draws attention to how censorship is always a matter of such mediality, and that anything which might be recorded or recalled is already a function of the mediality of the medium itself (an idea explored in the previous chapter). Censorship, both conceptually and historically, is a function of the technics of recording, storage, retrieval, circulation, and so forth; and, importantly, the connectability of archival records and archival materials of all kinds. This condition of censorship applies in the case of *Magic Bullet*, too: Öhrn's creative decision for the chronological sequencing of the material is inescapably a form of censorship in that it was a *decision* which excluded all other possible alternatives.

CENSORSHIP AND THE SUBJECT OF POWER

The conventional way of thinking of censorship is as the antithesis of free expression. This is reflected, for example, in Sweden's Freedom of Printing Act 1766, in the first amendment to the US Bill of Rights and the UN Declaration of Human Rights (Article 19). Liberal democracy envisions the protection of the citizen-Subject *from* censorship. We normatively suppose that modern liberal states, by virtue of being democratically accountable, are able to 'protect' their citizens against the harm done them by their *being subject to censorship*, and that this is achieved on the basis of a 'division' of powers – for instance, between the state and the law. However, in states where there is no 'official censorship', such as in the UK, in reality the division of powers is far more diverse and complex than this. In the UK there is no one power which censors film and officially no film censorship. However, there is a wide range of forces and legal provisions which contingently serve to impede the production, circulation and possession of images (and texts), just as there are, one might add, all other, broadly defined, forms of 'free expression'. There is in fact a plethora of controls: for instance, the Obscene Publications Acts 1959/84, the Criminal Justice and Public Order Act 1994, the Racial and Religious Hatred Act 2006, the Criminal Justice and Immigration Act 2008, Sections 63–7; as well as 'regulation' by the BBFC, the Advertising Standards Authority, the Office of Fair Trading, the Press Complaints Commission, the Public Sector Transparency Board; as well as norms such as the 'evening watershed' and countless other professional codes of practice – all of which come into play to some degree 'censoriously'. But to simply represent this censorial power nexus as, say, a 'repressive state apparatus', would be to forget something more fundamental: namely, that there cannot be any state, or condition of human subjectivity, or society, which is ever *wholly free* of censorship. This is so not because there is, or may always be a little bit (or a lot) of censorial practice left over here and there still needing to be challenged in the name of free expression. Nor is it because the mission of liberal democracy is in part defined by the ongoing attempt to balance the free expression of each against the harm it can cause to others (though this is no doubt a significant aspect of its self-understanding). It is, rather, because the very founding interdiction against censorship (as this is expressed in the kind of conventions just listed, as well as in more recent freedom of information acts) is itself a foundational restriction and a delimitation of *the meaning of censorship* which coincides with the production of a modern Subject who, at its birth, so to speak, concedes sovereign power to the state (or, in practice some aggregate of 'the state', the law and commercial powers) in exchange for the protection of its freedom so defined. As Judith Butler says:

> It's important to know what one means by 'censorship' (indeed, what has become 'censored' in the definition of censorship) in order to understand the limits of its eradicability as well as the bounds within which such normative appeals might plausibly be made.[6]

For this reason, we need to hold in mind that it does not make sense either to be for or against censorship per se: the pursuit of the complete freedom of expression and its defence in the name of the inclusivity of all, implicitly and inescapably involves the exclusion of others. It is thus, paradoxically, but nonetheless by definition, a totalising gesture.

Conventional accounts of censorship, as Butler notes, 'presume that it is exercised by the state against those who are less powerful. Conventional defences of those less powerful argue that it is their freedom that is being constrained and sometimes, more particularly, the freedom of speech.'[7] This remark invites consideration of the various consequences of thinking about censorship only in terms of the exercise of juridical power, and in terms of the right to free expression before the law. But 'before the law' in this context effectively means 'before censorship'. One of these consequences is that the freedom/censorship dichotomy requires that we concede the necessity of the institution of a regulatory agency.

This aporia of the 'necessary illegitimacy of foundation of the law' is particularly acute and pertinent today in relation to the emergence of a new general 'culture of offence' being played out in the context of our European multicultural societies, societies in which well-meaning anti-hate speech and anti-incitement to violence legislation aimed at protecting the vulnerable against abuse and attack, bears with it the unintended consequence of curtailing the freedom of expression of some in relation to others. The law is, in effect, the censorial regulatory agency that is tasked with censoring malicious free expression by insisting that *all expression be regarded as context specific*. Recent debate surrounding whether the 'right to offend' is superior to the 'right not to be offended' is a prime example of this. In the United Kingdom the recent extension of the law on hate speech to cover abusive references to a person's faith has been central to this.[8] Similar issues have arisen and excited controversy across Europe in recent years. At the height of the 'Danish cartoons affair,'[9] in the UK in 2005, the BBC, other national TV channels and British newspapers all decided not to show the offending cartoons in their reportage of the incident during the surrounding international furore, claiming that they feared that by doing so they would be in danger of literally repeating 'the offence', namely, an actual act of 'islamophobia'. Any viewers wanting to judge for themselves, or just to understand what was being talked about, had to turn to other sources – which was only too easy, given that the cartoons themselves could, and still can be, googled (so no need to cause anyone offence by reprinting them here!). The mainstream media were less willing, I suspect, to declare that they also feared they would be liable to prosecution; liable to be judged socially irresponsible for stirring up the violent protest that could follow; and, of course, liable to be subjected to some form of direct, retaliatory action themselves, by militant sections of the offended.[10]

The paradox I draw attention to here is that when we unquestioningly accept the modern, normative juridical idea of censorship, we falsely attribute to regulatory agencies (including the legislature itself) sovereignty of power – in other words, the power to do what they say. We mistakenly suppose that through such an agency, the state and civil society can, in principle and in fact, guarantee the defence of a set of putative shared cultural values, including the one about 'free expression for all'. But this is a fantasy: a fantasy that being-for and being-against censorship in the conventional juridical sense, does not involve a contradiction – which in reality it obviously does. This is the fantasy that freedom of expression is *universalisable*. The reality is, rather, that there is in society an unrelenting power struggle surrounding who censors whom; a struggle within which all manner of instruments and weapons are brought into play. The contradiction this fantasy would magically resolve, and which is normally invisible, arises because a certain 'censorship of censorship' has always already taken place. Censorship, in fact, always precedes and makes possible the intelligibility of any appeal to such a regulatory authority in the first place – just as the rules of grammar predetermine the intelligibility of any meaningful statement in language.[11] Censorship is, to all intents and purposes, what makes any form of expression intelligible in the first place – within a specific community, society or culture. It is only because there is censorship that anything meaningful can be said at all, in so far as it enables the distinction between what is and what is not allowed to be identified as such. For this reason censorship cannot be thought of simply as the repression of what is otherwise free. Censorship, rather, makes possible and conjures into being a certain kind of Subject, or citizen, or form of artistic expression, whilst rendering other kinds impossible. This could easily be shown to be evident across the landscape of culture and society, but I will briefly illustrate how this relates to the discussion of the first two sections of this chapter on the mediality of film and film censorship.

Any film is the product of a set of 'decisions' which can be viewed as acts of censorship in their own right. Take, for example, the decisions of the film director or editor in the cutting room to keep certain shots, sequences and frames and to remove others. There cannot be an 'original' film – a 'director's cut', as we say, without there being a cutting-out of something from something else. There must be an act of censorship, a (de)cision, at least in this sense, for there to be something we can identify as the 'uncut film' in the first place. But this is actually a misnomer: there is no such thing as an uncut film and, therefore, no such thing either as an 'uncensored film'. I am suggesting we should conceptualise the very notion of 'the film' itself as an original act and form of censorship: a film, so to speak, cuts-out some bit of the reality the film deals with and 'presents' it (makes it present) for the first time, as it were. This kind of deep originality is, in fact, what we conventionally prize in the context of film making. Of course, traditionally we think of film in terms of the re-presentational capacities of the medium and the essentially photographic image made of some external, ontologically independent reality. This traditional concept of filmic representation, however, is inadequate to the manner in which the 'cut of the real', which a film individuates uniquely and singularly, what it accomplishes and shows. Film is, in this way, no more subject to censorship than it is an original act of censorship; it is both censorship *and* a performative form of free expression. This example shows how the politics of censorship is not ultimately about the uncensored, or the right of access to the uncensored as the measure of freedom, but rather about the power of expression as a creative intervention in the world. The traditional conceptualisation of the relationship between film and the world in its thinking of the boundary between the two on the basis of a metaphysics of representation is, precisely, an example of how the 'censoring of censorship' serves to limit the way in which we can conceptualise the film–world relation. Censorship no more hinders expression than it makes it possible in the first place: the power expressed by censorship is, in its own ways, just as productive as any other power.

In her analysis of hate speech and hate speech legislation in terms of performativity, Judith Butler directs us to what she calls the 'implicit censorship' which is always at work determining the distinction between the permissible and the impermissible, noting that 'the regulation that states what it does not want stated thwarts its own desire, conducting a performative contradiction that throws into question that regulation's capacity to mean and do what it says, that is, its sovereign pretension'.[12] The 'sovereign pretension' of censorious power means, primarily, that censorship is always incomplete, or fails. It fails because it calls into being the forms of subjectivity that it desires to prohibit. Hence, generally speaking, we cannot think about freedom of expression without censorship. And in her analysis of the politics of hate speech legislation, Butler views censorious power (in the same way that Foucault does) as a productive force rather than a repressive force.

SELF-CENSORSHIP AND TECHNOLOGY

That the 'sovereign pretension' of the state as regulatory authority with regard to censorship is today clearly exposed for all to see, is, in effect, what the last director of the SBB, Gunnel Arrbäck, was touching upon when she noted that in the age of the Internet, the old idea of a regulatory censorship is redundant. There may well be dictatorial states, such as China and North Korea (and dictatorial impulses at play in democratic societies[13]), for example, which will attempt to censor access to and uploading of information and data of all kinds to Internet sites, and can do so with varying degrees of success. But, the specific technical nature of the digital infosphere is such that what one might, for brevity, describe as censorship of access and participation, cannot be imposed in the manner which was possible with modern traditional technologies and power structures. During the first weeks of 2009, for example, this was evident in the way Israel's denial of access to Gaza to all Western news agencies did not prevent the world from seeing many images, including live film, of the violence unfolding. The Israeli military-state machinery attempted to censor what was seen, but by way of what Butler calls a 'performative contradiction', its forceful prohibition was itself on full show, and effectively turned everything that was broadcast globally into examples of 'what Israel didn't want the world to see' – thus making Israeli censorship a significant part of the event itself.

I am not suggesting for a moment that the power of the state to prosecute what it identifies to be breaches of the law determining what is allowed or not allowed to be shown or said is a thing of the past: it is not. There is a litany of cases of one could point to; doors still get kicked down, computers are seized, records subpoenaed from Internet service providers (ISPs), websites can be taken down. The United Kingdom, for instance, has the Regulation of Investigatory Powers Act 2000, which can compel an ISP to track all data traffic passing through its computers and route it to the blithely named National Technical Assistance Centre for analysis. Anyone with a concern for civil liberties in democratic countries clearly should be concerned about such developments in 'the surveillance society'. Still, it can prove almost impossible for the state to halt the circulation of the material it would care to sanction from being published and aired in the first place. The reverse side of this situation is that no national news agency can expect to command the attention of its entire population any longer. Every node in the networked communications society is a potential editor, remixer, original source of information and producer of images. The revolutionary impact of this general situation is widely to be observed: in the use of social media in the course of the Arab Spring, or in its role in the UK riots of August 2011, or, say, in the cell phone filming of the police attack on Ian Tomlinson which led to his death, during the G20 protests in the UK. Such examples as these and countless others stand alongside the Israeli attempt to control the image record of the 2009 attack on Gaza. After the democratisation of the technologies of image making and circulation, the traditional power to censor is serially undermined.

New media phenomena such as these feed into the now widely held belief that the Internet represents a prima facie democratisation of communications and information, and thus signals yet another 'end' to censorship by virtue of its subversion of traditional forms of power of sanction. However, the truth is that we are living in a highly complex situation, one which demands a new analysis of the operation of power itself in the context of the newly configured digital mediascape. As the power of governments to censor has been weakened (as dramatically illustrated by the 'WikiLeaks phenomenon', for example), redress has been sought in the strengthening of the powers of governments to seize and subpoena data and information held on *any* recording device.[14]

In his short but highly influential essay 'Postscript on the Societies of Control', Gilles Deleuze anticipated the transfiguration of power structures the information society would lead to in a way which I believe is insightful for theorising the present state and prospective future of censorship.[15] He argues there that the transition from state power to what he refers to as 'corporate power' which characterises the information age, obviates the need to ask 'which is the toughest regime, for it is within each of them that liberating and enslaving forces confront one another'.[16] So, for instance, we can trace today the shift in the power of censure towards corporations such as, say, Network Solutions – one of the biggest and oldest Internet domain name registrars – which operates its site hosting business according to its own acceptable use policy. That policy states, for instance, that Network Solutions will not host 'material of any kind or nature that is obscene, defamatory, libellous, profane, indecent, or otherwise objectionable material'.[17] Another kind of corporate organisation is the Internet Watch Foundation, founded, as it says of itself, by the 'Internet industry' (in 1996) and sponsored by a long list of other corporations, many of which are familiar high-street names, including the likes of Tesco, Vodaphone and News International. The declared mission of the IWF is to be a 'hotline for the public' to report suspected illegal content, especially 'online child sexual abuse content hosted anywhere in the world and criminally obscene and incitement to racial hatred content hosted in the UK', and it makes clear that it 'works in partnership with the police, government, the wider online industry and the public to combat' such (possibly) criminal activity.[18]

I do not cite the IWF's declared mission here in order to question its specific aims as such (though its scope is clearly greater than the sanctioning of 'internet paedophiles', which is its headline activity), but rather to point out the way in which the power it and other corporations wield produces a new form of subjectivity, one which is now characterised by *self-censorship*. Such self-censorship is the modus operandi of the Subject in the context of the self-regulating techno-cultural system. A simple illustration of this is the way YouTube may choose to censor the content it carries by removing (rather than by preventing the uploading of) video material posted by the user, if it receives a certain number of complaints from other users that the video is offensive. So great is the quantity of material posted on YouTube that it actually depends on users to spot such 'offensive' (and possibly illegal) material. However, those complainants do not constitute a 'public' in the traditional sense of the term – for there is no discussion, no argument made in public and no apparent need for a public sphere at all for a decision to censor to be actioned. The complainants are a disparate set of individuals, each of whom has already 'self-censored' in what could be described as a 'YouTube-corporate-style', and they are rewarded for doing so with the apparent power of censure over others. YouTube might take a corporate decision to actually reinstate a particular censored video following the submission of a further set of complaints from users that such action constitutes unacceptable censorship of free expression. In order to gain full access to 'the system' – in other words, to use it fully as a YouTube member – one is required to individually internalise the principle that at any moment an 'exclusion mechanism' can be automatically initiated, or rather triggered, by interactions with the system as a whole. At least in the age of censorship under the law, the law could be appealed in public. In the age of corporate censorship – despite all of the 'corporate public statements' made, censorship 'by proxy' is, rather, Kafkaesque. The model I describe shows how the subjective intentionality traditionally serving as the foundation of a public sphere is slipping away. It illustrates the manner in which censorship is already becoming an internal feature and control mechanism of socio-technological systems of governance. According to Deleuze, the emergence of a power structure that operates along these lines coincides with the production of the 'continuously modulated' Subject. The replacement of the kind of institutions that traditionally 'moulded' the Subject (such as factories, schools, hospitals or the military) by the corporations which 'modulate' it are simultaneously perceived as what both threatens freedom of expression at the same time as facilitating it. The ubiquitous incorporation of the 'status update' in the context of the social mediafication of everyday life is perhaps an iconic example of how the censorship/freedom of expression dichotomy has been redefined (or 're-censored') in the contemporary context of digital culture, and of how such modulation subjectifies the Subject.

LEST WE FORGET: THE ETHICS OF CENSORSHIP IN THE AGE OF TOTAL RECALL

Finally, lest we forget: in what sense is censorship an ethical issue as well as a political one? The final section of this chapter aims to indicate the manner in which it is so. That we might forget this entirely is something Derrida cautions us against in his *Archive Fever* (*Mal d'archive*) in the context of his remarks about the relationship between censorship and *archivisation*. Obviously the French word '*mal*' in Derrida's original title maintains a reference to 'evil' throughout, as well as to sickness, or 'malady'; and in drawing this chapter to a close, taking my lead from that text, I shall examine how archivisation and the technicity of memory and recollection figure in relation to censorship as an ethical issue (beyond its being viewed as a purely political one). This involves identifying the point at which, or the extent to which, subjectivity and censorship are inseparable from one another, or can be seen to be bound up with one another, and how this relationship between them calls for ethical caution.

The word 'lest' in the expression 'lest we forget' is an archaic English word; it is a conjunction meaning 'for fear that; so that one should not'. It is used to introduce a clause expressive of an action or occurrence requiring caution. It is perhaps most familiar to us today because it is inscribed on war memorials everywhere in Britain, usually at the bottom of the obelisk monuments bearing the long lists of names of fallen soldiers. 'Lest we forget', the inscription reads, not, in fact, 'Lest we forget *them*', these particular, named individuals – though undoubtedly they are each being called to mind. The inscription 'lest we forget' also calls to mind all those other victims of mass death who are unnamed, perhaps unnameable, and yet further still, I suggest, it calls to mind the madness, or malady, of war and mass death itself, *beyond* the historical and political arguments about the origins of war and so forth. I bring this image of the war memorial to mind at this point, to draw attention to how it can stand as an example of the material nature of the archive in general, and the ethical caution the archive specifically demands: a war memorial is a kind of archive by virtue of the inescapably technological nature of the inscription it bears. Without the impression of 'words in stone', or in some material form or other (be this organic or inorganic), there is no psychic impression of the words 'lest we forget'– one could add, 'lest we forget' that too. As well as marking the commemoration of sacrifice, suffering and death, war memorials also lend themselves, by virtue of their publicity, to uses and abuses that their original builders could not anticipate. For instance, they are frequently used as a focus for displays of militarism, or they might conversely be the focus of anti-war protests; they may even become objects of desecration. Indeed, wherever there is, to use the word privileged in the previous chapter, a 'recording' of events, in whatever medial form, a certain censorship is always at work. And it is because censorship is always a matter of *both* forgetting and remembering that it always calls for caution too.

Firstly, just to indicate the *conventional* senses in which the caution censorship demands might be regarded as an ethical matter: every time we say we agree or disagree with censorship in general, or dispute a particular instance of censorship in terms of its rightness or wrongness – be this in the context of totalitarian, democratic or theocratic political regimes, and in view of whatever legislative authority applies – then a certain implicit understanding of the ethical capacity of the Subject is always also being expressed. Irrespective of what in particular is forbidden or allowed, there is already at work a certain concept of the Subject as capable of both adhering to the law *and* capable of its transgression. A certain freedom is being affirmed even as it is being denied. As argued above, as far as the modern Subject is concerned, whether it is for or against censorship in a normative sense, in general or in a particular instance, it is generally assumed that the strength of any argument for or against it is ultimately a matter of the evidence brought to bear on any case. There might be disagreement as to when and where the right to free speech is conflicted by the outlawing of hate speech; or as to the tolerability of the harm caused to some by the freedom of expression afforded to others, but, metaphysically speaking, such disputes are grounded in their entirety on a notion of the autonomous, rational Subject who, in principle at least, by virtue of its share in 'humaneness', is simultaneously both subject to the law *and* entitled to its protection. That includes, as an ideality at least, protection *from* whatever authority administers the law, as well as from others when their actions threaten its free expression. In practice, however, adherence to the ideal principle of the freedom of the Subject is necessarily imperfect. Those practical reasons which compromise the capacity of the juridico-political system to dispense justice, are considered, by and large, to be 'human failings': for instance, the prejudices of judges and juries; the faultiness of evidence and argument, ambiguous statements, flawed statutes, and so forth. Alongside such a representation of the relationship between a necessarily restricted ideality and the 'imperfect nature of the human', however, there are also technological considerations which are equally significant. The point I want to make here concerns how the Subject comes into being always in conjunction with a certain technical apparatus of remembrance, recollection and memory; how neither censorship nor ethical subjectivity is independent of technologies of such memorialisation.

For instance, the ideality of the law, in reality, is dependent on its being *enregistered* in some form or another. There can be no recall of or recourse to the law (in general) at all without this. The law has to be remembered, and to be remembered at all it has to be materially fixed in some form or another. This refers not merely to the obvious empirical fixing that printed words on paper pages achieve – though this is historically a key component of such enregistering in general – but fixed, first of all, in language itself; fixed also in institutions, in the administration of legal qualifications, and so forth as well as in statutes and, perhaps especially important in practice, in accumulated case law. All of which together, 'record' the law as such in the first place. Paradoxically, without recording devices of a material nature, the ideality of the law would have no chance at all. (There could be no judgment 'according to the law' and hence no justice.) The recollection of the law and the recorded history of its constitution have always been dependent on technical apparatuses of inscription of one kind or another.

The *political* subject/Subject of censorship and its relationship to freedom of expression, I have already argued, is to be understood in conjunction with recorded and recallable 'legislative heritage'. This archivial cultural memory is what at once expresses and supposedly secures the *ideality* of the Subject as being free and that which would protect its freedom of expression. But, as has also been argued, there cannot be *in practice* a condition of human subjectivity which is ever wholly free of censorship. I now want to suggest that to fully understand the nature of this tension between censorship and freedom of expression, it must not be forgotten that this 'act' of definition is never a purely intellectual project; it is itself enrooted in the materiality of the technological conditions of archival recall. As Timothy Clark reminds us: 'the modern self as an individual, as subject of representation and space of private interiority' only became possible 'in the context of a mass print culture' and within the public sphere constituted by that.[19] What I have sought to do in this chapter is to insert the subject of censorship into such a general account of the material-technological condition of subjectivity as a function of its techno-cultural situation as a whole. Today that is increasingly characterised by peer-to-peer communications and the extensive networking of archives and data-bases of all kinds (viz. entertainment, learning, socialising, publishing, crime-solving, self-expression, and so forth). In this new technocratic situation, I have already argued, 'old-style' censorship becomes redundant in several senses. The question I want to address in drawing this chapter to close, concerns what could be termed the Subject's post-censorial responsibility under conditions of the new archival culture.

Just as the techno-juridical apparatus renders the law (including the laws on censorship) recallable and hence accessible and applicable, today's techno-cultural forms of recall and memorialisation are determinative of new forms of subjectivity. What this whole example of 'the law' and the technical conditions of its recallability illustrates, is how the very idea of the free Subject (whose freedom might be infringed, denied, alienated or subjugated) is dependent on its *reiterability as inscribed in 'the law'* – and yet it is the technological form of this inscription which threatens the very ideality it enables.[20] It is the technological system facilitating reiterability itself, therefore, that could be said to be what demands *ethico*-political, rather than purely political, caution. This *mal*, evil or malady of archivisation is thus identified, by Derrida, as an ethical matter in the deepest sense: the central issue of archivisation 'is the violence of the archive itself, *as archive, as archival violence*'.[21] What this draws attention to – to go back to my example of the war memorial – is the relationship which exists between the technics of remembrance and the violence of war itself. It is the 'ambivalence' of the repetition and the 'memorialisation' the archive gives rise to which bears with it the ethical danger of what is both denied (that is, censored) and commemorated at one and the same time. The distinction and relationship between the event and its mechanical recollection is fundamentally a matter of the technics of the archive; and this is the background against which the Subject 'experiences' the future as being at stake and thus as a matter of ethical concern. The (material) technical basis for recollection will figure in not only 'how' but also 'what' we remember. The 'how' and 'what' are inseparable. In his essay *Typewriter Ribbon* (1998) Derrida poses the question:

> Will we one day be able . . . to join the thinking of the event to the thinking of the machine? Will we be able to think . . . at one and the same time, *both* what is happening and the calculable programming of an automatic repetition? For that it would be necessary in the future (though there would be no future except on this condition) to think *both* the event and the machine as two compatible or even indissociable concepts.[22]

Considering Derrida's deconstruction of the distinction between the human and the machine and his demonstrations of the co-originality of the human and technology, his question here might seem rhetorical, save for the fact that the future is *always* at stake and the specific character of the exteriorisation of memory constantly changes – and in the context of digital culture has done so dramatically. This cautioning serves at least to recall, and to make a 'live issue', how recollection of the past in the present, always by means of the present's technological capabilities, is a profoundly ethico-political matter.

The ethical significance of this Derridean techno-logics of memory and recall – the *mal*, evil or malady, which is inherent to archivisation, and which Derrida reminds us at the outset of *Mal d'archive* takes the form of violence, is to be measured, ultimately, in terms of the threat it poses – namely, the threat of totalisation. But we are still left with the question of just what this means: what exactly is this 'violence', and who or what is being threatened or suffers it? To say that it implicitly poses a threat is to recall once again, to reiterate in fact, that recollection itself always bears with it a hitherside of denial and suppression. It is a circular argument, perhaps, this cautionary 'lest we forget'. We have to proceed, precisely, with ethical caution for fear, that is, to use one possible formula, of censoring (or denying) the otherness of the Other. We must consider whether a particular act of 'censorship' (which effectively should be seen now as synonymous with 'denial', 'exclusion', 'suppression', 'subjugation', and so forth) is a violation of a singular and unique Other. Does censorship repeat, risk repeating or add to, an original instance or an 'event' of violence? One might ask oneself, for example in a psychoanalytic context, 'what is it for this individual to recall and relive a traumatic experience?' Or in the context of a TV news programme: 'is it responsible to re-present and make public someone's experience of offence or suffering; is it ethical or unethical to do so?' These are banal enough examples – so banal in fact there are long-established professional rules/codes (laws, if you will) of conduct for psychoanalysts and news editors to bear in mind when deciding such issues as these. It is important, though, to look beyond such a narrow code-oriented way of thinking about the ethical and ethical caution. The situation has to be theorised, for a start. Just to illustrate with reference to these two particular examples: is enough known about the role psychic repression plays in making a traumatised life bearable, or, to what extent the stability of Western democratic capitalism is dependent on the general suppression of the truth about the violence on which it is founded? I have to ask myself: what is the nature of my own personal relationship to the 'collective unconscious repression', for example, whose spell is broken every time it occurs *to me*, consciously, that everywhere in the world others are suffering right now but *I* do not act? Who or what censors the account I have of the limits of my ethical responsibility, to which I casually subscribe *without even thinking*?

'Recollection', remembrance, anamnesis, however it is to be named, is in the ways described here (a) key to contemporary ethical subjectivity, and archival technologies of recollection are central to the possibilities of the becoming ethical of the Subject. The 'evil' or 'malady' of 'the archive', as the name of an inherent threat, stems from the technical possibility that the protocols and algorithms of recall (the archive's functionalised organising principles) which are already, today, largely decided by corporations such Microsoft and Google, might in the future be decided by no one at all, but rather by the archival machine itself. In view of such a prospect, finally, one might ask: should we be worried? The answer, in my view, is both yes and no. No we should not, because this externalisation of 'decision making' into the 'recall machinery' of culture and society, has always been with us: the human and technical are hetero-genetic. Yes we should, to the extent to which it is unthinkingly supposed that new mediatised forms of communication bring about a *purely* technological, de facto end of censorship; after which there is nothing to do except join in the cultish 'end-of-censorship' party celebrating the latest technicised experience of free expression and uncontrolled mediatised interactivity. What is ethically dangerous about this perspective is that it forgets to address the issue of how the transformation of the subject of censorship is a transformation of ethical subjectivity too.

NOTES

1. Derrida, *Eyes of the University*, p. 47.
2. Swedish Media Council, 'Film Classification'.
3. See BBFC website at <http://www.bbfc.co.uk/about/mission-statement/> (last accessed 10 August 2012).
4. At this point it is clear I am side-stepping a host of other issues such as whether the contemporary easy availability of, say, pornographic imagery, often of an illegal or borderline-illegal nature, has what might be considered an undesirable effect on social attitudes and sexual behaviours. I am not at any point suggesting such matters are not of legitimate concern.
5. An ironic reference to the largely discounted media effects theory associated with Harold D. Lasswell's theories of how media content and messages penetrate and act directly upon the audience's consciousness 'causing' them to respond in certain ways. See his highly influential

Propaganda Technique in the World War (1927). See also Sproule, 'Progressive Propaganda Critics'.

6. Butler, *Excitable Speech*, p. 140.

7. Ibid. p. 128.

8. See the UK Racial and Religious Hatred Act 2006, available at <http://www.opsi.gov.uk/acts/acts2006/ukpga_20060001_en_1> (last accessed 10 August 2012).

9. The Danish newspaper *Jyllands Fasten* originally published, on 30 September 2005, several cartoons, including one of the prophet Muhammad wearing a bomb-turban on his head. On 6 February 2006 the French satirical magazine *Charlie Hebdo* reprinted the cartoons, claiming they lampooned Islamic fundamentalism.

10. An attempted prosecution against the publisher of *Charlie Hebdo* based on alleged breaches of laws pertaining to racism failed. The magazine was fire-bombed in November 2011.

11. Butler, *Excitable Speech*, pp. 129–38.

12. Butler, *Excitable Speech*, p. 130.

13. The recent introduction of Internet filtering in Australia, involving agencies such as the Australian Communications and Media Authority, and ISPs Telstra and Optus, are testimony to this.

14. The UK Terrorism Act 2000, for example, reserves the right to determine whether images stored on any device 'are of a kind which could be used in conjunction with terrorism'. Available at <http://www.legislation.gov.uk/ukpga/2000/11/contents> (last accessed 29 October 2012).

15. Deleuze, 'Postscript on the Societies of Control'.

16. Ibid. p. 4.

17 <http://resellers.networksolutions.com/aup/index.html> (last accessed 9 October 2012).

18 <http://www.iwf.org.uk/> (last accessed 9 October 2012).

19. Clark, 'Deconstruction and Technology', pp. 242–3.

20. See ibid. pp. 242–3.

21. Derrida, *Archive Fever*, p. 7.

22. Derrida, 'Typewriter Ribbon', p. 72.

8. *Suffering*

It could be argued that suffering is the *sine qua non* of all ethical subjects and of ethical subjectivity itself; the problem of suffering is the motivation of the ethical Subject and the subject matter to which all ethical concern must ultimately be referred. It is the provocation to which the Subject's becoming ethical is the response. Yet suffering is repugnant to the life of the Subject itself; suffering is precisely that from which life distances itself in order to live and to flourish. The relationship to suffering is thus profoundly ambiguous: in distancing itself from suffering, life remains fascinated by it; it provides the measure by which well-being comes to know itself as such and in terms of the absence of suffering and its distance from it. A relationship with suffering is thereby maintained across that *distance* opened up between the Subject and suffering, whilst suffering serves as a constant reminder to it of the fate that can befall it. That suffering persists and 'demands' alleviation across the distance between the suffering and the non-suffering Subject, suggests both a connection and a disjunction between the very existence of the Subject and the demand for alleviation from/of suffering to which it has already responded in its aversion to suffering.

THE AMBIGUITIES OF MEDIATED SUFFERING

That suffering is, ambiguously, both repugnant and attractive at the same time, neither entirely internal to the Subject nor entirely alien to it, I suggest, is reflected in various cultural forms expressive of the ambivalence to suffering. There is a thin line, for example, between horrification at witnessing suffering and the pleasure of the 'entertainment' it provides. This is evident, for example, in spectacles of suffering; from the days of the Roman Colosseum to Samuel Pepys pushing his way through the 'joyous' crowd at Charing Cross to see the hanging, drawing and quartering of Major-General Harrison (before 'oysters and to bed');[1] from the popularity of YouTube road accident compilations to the appetite for medical documentaries detailing extreme suffering in illness – such as 'The Boy Whose Skin Fell Off', or bearing some other such similarly enticing title.[2] The relationship to suffering, in the broadest terms, is culturally mediated. In the globalised media culture of the twenty-first century images of actual or fictionalised suffering abound and are enthusiastically consumed. From daily news reports of the latest massacre to home-made splatter movies; from terrorist beheadings to Tarantino ear-jobs and shoot-outs, and so forth, the 'unspeakable' horrors of the world and the suffering which can befall the human being are repeatedly played out across the landscape of popular culture, and are at the centre of popular explorations of the relationship between good and evil. These are all examples of how contemporary culture could be described being 'obsessed' with images of the pain of suffering. (See the discussion of Bataille in Chapter 4.) The normative moral abhorrence of suffering which is inflicted (as opposed to that which is incurred accidentally) does not appear to diminish the fascination with suffering per se, it is rather subsumed by it. This is, at least in part, because we recognise suffering as the universal possibility of the sensate creature and the cruelty to which it is exposed.

In view of this, in this chapter I shall attempt to show how, in order to lay claim to the properly ethical dimension of suffering *as* the responsibility for its alleviation, the responsibility–suffering relationship has to be understood beyond the normative moral assessment of the question as to whether inflicted suffering is ever justifiable (for example, as 'punishment') on the one hand, and how this differs from accidental suffering, on the other. Suffering also needs to be thought beyond the psychological fascination of the 'horror' the scene of suffering produces in the forms of pleasure and disgust. In other words, we have to think the phenomenon of suffering beyond the moral normativity shaping the distinction between the suffering which is considered to be deserving of *pity* and that which is not.

THE MEDIATION OF THE EXPERIENCE OF PITY

In the context of our contemporary global mediatised culture it is largely through the televised spectacle of suffering, in any of its forms, that extreme suffering is brought into the lives of the vast majority of the non-suffering. It is also by such means that the experience of suffering becomes available as an object of ethical and political concern. The mediation of suffering closes the gap between suffering and non-suffering, such that the non-suffering Subject is touched, moved or affected by the suffering of the other at a distance. By means of media technologies, the pain of the suffering of others is transmitted and communicated to the non-suffering. In this, essentially cultural, context, as Clifford Geertz argued long before the incorporation of *tele*-visual media into most aspects of everyday life, the aesthetics of media representation 'are not mere reflections of pre-existing sensibilities, they are positive agents in the organisation of a sensibility'.[3] The viewers' experience of the suffering of others is structured and organised by media, not merely at the level of its narrativisation, how its story is told, but also in the context of the 'total media environment' within which suffering is encountered and 'consumed'. Consequently, mediated suffering solicits a range of responses according to the way in which the visibility of distant suffering is managed, and how the perception of vulnerability to the danger of being included in suffering, by way of getting 'too close' to it, and association and disassociation with sufferers, is actively shaped.[4] This shaping is of course broadly to be understood as political in the sense that it is always selective, and the selection and representation of suffering is politically motivated and manipulated in the context of the prevailing political determination of 'friends and enemies' by various power blocs and elites. Which suffering or whose suffering matters, and to whom, and the individual and public responses various representations of suffering solicit, can be claimed, I believe uncontroversially, to be a function of the mediation process itself. I am not concerned here with the details of how, precisely, media power operates or who benefits most from it. But clearly how a desired response to suffering is produced in an audience is a matter of as much interest to charity fund-raisers as it is to global power brokers, despite their usually different interests with respect to the suffering represented. The politics of pity and compassion for suffering and its mediated representation are, in any case, inseparable: how 'we' the non-suffering feel and what we are able or made to feel; even what it is 'to feel', or to be touched or moved by way of the relationship to distant suffering facilitated by media, is a function of the mediality of the system of representation, and the structuring of our encounter with it.

The commonplace mediation of suffering, however, does not in any way resolve the ambiguity of the relation to suffering as such; it simply gives further expression to it. For example, anxieties about 'desensitisation' to cruelty and violence and 'compassion fatigue' in the context of debates about how the alleviation of suffering might be promoted, are matched by concerns that the representation of these things might be dangerously too explicit and 'too disturbing'. This is especially the case where the cruelty often associated with suffering is concerned. And yet it is widely recognised also that the suffering of the anonymous 'starving millions' or the mass victims of natural disasters and genocidal violence, is best 'brought home' to the audience by representing the experience of suffering of a single individual; a suffering *someone* with a name or a face. I suggest we can discern in this tension between the problem of suffering in general and the singularity of the demand for its alleviation most recognisable in a singular instance, the entire problematic of the relationship between the ethics and politics of suffering.

THE POLITICS OF PITY

It is in relation to the, in one form or another, always culturally mediated distance and proximity to the suffering of the Other, that I want to note one further aspect of the ambiguity of suffering. If the rational autonomy of the suffering/non-suffering Subject is assumed, then the 'distance' between the suffering and the non-suffering Subject is already absolute by definition. No *one* suffers the *Other*'s suffering: the one feels pity for the Other in his or her suffering. I empathise with the Other when I feel pity or compassion, and I am able to do so because I can *imagine*, as a creature with the capacity to suffer, what it feels like to be in the Other's place. Rousseau famously argues that it is precisely such a *sentiment* of pity which constitutes the basis on which empathy for the Other in his or her suffering is possible ('there but for the grace of God go I'). Pity is in this way always self-interested; one might even say pity is always 'self-pity'. This would be the condition of *both* the wilful capacity of the rational autonomous Subject *to act* to alleviate the suffering of the Other and of its *perception* of the practical, empirical limits placed on its ability to do so. Its *own* discomfort at the Other's suffering is the measure by which it assesses what 'needs to be done'. Compassion, on the other hand, strictly speaking as *passion* rather than *reason*, represents for Rousseau a dangerous over-identification with the Other's suffering, and as such can be self-destructive. For Rousseau the twin sentiments of self-interest and pity for the suffering other are considered to be *natural* and in thinking of pity as natural, Rousseau also *assumes* the rational autonomy, or freedom, of the Subject who pities, and to whom the suffering of the Other represents the threat of its destruction by virtue of the fact that it may induce excessive compassion.[5] A political project aimed at alleviating suffering in the world in general would therefore not be best served by the abdication of reason in the matter as it calls for rational calculation. However, as is brought

out in the course of Derrida's reading of Rousseau's thinking on this
theme, pity also only arises in the rational Subject in conjunction with,
or as a *response* to, the suffering of the Other:

> In the experience of suffering as the suffering of the other, the imagination,
> as it opens us to a non-presence within presence, is indespensible: the suf-
> fering of others is lived by comparison, as our non-present, past or future
> suffering. Pity would be impossible outside of this structure . . .[6]

Two points to be noted here are: firstly, that pity in Rousseau is thought
of as a form of auto-affection within *thought itself*, but its origin is logically exterior to this; it is, in reality, already an *affective* response to the
alterity of the Other's suffering. Secondly, in its being thus motivated by
what is exterior to it, pity is not, also on Rousseau's own understanding
of the term, 'natural' to the rational autonomous Subject, it is rather
necessarily mediated – and it is mediated in its most general form by
'culture' (by the same argument, the distinction between nature/culture
would itself lack any transcendent ground). Whatever difference, 'gap'
or space there is between pity in the Same and the suffering in the Other
that motivates it, it cannot be thought of simply as 'natural' because
the relation to the suffering other spatialises the 'space of suffering'
between the Same and the Other in the first place. I might be more
intensively piteous in myself when directly confronted by the suffering
other; I might be more inclined to act compassionately and actually do
something in that moment of encounter with suffering, but the structure
of pity/compassion remains the same. On the one hand, for Rousseau
there is a danger of pity 'degenerating into weakness'[7] in the face of the
particular instance of suffering; it can only become 'just', in his view,
if my response can be universalised by my distancing myself from it; in
effect by resisting any urge to compassion. On the other hand, to pity
the whole of suffering mankind is not a recipe for any particular action.
At one and the same time, therefore, pity produces an ethos of benevo-
lence which rationalises and naturalises suffering as a part of the world
and 'the human condition', and it emphasises the limits of 'what can
be done' to alleviate suffering in general. One could say, for Rousseau,
suffering is above all a moral philosophical problem and is destined to
remain so. The problem is, in a nutshell, that of the universalisation
of what is essentially understood as *my own* sentimental response to
the Other's suffering; and to enshrine it within the moral code or law.
Derrida's reading of Rousseau shows that the tension between what is
both necessary and impossible is an aporia already to be found at work
in Rousseau: 'The condition of morality is that through the unique
suffering of a unique being, through his presence and his empirical

existence, humanity gives itself to up to pity. As long as this condition is not fulfilled, pity risks becoming unjust.'[8]

Between the forces of universality and particularity in tension with one another, in Rousseau, Derrida then says pity is presented as being 'contemporary with speech and representation'.[9] In other words, it is no more natural than it is cultural, or, in terms of the discussion above, the prevailing moral code will be informed by culturally mediated public perceptions of suffering and the prejudices with regard to the suffering which is and which is not, *on reflection*, considered to be deserving of pity. Such reflection cannot but be informed by the prejudices which give rise to the sentiment of pity in the first place. And as soon as it is accepted that pity is not a purely natural sentiment but arises, rather, always in a given cultural context of 'speech and representation', then the value attached to pity and the morality and politics of pity lack any properly ethical ground.

I shall now move on to analyse this ambivalence and the ambiguity of suffering further on the basis of the relationship between Nietzsche's and Levinas's accounts of the ethical. And I shall consider the sense in which for each of them thinking the ethical involves thinking suffering beyond the politics of pity in its conjunction with normative moralities, and requires negotiating the impasse the ambiguity of suffering represents.

NIETZSCHE, LEVINAS AND THE AMBIGUITY OF SUFFERING

That such an ambivalence towards suffering is key to the cultural origins of ethical subjectivity is superficially reflected in the apparent polar differences between the Nietzschean and Levinasian accounts of its ethical significance:

> To see suffering does you good, to make suffer, better still – that is a hard proposition, but an ancient, powerful human-all-too-human proposition . . . No cruelty, no feast: that is what the oldest and longest period in human history teaches us . . .[10]

> For pure suffering, which is intrinsically meaningless and condemned to itself without exit, a beyond takes shape in the inter-human.[11]

The possibility that these positions are not necessarily mutually exclusive and, perhaps, only to be perspectively differentiated, is raised by their both placing suffering and the vulnerability to cruelty and violence at the centre of the respective accounts of morality and moral value of which they are a part. Suffering in each case is decisive for the formation of the ethical Subject. For Nietzsche it is through the refusal of the meanings attributed to suffering by 'the herd' (the slavish, unthinking mass) that the 'sovereign noble' (the masterly, superior type) both differentiates him- or herself from the herd and contemplates a reversal of the will, which has become mired in forms of ascetic idealism which are 'hostile to life'. For Levinas ethical responsibility is premised on the radical differentiation of suffering in the Same from the suffering of the Other; it is the condition of the ethical Subject's openness to the other *qua* absolute Other. In the context of a critical exegesis of the relation between these, in some respects antithetical and in other respects conterminal, philosophies of suffering, a key point of contact between Nietzsche and Levinas on suffering is the significance attached by each of them to the materiality of sensation and embodiment in their accounts of subjectivity. For both them, however different the destinations of their thinking may be, the passage of thought 'beyond suffering' is crucial – for Nietzsche to what he refers to as 'the affirmation of life'; for Levinas to the claims he makes concerning 'infinite responsibility'.

Richard Cohen has written that Nietzsche was troubled by the 'meaninglessness of suffering' and that he 'rejects all interpretations whatsoever for suffering', finally offering only a 'brave but fantastic heralding of the heralding of yet another messiah: Zarathustra, heralding the Overman'.[12] It has to be remembered, though, that it is only from the perspective of herd morality that the meaninglessness of suffering is an issue according to Nietzsche; it is only the 'lower type' of human being which suffers from the 'meaninglessness of suffering', moreover by virtue of bringing it upon him- or herself. Of course, this entire discourse might be judged highly objectionable, even proto-fascistic, nonsense, were it not for the simple fact that the noble and the herd are also to be understood as twin aspects of every individual. And, for that reason, everywhere there is tension and loathing between these 'two' in Nietzsche's genealogical account, we are effectively referred back to the internal struggle between them. Most significant, when reading Nietzsche's genealogy in conjunction with Levinas's ethical metaphysics, are their respective rejections of anti-*thetical* thinking per se.

Suffering, I suggest then, is a point of condensation for Nietzsche's and Levinas's respective philosophical positions *tout court*. It is fundamental for Nietzsche's project, expressed in such terms as 'becoming', 'overcoming' and 'the affirmation of life', and for Levinas's project of ethics expressed in terms of the 'humanism of the other' and 'transcendence'. Both of them present responses to the problem of 'the meaninglessness of suffering' from *within* suffering itself. My own questions in this context concern the sense in which Nietzschean affirmation and

Levinasian responsibility are accessible only 'beyond suffering' and what is at stake in deciding between them.

There is, of course, no denying these thinkers generally present us with radically differing perspectives on suffering. For instance, in Nietzsche we read:

> You want if possible – and there is no madder 'if possible' – *to abolish suffering*; and we? – it really does seem that *we* would rather increase it and make it worse than it ever has been! ... And do you understand ... that *your* pity is for the 'creature in man', for that which has to be formed, broken, forged, torn, burned, annealed, refined – that which has to *suffer* and *should* suffer?[13]

And in Levinas we read:

> The vortex – suffering of the other, my pity for his suffering, his pain over my pity, my pain over his pain, etc. – stops at me. The I is what involves one movement more in this iteration. My suffering is the cynosure of all the sufferings – and all the faults, even of the fault of my persecutors, which amounts to suffering the ultimate persecution, suffering absolutely.[14]

This juxtaposition illustrates the difficulty of trying to think with Nietzsche *and* Levinas on suffering: the strategic and fictitious 'we', the voice of Nietzsche's aristocratic noble at pains to differentiate itself from the 'you' of the herd, cannot strictly be compared to the actuality of the inclusive Levinasian 'me' – which includes Levinas himself, me, you and every other singular Subject, for whom, on the matter of the responsibility for suffering, Levinas's last word will always be 'the buck stops here'. The initial difficulty I identify, then, concerns the matter of the 'who' or 'what' of suffering, and this in turn points to a set of questions concerning various relationships: for instance, the relationship between the self and suffering – both myself in relation to my suffering and my relation to the Other in his or her suffering, and not forgetting his or her relation to me in my suffering. The way I shall approach these relationships now is along the line of connection they suggest between Nietzsche's and Levinas's thinking of 'individuation' and 'separation',[15] respectively, and the roles they play in their discourses on the *pain* of suffering.

PAIN AND INDIVIDUATION

One of Nietzsche's earliest and most abstract figures of suffering can be found in his early work, *The Birth of Tragedy*, in the sufferings of the God Dionysus. As Keith Ansell-Pearson notes, Dionysus experiences the sufferings *of* individuation as such, as it gives us a profound and pessimistic way of looking at the world: what exists is a unity and primordial oneness: individuation is mere appearance and is the primal source of all evil; art offers the joyous hope of that the spell of individuation can be broken and unity restored. We suffer from life because we are individuals alienated from nature and because consciousness of this separation afflicts us.[16]

If this may be allowed to stand as a sketch of the early Nietzschean project of thinking, then it could be said that it is generally aimed producing a reversal of this metaphysics of individuation and at a re-aestheticisation of life. The re-aestheticisation of life requires the fostering of the irreducible play of forces characterising life itself, and sets the stage for the later genealogical critique of the antithetical representation of those forces. On this basis the will can become truly capable of the affirmation of life as it is lived. In contrast to such a reorientation of thought towards the restoration of a 'unity', the orientation of thought 'beyond being' in Levinas, as seen in previous chapters, is actually premised on an account of individuation as the 'substantive' Subject's separation from existence in general. Levinas's phenomenological discourse claims it to be 'solitary', 'at home with itself' in 'enjoyment' and in satiating its needs. Such an existent can suffer, but its 'suffering is the failing of happiness; it is not correct to say that happiness is an absence of suffering'.[17] Phenomenological descriptions such as these and others offered by Levinas are not of moments of a consciousness but rather of 'instants' of the existent's life.

The achievement of aestheticised life in its highest form for Nietzsche, then, is premised on the prior accomplishment of a certain *dis*-individuation rather than on individuation, as this figures in Levinas's account of subjectivity. Moreover, the dis-individuated aestheticised life would appear to be a form of what Levinas calls the 'dissolution of Subject'.[18] But where these two accounts of suffering touch, I suggest, is in terms of a suffering which causes, or threatens to cause, the *failure* of a certain projected fulfilment – for Levinas that of the 'satisfaction of needs' of the existent; for Nietzsche in life's quest for 'unity', or the reunification with nature. Though Nietzsche equates Dionysian 'joy' with such *dis*-individuation, and 'enjoyment' is said to secure separation for Levinas, and though Nietzsche valorises a return to 'unity', whereas the accomplishment of 'ipseity' is the condition for transcendence for Levinas, in both cases, with suffering we are in the presence of a certain less-than-wholly-individualised Subject: a Subject which is either halfway to coming into being or halfway to becoming unified – depending on the direction one supposes it to be moving in. In both cases it is the suffering of such a Subject which threatens to forestall the process at hand, and what is called for is the unblocking of its movement. In this way subjectivity is connected with the possibility of a philosophical revaluation of suffering – but this is not in any sense guaranteed in advance.

Now, however different the destinations of Levinasian ethics and Nietzschean aesthetics may be judged to be, they each privilege suffering in their respective accounts of how thought (which is always that of some *body*, if not a *somebody*) can be redirected beyond itself. One way to approach the relationship between the two is thus to consider how they each understand the relationship between suffering and what lies 'beyond suffering'. Intriguingly, both of them address the problem of the 'meaninglessness of suffering', but neither of them supposes the 'abolition of suffering' to be a meaningful goal: suffering is approached by both of them, rather, as a given feature of the subjectivity of the Subject, or 'the human condition'. Any 'justification' or 'theodicy' of suffering, is not only impossible due to the disproportionate degree of suffering in the world (the paradigm of which, today, is the excess of suffering represented by the Holocaust),[19] it is just as much so due to its 'lateness', in the sense that it comes always 'after the fact' of suffering and hence always deals with its representation. Having rejected theodicy from their differing perspectives, Nietzsche and Levinas both direct their thought to the question of how we might *live* our proximity to suffering.

SUFFERING AND THE BODY

Even though *The Birth of Tragedy* presents a highly abstract image of suffering, one apparently far removed from the suffering experienced in the body and the banality of physical pain, it is important to remember that such 'high-mindedness' is ultimately grounded in the materiality of sensation. In a note at the end of the first essay of the *Genealogy*, Nietzsche says, for instance: 'Every table of values, every "thou shalt" known to history or the study of ethnology, needs first and foremost a *physiological* elucidation; rather than a psychological one.'[20] And, at the root of the *Genealogy*'s account of how modern moral indignation over suffering is aimed not 'at suffering itself, but at the meaninglessness of suffering',[21] is a recollection of how punishment in the form of the infliction of bodily pain in torture, since antiquity, has been a 'physiological' matter. The cultures of the Greeks, Romans, Egyptians, and more recently even the medieval Germans, Nietzsche notes, lived by penal codes which were practised, quite literally, on the body of the miscreant. He mentions, for instance, the old German punishments, such as stoning (– even the legend drops the mill-stone on the guilty person's head), breaking on the wheel (a unique invention and specialty of German genius in the field of punishment!), impaling, ripping apart and trampling to death by horses ('quartering'), boiling of the criminal in oil or wine (still in the fourteenth and fifteenth centuries), the popular flaying ('cutting into strips'), cutting out flesh from the breast, and, of course, coating the wrong-doer with honey and leaving him to the flies in the scorching sun.[22]

By showing how such punishments are, in fact, entirely 'meaningful', Nietzsche presents his evidence that 'meaningless suffering' is actually a recent invention. In his genealogy of the concept of 'suffering as meaningful', such literal 'pound of flesh' punishments are for Nietzsche located at the 'halfway' stage of individuation (in the sense indicated above) between the characterisation of a relation to suffering as pure 'joy' and 'festivity' and the transformation of the concept of debt (*Schulden*) into that of guilt (*Shuld*). They are indicative of a point where 'compensation is made up of a warrant for and entitlement to cruelty'.[23] There is no need here to recall the full trajectory of Nietzsche's account of how the 'negative' value assigned to suffering emerges through various stages of the reversal of its origin in 'the joyous life', culminating in Christianity's seeking 'to abolish suffering altogether' – and along with it, according to Nietzsche, the joy of life itself. I wish rather at this point to emphasise and to stick with the idea implicit to the *Genealogy* that the 'superior type', the noble, accomplishes individuation in the form of his or her *response* to the suffering of *pain*. Nietzsche's texts frequently invoke examples of the life subjected to extreme suffering, in the pain of tortures and punishments – as in the passage cited above – or, alternatively, in the pains of illness. In either case, the suffering of pain forces the sufferer *back* into the sensual dimension of bodily existence, a force against which the body itself can offer no resistance; it can do nothing (other than suffer) and its becoming thus falters in such pure suffering. However, Nietzsche views such a condition of life positively; as the occasion for a revaluation of suffering, and thereby of life itself. He imagines that amidst such suffering and in such a moment of 'general disappointment and enlightenment over the delusion of his life', there arises for the sufferer, an opportunity for self-reinvention and a transformation of his vision and 'a sobering-up' from the world as he has hitherto 'fantasised' it.[24] The suffering of extreme physical pain is thus regarded as the possibility of liberation from another mode of suffering, namely, intellectual suffering, or rather anxiety. Nietzsche unequivocally regards the latter form as the worse and more damaging of the two. On the face of it, this sounds utterly implausible (one thinks: 'ask anyone in such physical pain'!). However, it has to be remembered (as noted above with respect to the noble and the herd distinction) that for Nietzsche suffering is not, in reality, divisible into 'two' in this way. This is evident in what he says about how the ascetic, and in particular the Christian 'cult of suffering', seeks to heap suffering upon suffering so as to allow the herd to indulge itself further in its self-pity, and at the same time to contaminate the noble with its 'disease' of pity. If it were not the instinct of the herd to do this, according to Nietzsche, then the overall degree of suffering would actually be less. In this context the difference between the noble and the herd can be expressed in terms of the noble's knowing how to say 'yes' to pain. The noble's 'yes' to pain is thus held not to increase the amount of pain, whilst the herd's 'no' to pain is claimed to increase the burden of pain for all. What happens, in either case, is a shift in the balance and distribution of forces. Nietzsche's reader just has to weather this paralogy as Nietzsche does his own pessimism whilst railing against the unquestionable triumph of reactive forces throughout the *Genealogy* (to which, incidentally, Deleuze, says, the entire book is devoted).[25] Nietzsche's genealogy clearly does not anticipate a reversal of ascetic idealism in its near future, but its revaluation of suffering does still serve to counteract its 'deadening of life forces'. According to Nietzsche any thesis of individual becoming can only ever be articulated in the context of the prevailing structure of 'forces'. These forces govern not only thought, or *cognate* life, but also individual becoming understood as *carnate* life. Individuation (or individual becoming) is a matter of differentiation in both of these senses and dimensions of life, and it is, therefore, always as much a matter of sensate being, or carnality, as it is a matter of meaning, or cognition.

In their thinking on suffering, Nietzsche and Levinas overlap most significantly, I suggest, in their respective accounts of the formation of morality as it emerges from the experience of the body. Nietzsche emphasises this in many places, for example in Zarathustra's 'I am body and nothing beside'[26] (a sentence uncannily echoed in Levinas's remark that I am 'entrails in a skin'[27]), and, for instance, in the late remark from *The Will to Power* (cited earlier in Chapter 3): 'Our most sacred convictions, the unchanging elements in our supreme values, are judgments of our muscles.'[28] Similarly, the suffering of the sensate Subject for each of them, as noted above, is an 'undergoing' rather than *conatus essendi*, and the meaning of suffering as such has its origin in the *response* to pain undergone at the level of sensation. The manner in which they each articulate their thinking on this point may differ greatly, but the rootedness of the 'pained-Subject' in material life and embodiment in general, is crucial to each. In neither case, let us be clear, are we referred to the body as it is objectified in the sciences of biology, physiology and anatomy, all of which deal with *representations* of the body: they both direct us, rather, to the not-yet-represented materiality of sensation. For Nietzsche, as just noted, the sensibility of the body is the origin of 'our most sacred convictions', and the suffering body signals the possibility of overcoming the individuation it suffers in its very suffering of extreme pain. Even Christ himself, in the most painful moment of his suffering on the cross, Nietzsche speculates, may have discovered the 'complete disillusionment and enlightenment in regard to the deceptions of life' and thereby 'insight into himself'. This is perhaps evident, suggests Nietzsche, if the words '"My God, my God, why hast thou forsaken me?"' are 'understood in their deepest sense'.[29] Extreme pain, for Nietzsche, is the occasion for self-mastery and self-insight, the production of something new, growth and the affirmation of life. It is because of the transformative power of sensate suffering that it is deemed to be both necessary and desirable. The difference between aristocratic and ascetic sensibilities is that the former appropriates and directs the energies of suffering 'inward', such that the self reinvents itself, whereas the latter directs them 'outward' in a gesture of pity for all those whom it recognises to be *the same* as itself – to all 'humanity'. Pain thus places the sufferer in a situation where 'it could go either way' – a discovery, as has been noted (in Chapter 4), Bataille could also be considered to have made. That Levinas also directs us to this same point of 'decision', is most clearly to be seen in his account of ethical subjectivity where he speaks of this Subject in terms of its being a 'being-in-a-skin', as he does throughout *Otherwise than Being*. And, as discussed in previous chapters, the skin, in this text, is a figure of *liminality*: it is the boundary maintaining the distinction between the me and the not-me; it is the surface of my contact with the other person; it gives me the sense of my own interiority, and at the same time it is the surface of my exposure to exteriority and hence to wounding and violence. The skin is the surface of all possible 'contact' and the exposedness to injury, wounding and violence – and physical pain itself; 'as a passivity, in the paining of the pain felt, sensibility is a vulnerability'. [30]

Levinas holds fast to this moment of undecidedness of pain in his phenomenological discourse in order to reveal the manner in which 'the possibility in suffering of suffering for nothing prevents the passivity in it from *reverting into an act*'.[31] Where Nietzsche's thinking goes outward from pain in the direction of *dis*-individuated 'unity', Levinas's thinking goes towards what he calls the superindividuation of the substantive Subject as a being-in-a-skin: 'The individuation, or superindividuation, of the ego (*le Moi*) consists in being itself, in its skin' but, take note, this is 'without sharing the *conatus essendi* of all beings which are beings in themselves'.[32] Is it not possible to say here that Nietzschean *dis*-individuation directed at the accomplishment of 'unity' and Levinasian superindividuation of the substantive 'being-in-a-skin' directed at the openness to alterity, share a common starting point, if we understand this starting point to be the rejection of a certain egological interiority? In other words, both Nietzsche's and Levinas's projects are premised on a certain notion of dis-individuation and a refusal of the naturalness of the psychological notion of 'the ego' or 'self'. For Levinas this is the moment in which there is an *ambiguity* of which the 'body is the very articulation'; the moment in which 'it frees itself from all the weight of the world, from immediate and incessant contacts' and is 'at a distance'.[33] All of this pertains to the Subject as an 'I' viewed from the perspective of the 'I'. In Nietzsche it corresponds to a point at which there is a tentative balance of the forces which he names as the noble and the herd: at this point, the herd becomes self-obsessed and its pity for the suffering of the Other is simply an inversion of its own self-pity as it turns outward. The noble, on the other hand, is presented as the disruption of this equilibrium through the articulation of its contempt (*Veracht*) for the herd, as it turns inward. And just as these two perspectives are in reality aspects of a 'play of forces' at work within one individual Subject, Levinas's 'I' emerges through a process of differentiation from what is other (*autre*) played out through the satiation of its material needs (for example, in the satisfaction of the hunger it suffers). This accomplishment of its independent existence, its interiority or 'ipseity', which, as already suggested, could just as well be called the 'becoming of the Subject', is the necessary precondition for its orientation towards a wholly other alterity.

The significant difference between Nietzsche and Levinas, to which I will now turn, concerns 'what happens next'.

MEANINGLESS SUFFERING AND USELESS SUFFERING

For Nietzsche the theological conundrum of the 'meaninglessness' of suffering, in response to which the herd resorts to theodicy, marks the point of its entrapment in a cycle of 'bad repetition'; for Nietzsche it represents a certain figure of the 'eternal return of the same', but a negative one. Such a negative figure is to be discerned in the structure of the pity (*Mitleid*) which is redoubled in the pity expressed *for* suffering and multiplied further in the pity for that pity. The herd is caught in a downward spiral of pity. It wills suffering upon itself in order to indulge itself further; it embraces, even celebrates, its victimhood and becomes a neutered will to impotence. It would be only too easy (and short-sighted) to view Levinas's discursive deployment of the biblical figure of 'the widow, the orphan and the stranger' in his articulation of responsibility for the other human, moreover his suggestion that the other person is 'a value'[34] as the insignia of Nietzsche's ascetic priest. But to do so would be to disregard the manner in which 'what happens next' comes after his account of the 'substantive' Subject on the basis of what I have referred to throughout this book as his materialist phenomenology.

If we accept the discoveries of this phenomenology, worked through in extraordinary detail throughout Levinas's writings, and which culminate in his claim that 'suffering sensibility . . . is an ordeal more passive than experience',[35] then we have to accept that the suffering which is a pure 'undergoing' (of pain) is of a radically distinct order than 'suffering as meaningful'. It is on the basis of his phenomenological studies that Levinas can insist on such a 'splitting' of suffering into 'two' as an irreducible fact, and mark 'meaningless suffering' as simple tautology: it has the descriptive value of 'suffering suffers'. Nietzsche's discourse does not make this discovery. It does not do so only because he has no recourse to phenomenology, but because he is preoccupied with the struggle between two *impersonal* perspectives on suffering occurring within *the same* individual, whose ideal resolution (in both senses of 'whose') he conceives of as a re-turn towards a primordial unity. Levinas's description of the suffering of pain as 'unassumable' by the Subject, is of the pain which 'results from an excess, a "too much" which is inscribed in a *sensorial content*'.[36] As such it neither lacks nor awaits *a meaning*; it is said, rather, to 'penetrate' the dimension of meaning, which is 'grafted on to it':

> What counts in the non-freedom of the undergoing of suffering is the concreteness of the *not* looming as a hurt more negative than an apophantic not. This negativity of evil is, probably, the source or kernel of any apophantic negation. The *not* of evil is negative right up to non-sense. All evil refers to suffering. It is the *impasse* of life and being. The evil of pain, the harm itself, is the explosion and most profound articulation of absurdity.[37]

This could perhaps be viewed, mistakenly, as an *identification* of suffering with evil (*mal*), and hence as making a comparable error to that made by the herd in Nietzsche, were it not for the fact that this does not amount to the same thing as identification of the *meaning* of suffering with evil. The coincidence of evil and absurdity in suffering means, rather, that suffering is 'for nothing'. There is nothing to be said about suffering qua suffering. By itself suffering is without any moral implication. However, Levinas's 'positive' thesis is that for the

> pure suffering, which is intrinsically meaningless [i.e. 'useless'] and condemned to itself without exit, a beyond takes shape in the inter-human . . . the suffering of suffering, the suffering for the useless suffering of the other person, the just suffering in me for the unjustifiable suffering of the Other, opens upon suffering the ethical perspective of the inter-human . . . Properly speaking, the inter-human lies in the non-indifference of one to another, in a responsibility of one for another.[38]

The brazen 'no cruelty, no feast' of Nietzsche's noble is effectively challenged, though obliquely, by Levinas's 'no suffering, no ethics'. Levinas's 'ethical perspective', that of 'responsibility', is no more *assumable by me* than is my own suffering, and to be ethical is thus not *my decision*: it is not a matter of my good character or my personal qualities, but rather the matter of what intransitively articulates my very existence; my entry into existence as such. This 'thesis' is, in fact, a 'perspective' – and in this respect Levinas's discourse maintains a similarity with that of Nietzsche: *in (my) suffering* I am not concerned with the distinction between myself and the other person. The perspectives which Levinas switches between in his discourse are not what he calls 'supra-sensible perspectives' of the kind which theodicy appeals to in its attempts to provide a transcendental meaning for suffering. That I am responsible is not the *judgement* of anyone (nor even of God). Putting this the other way around now: it is not that I am responsible *in my being* – which would amount to an ethical ontology, but, rather, that any 'justification of the neighbour's pain is the source all immorality': ethics, or responsibility, is thus held to precede (my) existence, such that 'the very phenomenon of suffering in its uselessness, is in principle the pain of the Other'.[39]

As it is claimed repeatedly in *Otherwise than Being*, my responsibility for the suffering of the Other is a matter of *accusation*. It comes to me prior to any subjective interpretation placed upon it: I may regard it as a matter of my shame, guilt or conscience; I may 'walk away' from the suffering of the Other in fear, but this does not diminish its objective ethical implication for me. That such an absolute alterity and 'ethical objectivity' escaped Nietzsche is illustrated well by the following passage:

> If we love someone [who] . . . is suffering . . . our feelings of love change: they become tenderer; that is, the gap that separates us seems to be closed . . . We endeavour to ascertain what can best ease his pain, and we give it to him . . . but, if he would like to see us *suffer at his suffering*, we pretend to suffer, for this gives us *the enjoyment of active gratitude*, which is, in short, *good natured revenge*.[40]

Nietzsche here views 'tenderness' towards the suffering of the Other as an inverted form of self-interest, and the scene of suffering as the continuation of a struggle of wills. The Levinasian notion of the Other's 'absolute otherness' (*Autrui*) – the coincidence of 'the Good beyond being' and other person who suffers – remains invisible to Nietzsche. This is not, however, the consequence of a truly vengeful, malevolent or sadistic philosophy of suffering; it is, rather, a consequence of Nietzsche's *theoretical* insistence on the other as an individual, who, still rather like Rousseau's rationalist Subject, *always calculates* his or her own interests, even in their moment suffering. Levinas's phenomenology of suffering shows to the contrary that in moments of extreme suffering the 'I' can no longer even constitute itself so as to be so self-pitying: hence his idea of an infinite responsibility which is 'all mine' with no scope for 'pretence' at all. In contrast to Nietzsche's thought in the above citation, the 'tenderness' of my proximity to the Other in his or her suffering is expressed in terms of the 'tenderness of skin' which '*is* the very gap between approach and approached, a disparity, a non-intentionality, a non-teleology' and 'I can enjoy and suffer . . . because contact with skin is still proximity of a face'.[41] We might therefore say that Nietzsche's account of 'tenderness' is of the psychological 'tenderness of the heart', whereas Levinas's 'tenderness of the skin' points, in his own terms, to the precedence of my ethical obligation as an empirical reality.[42]

Nietzsche's paragraph 'On tenderness' in *Daybreak* is consistent with what the *Genealogy* expresses concerning the undermining of the strong by the weak. It is very shocking, in the first instance at least, to be told that the equation of suffering with evil in the Judaeo-Christian tradition must be rejected because it is the result of the victory of the weak, the vulnerable, the sick over 'us' (those to whom his thinking always addresses itself) who aspire to strength, and who would actually be stronger than we are were it not for the undermining *we suffer* at the hands of the weak as a consequence of how 'they' live 'their' suffering. And, that the only suffering that really matters in a world-historical sense is that which is caused to 'us'. On the other hand, the perspectival differentiation of suffering, between my suffering and the suffering of the Other as such, is just as important to Levinas's ethics as it is to Nietzsche's notion of affirmation. Though Nietzsche's and Levinas's aims may differ, they both nonetheless confirm that the necessity for thinking 'beyond suffering' needs to be understood in its own right.

PITY AND/OR COMPASSION AND THE AMBIGUITY OF LANGUAGE

The Judaeo-Christian discourse of pity (*Mitleid*) is so culturally dominant that Nietzsche's rejection of it must struggle against the determining force of language itself, which forces 'us' to speak in its terms – as must Nietzsche in order to get through to his reader. This situation is compounded somewhat further by the fact that the term *Mitleid* in German connotes both 'pity' and 'compassion'. In *Beyond Good and Evil* he unravels the structure of *Mitleid* so as to distinguish between the pitying of the pitiful (essentially for themselves and their kind) and the pity the strong feel *for* the piteous attitude of the weak towards the world whilst, at the same time, 'blaming' the weak for infecting the strong with such doleful piteousness:

> [A]nyone conscious of creative powers and an artist's conscience will look down on [the herd] with derision, though not without pity. Pity for *you*! That to be sure is not pity for 'social distress', for 'society' and its sick and unfortunate, for the vicious and broken from the start who lie all around us; even less is it pity for the grumbling, oppressed, rebellious slave classes who aspire after domination – they call it 'freedom'. *Our* pity is a more elevated, more far-sighted pity – we see how *man* is diminishing himself, how *you* are diminishing him![43]

This is just one of Nietzsche's many attempts to distinguish noble and herd understandings of *Mitleid*. Speaking from the perspective of noble *Mitleid*, Nietzsche expresses contempt (*Veracht*) for this wallowing in the reciprocity of piteous sympathy for the suffering of the herd. He is at pains to distinguish noble *Mitleid*, then, as 'contemptuous pity'. Elsewhere he says that what the herd cannot appreciate is that 'to offer pity is as good as to offer contempt'.[44] All of this is articulated within a *discourse of antithesis* forced, as it were, upon the noble (and Nietzsche), who responds to *the concept of pity* by stridently calling for an *intensification of suffering* as an antidote to the sentiment ultimately directed at its elimination. Why? Because when pity remains unopposed then it does not merely serve to define the moral identity and the morality as such of the herd. If this were so, it would be safe to let the herd go off on its self-piteous, suffering way. But such pity represents a threat to the health of the noble – it is a contagion, and the sick are viewed as the greatest threat to the strong. The noble's perspective on the herd does not merely envisage the reversal of the herd's value system, though, it also serves to diagnose the herd's self-deception. The herd has no conscious inkling of how its identification with *Mitleid* is in reality the most perverted form of individual self-interest: it is content to seek its salvation and the reward of heaven. Hence its super-valorisation of the example of Christ, whose self-sacrifice and suffering is 'for the sake of all the others'. This is why even the suffering of the 'loved one' or 'friend', to the extent to which it diverts 'us' from the project of the affirmation of life, should be countered with noble *Mitleid*: no matter the circumstances, no matter who the suffering other is, such 'good natured revenge' should be deployed to guard against the corrosive effects of pity.

Nietzsche's legitimate critical concern – 'beyond suffering' and the form of *Mitleid* that suffering demands in all of this – is clearly with *the fate of culture as a whole*. It is not with the relationship between anyone in particular in their relation to any particular other. Levinas's thinking 'beyond suffering', on the other hand, returns us to the primal scene of a certain 'intimacy'; something which cannot be 'given as an example' of some greater whole (such as culture) 'or be narrated as an edifying discourse'.[45]

MORAL VALUE AFTER 'THE DEATH OF GOD'

The discussion so far has concentrated on how, from a point crossed by both Nietzsche and Levinas, the former's thinking heads off towards 'unity' by way of the dis-individuation of the self, and the latter's, so to speak, goes in the opposite direction towards 'uniqueness' or 'singularity': these have been presented, respectively, as the conditions for the 'affirmation of life' and 'responsibility for the other'. It has been shown how each of these movements of thought is based in the materiality of suffering as something lived at the level of the body and its sensate being. I now want to look more closely at the suggestion – voiced by Richard Cohen, for example – that Levinas specifically takes up 'Nietzsche's challenge',[46] which I take to generally refer to the problem of moral value after the 'death of God'. Bearing in mind the discussion so far, in drawing this chapter to a close, I shall briefly return to its opening theme and to their overlapping interpretations of the *ambiguity* of the suffering of the Other in its relation to the perspectivist strategies of each.

Firstly, there is a sense they each *refuse* the suffering of the Other, but for different reasons. For Nietzsche it is because it signifies a manipulative demand for pity; for Levinas it is because the 'I' cannot literally suffer the Other's suffering any more than it can *be* the other. The Other's suffering is ambiguous for Nietzsche because the Other (the herd, for example) prevails within me, it is in fact a part of me, and without this 'other's' suffering 'in me' I could not contemplate the prospect of overcoming the self which I already am. The other's suffering is ambiguous in Levinas because the singular other is the one who 'obliges' me to be responsible; the Other is the one who calls me to my responsibility, such that responsibility is the very modality of my subjectivity. In both cases ambiguity is a matter of the coarticulation of (their respective senses of) self and other. In Nietzsche this takes the form of the play of opposing forces 'present within one soul', and in Levinas this corresponds to the precedence of the ethical obligation to the other person over the egological relation of the self (*le soi*) to itself. Secondly, it is now clear that the ambiguity of suffering is a matter also of the *ambiguity of language*, and specifically, related to the limitations imposed by the subject/predicate structure of language. Both Nietzsche's and Levinas's philosophical responses to this utilise forms of perspectivism in the formulation of their respective theories of value. This is evident in Nietzsche's *Genealogy* as a whole being forced to express itself in the language of the herd whilst simultaneously asserting the noble's 'seigneurial privilege of giving names'.[47] It is precisely because of this privileging that Nietzsche can be too easily read as an enemy of 'compassion' in his critique of 'pity'. But his negative account of pity does not imply this, or for that matter even an insensitivity on his part, to the value of, or need for, what is ordinarily understood by compassion in the face of actual suffering. All one can say is that the danger Nietzsche highlights is that of over-identifying with the suffering of the other which leads to a deleterious effect on 'oneself'. The 'dead God' of salvation, let us recall, died 'of his pity for Man'.[48]

The ambiguity of language in Levinas's ethics comes to the fore in his attempts to articulate the difference and the asymmetry of the I/Other conjuncture, and to give expression to the *unthematised* situation of suffering. It is evident in every attempt he makes at 'unsaying' (*dédire*) the objectification effectuated by 'the said' (*le dit*). Turning once again to just how this plays out in Levinas's account of suffering: in the instant of physical pain, the very existence of the 'I' 'merges with impossibility of detaching oneself from suffering';[49] this pain 'in its undiluted malignity' is described as 'useless' and 'for nothing'.[50] Richard Cohen in his summary on this point says: 'Just as a bodily being enjoys enjoying, it suffers suffering. The unwanted and at the same time inescapable character of pained corporeal reflexivity is what distinguishes the phenomenon of suffering: one suffers from suffering itself.'[51] The 'reflexivity' of the substantive 'I' in its suffering is, emphatically, through and through 'corporeal' and not a consciousness. In speaking to us from within the discourse of phenomenology, of the pain lived by the 'me' from the perspective of the pain of the other person considered as *a* 'me', this voice has to express such a 'saying' in defiance of the subject/predicate structure of language. Whilst 'compassion' is perhaps the word which in its ordinary usage is best suited to express what I 'feel' for the suffering other – and Cohen uses this word to name what Levinas calls 'the only meaning to which suffering is susceptible'[52] – Levinas's discourse of obligation and my being 'hostage' to the Other, in the discourse of *Otherwise than Being*, emphasises better the absence of any volition on my part with respect to what he calls my responsibility for the Other's suffering. From a transcendent perspective, there is the sense in which I and the other person are 'united' in his or her suffering, but this term 'united' here refers always to *relatio* rather than *res*. It is, as he says of it at one point, a 'relation without relata'.[53] 'Perspective', for both Nietzsche and Levinas, is always a matter of *relatio* rather than *res*. As far as my relation to the suffering of the Other is concerned, then, this means that I do not, indeed cannot, suffer the Other's suffering for him or her, but, without ever willing it, I suffer *for* the Other's suffering in me:

> In this perspective a radical difference develops between suffering in the Other, which for me is unpardonable and solicits me and calls me, and suffering in me, my own adventure of suffering, whose constitutional and congenital uselessness can take on a meaning, the only meaning to which suffering is susceptible, in becoming a suffering for the suffering – be it inexorable – of someone else.[54]

Despite its explicit origins in the physiology of the body and its experience of pain, as discussed above, one wonders whether Nietzsche's diagnosis of the general health of culture could ever be united with the reality of *individual suffering*. In contrast to the remoteness of the everyday to the Nietzschean project of 'revaluation of all values', Levinas's ethics never departs the everyday world of individual suffering, and this illustrates the manner in which Levinas's account of the ethical warrants the description of 'ethical realism', as suggested earlier. The other's suffering, his or her 'pure pain', directs me to 'the problem which pain poses '"for nothing": the inevitable and pre-emptory ethical problem of the medication which is my duty'.[55] This particular formulation may be awkwardly Kantian rather than Levinasian, but 'duty' is the way we tend to *think* and *represent* to ourselves the obligation the suffering Other brings to me by virtue of his or her 'absolute alterity'. So for Levinas I have no excuse and no judgement to make vis-à-vis the suffering of the Other: *after* the death of the God of salvation, waiting any longer for His 'saving actions' is 'impossible without degradation'.[56] I am obliged to act *now*.

NOTES

1. See Pepys, *Diary*, 13 October 1660.
2. One of a long-running, occasional TV series by Channel 4 TV entitled *Bodyshock*. Episode first aired 2004; other titles include 'Born with Two Heads' and 'The Man Who Ate His Lover'.
3. Geertz, *Interpretation of Cultures*, p. 451.
4. See, for example, Chouliaraki, *The Spectatorship of Suffering*; Boltanski, *Distant Suffering*; Tester, *Compassion, Morality and the Media*.
5. See Derrida's discussion of Rousseau in *Of Grammatology*, pp. 186–92.
6. Derrida, *Of Grammatology*, p. 191.
7. Rousseau, *Emile*, cited in Derrida, *Of Grammatology*, p. 191.
8. Derrida, *Of Grammatology*, p. 191.
9. Ibid. p. 191.
10. Nietzsche, *On the Genealogy of Morality*, pp. 42–3.
11. Levinas, 'Useless Suffering', p. 158.
12. Cohen, *Ethics, Exegesis and Philosophy*, pp. 270–1.
13. Nietzsche, *Beyond Good and Evil*, para. 225, p. 136.
14. Levinas, 'Substitution', p. 122 fn.20.
15. The Levinasian notion of separation is also discussed in Chapter 2 in relation to Deleuze's thinking of individuation.
16. Ansell-Pearson, *How to Read Nietzsche*, p. 12.
17. Levinas, *Totality and Infinity*, p. 115.
18. See ibid. p. 298.
19. See Cohen, *Ethics, Exegesis and Philosophy*, ch. 8, for a detailed discussion of this aspect of Levinas's account of suffering.
20. Nietzsche, *On the Genealogy of Morality*, p. 37.
21. Ibid. p. 48.
22. Ibid. p. 42.
23. Ibid. p. 45.
24. Nietzsche, *Daybreak*, para. 114, p. 114.
25. Deleuze, *Nietzsche and Philosophy*, p. 57.
26. Nietzsche, *Thus Spoke Zarathustra*, p. 61.
27. Levinas, *Totality and Infinity*, p. 77.
28. Nietzsche, *Will to Power*, p. 173.
29. Nietzsche, *Daybreak*, para. 114, p. 114.
30. Levinas, *Otherwise than Being, or, Beyond Essence*, p. 55.
31. Ibid. p. 74 (emphasis added).
32. Ibid. p. 118.
33. Levinas, *Totality and Infinity*, p. 116. In Levinas's *Existence and Existents* this is described as the solipsism of the 'I'.
34. Levinas, 'Contemporary Criticism', p. 187.
35. Levinas, 'Useless Suffering', p. 157.
36. Ibid. p. 156.
37. Ibid. p. 157.

38. Ibid. pp. 158–65.
39. Ibid. p. 163.
40. Nietzsche, *Daybreak*, para. 138, p. 87 (my translation; emphasis added).
41. Levinas, *Otherwise than Being, or, Beyond Essence*, p. 90 (emphasis added).
42. See discussion of Levinas's thinking of the empirical in Chapter 2.
43. Nietzsche, *Beyond Good and Evil*, para. 225, p. 136.
44. Nietzsche, *Daybreak*, para. 135, p. 86.
45. Levinas, 'Useless Suffering', p. 157.
46. Cohen, *Ethics, Exegesis and Philosophy*, p. 270.
47. Nietzsche, *On the Genealogy of Morality*, p. 13.
48. Nietzsche, *Thus Spoke Zarathustra*, p. 114.
49. Levinas, *Time and the Other*, p. 69.
50. Levinas, 'Useless Suffering', p. 158.
51. Cohen, *Ethics, Exegesis and Philosophy*, p. 272.
52. Levinas, 'Useless Suffering', p. 159.
53. Levinas, *Totality and Infinity*, p. xxx.
54. Levinas, 'Useless Suffering', p. 159.
55. Ibid. p. 158.
56. Ibid. p. 159.

9. Hospitality, Friendship and Justice

Hospitality is culture itself and not simply one ethic amongst others. In so far as it has to do with *ethos*, that is, the residence, one's home, the familiar place of dwelling, in as much as it is a manner of being there, the manner in which we relate to ourselves and to others . . . *ethics is hospitality*; ethics is so thoroughly coextensive with the experience of hospitality.[1]

Not only is there a culture of hospitality, but there is no culture that is not also a culture of hospitality. All cultures compete in this regard and present themselves as more hospitable than others. Hospitality—this is culture itself.[2]

Ethics is hospitality, hospitality is culture: it would appear to be a small syllogistic leap to the proposition that ethics *is* culture itself (or indeed vice versa.) This would be no more a conclusion though than it would be a starting point; one could only expand outward from such a statement to a multitude of cultural examples of one kind or another, scrutinising each one to investigate and to discover its ethical dimension and thereby to confirm the proposition. Rather than wondering whether or not there is a 'ethical turn' in Derrida's thinking, taking these remarks in isolation, it might be more accurate to say that ethics is conceived by Derrida as the precondition of the cultural universe in its entirety; which begins with a kind of ethical 'big bang'. Culture as religion, as philosophy, as art, as science, as technology, as customs and habits, sacred texts or popular culture, language itself – indeed everything that can be thought of as culture, would in some form or other bear the trace of this common origin, pointed at, triangulated as it were, at least in the two texts cited above, by 'hospitality', 'ethics' and 'culture'. None of these words is any easier than the others, and in any case they are presented by Derrida as being in some way synonyms or modalities of the same thing. Their conjunction is both surprising and yet vaguely familiar at the same time.

One does not need to know about the shared Abrahamic origins of the world's monotheisms and the place of hospitality in their sacred texts (or to have read a single word of Derrida on the common sources of hospitality in so far as it can be traced in various sacred texts) to have a sense of the ubiquity of contemporary cultural discourses or forms of 'hospitality' – people make their careers 'in hospitality' (in the likes of catering, hotels or the sex industry, to name just three). Hospitality is highly commodified and institutionalised: Tesco sells 'Welcome' door mats; the 2012 Olympics, we endlessly hear, have shown the world what British hospitality is 'all about'; the public hospital is a widely treasured modern institution. Hospitality is 'difficult' though, in both of these registers of culture, the philosophical and the everyday. It is difficult to think it because, as Derrida shows, like any other concept it is not pure, and so neither are any of the cultural forms it appears in; it is always contaminated by its opposite, 'hostility': unconditional hospitality is impossible and irrational. It is difficult to live it because only if it is restricted in some way does the very idea and ideal of hospitality seem liveable, or reasonable, at all. Contemporary culture is shaped by a broad and diverse politics of hospitality, governing numerous institutions of hospitality, anything from public house opening times to the treatment of asylum seekers. Whilst the first of these might seem trivial (and it is), I point to it because if we are to *think* of hospitality/culture/ ethics *as one*, then there is a sense in which the thread binding these together must also pass through every little cultural encounter with others. In *Totality and Infinity* – a work Derrida describes as being 'an immense treatise on hospitality',[3] Levinas says:

> [I]nevitably across my idea of the Infinite the other faces me – hostile, friend, my master, my student. Reflection can, to be sure, become aware of this face to face, but the 'unnatural' position of reflection is not an accident in the life of consciousness. It involves a calling into question of oneself, a critical attitude which is itself produced in the face of the other under his authority . . . The face to face remains an ultimate situation.[4]

Hospitality to the Other puts the 'oneself' into question in each instance. If hospitality is just as much 'there' in each and every encounter with the Other, the register, and the form of culture in which hospitality might be approached, theoretically and critically, is entirely open. In principle one could start from anywhere. No discipline of cultural inquiry has privileged access or claim to it, and intellectual work and critical study itself, as a part of culture, is just as much subject to prevailing norms of hospitality as any other form of culture. (See Chapter 1.) Indeed, Derrida's reflections on the aporias of hospitality have been carried through into several cultural spheres and into discussions of political culture, human rights, religion, world affairs, war, law, racism and cultural identity, amongst many other 'cultural matters', dealt with by a diverse range of disciplines. And given this thinking of hospitality explicitly calls for it to be thought in conjunction with both ethics and culture in all its dimensions, there is no ground to suppose its reach could not be extended indefinitely. The cultural *example*, or the context, to which it might prove to be relevant, and through which this suggested conjunction of ethics/culture/hospitality might be deemed to be instructive, valid and validated, will itself always be the test. By 'test' I do not mean that the proposition 'ethics is hospitality is culture' needs to be *proved*; I mean, rather, that it matters that we attempt to understand how the normative idea of hospitality shapes cultural practices of both welcome and exclusion. To whom or to what, as a particular figure of 'the Other', is the prevailing 'culture of hospitality' *in*hospitable? In this sense, it is always hospitality itself, in its various cultural manifestations, which is put to the 'test' by its 'others'.

Whether or not one concurs with Levinas's claim that the face to face is the 'ultimate situation' in which hospitality might be tested (would 'I' welcome the Other – the homeless, the asylum seeker, the criminal, the 'madman' or any other figure of alterity – into my own home?), it at least serves to remind us that the question of hospitality pertains to both the 'inter-personal' situation as well as to other structures of culture as a whole; it is as much an aspect of the microcosmic as it is the macrocosmic dimensions of culture understood *as* hospitality. With this in mind, the context and 'example' this chapter will discuss approaches to the subject of hospitality, drawing together the themes of reason and unreason, friendship, fidelity and justice as well as madness as a figure of absolute alterity which 'tests' hospitality – and there is a certain madness to the approach adopted here itself!

This entire chapter is, to tell the truth, a bit of story, so it will begin in earnest with a prologue.

Two old friends meet. The purpose of their rendez-vous is to readdress an old dispute between them. It is a difficult meeting for many reasons, not least because one of them has been dead for many years and must for this ghostly reunion rely on the memory of the other. Fortunately, this reliance on memory is underwritten by the fact that the matter up for discussion is also a matter of public record. What was said between them once, concerning madness, though in part in the form of personal exchange, was also published and widely disseminated and read, indeed discussion and disputation of their 'disagreement' was widely debated. The dispute between them, revisited now after many years have passed (and from one side only), is approached from a different angle and in another age. This other, new angle is, so to speak, a triangulation, a new position subtended from an alternative, third point, present but marginal in the early work of the dead friend, but, no less for that, anchored by it. In this sense, 'the work in question' itself calls for the rereading and the new commentary it is given; the new critique returns to the work from its own future. For reasons that will become clear, I will imagine the venue for this meeting as a hotel: it will not take place in the home of either protagonist, because one can never be truly at home in the idiom of the other.

OLD HOSTILITIES, NEW HOSPITALITIES: DERRIDA'S RETURN TO FOUCAULT

The subject of hospitality will be approached in this chapter by way of a restaging of a critical exchange that took place between Derrida and Foucault around the theme of what it means to be 'hospitable to madness'. The work in question around which this chapter itself will revolve is Foucault's *Folie et déraison* (FD)[5] and Derrida's return to it on the occasion of a thirtieth anniversary commemoration of its publication at which Derrida presented a lecture entitled '"To Do Justice to Freud": The History of Madness in the Age of Psychoanalysis' (TDJF).[6] This was an occasion, too, for Derrida to reflect on the contamination of the personal by the intellectual, recalling the once hostile exchange between them concerning the relation of Reason to madness as a figure of absolute alterity. The chapter will centre on Derrida's post-mortem of the ambiguous place of Freud in Foucault's thought, and argue that Derrida's rereading of Foucault's celebrated text in relation to psychoanalysis can itself be understood as a discursive gesture of 'hospitality', as this has been thematically explored in various of Derrida's later works, and as it bears on Foucault's understanding of what to be 'hospitable to madness' means. In the course of the chapter I shall aim to show how the critical practice of 'deconstruction' can be viewed as a form of culture which exemplifies the conjunction of ethics/hospitality/culture, rather than just abstractly theorising it. In what might be described as a form of 'hospitable reading', Derrida's text revisits and critically reassesses the difficult intellectual proximity to his 'dead friend' – whilst being commemoratively responsive to the alterity of madness to which Foucault's text gave, and still gives, expression, beyond his death.[7]

Not least, though not only because, death figures in this post-mortem of a dispute, these two friends will not meet (as friends might be expected to) in the 'intellectual home' of either one of them (for neither can ultimately offer hospitality to the other in that sense). The meeting is instead staged here, courtesy of an institution – a form of critical discourse – where intellectual hospitality can be arranged so as to provide a place of neutrality; a place where no one is on his own turf. For the sake of the argument elaborated below, I invite you to think of this as a kind of 'hotel', to which I shall give the name *Chez Freud* – I shall take you there later.

In TDJF Derrida revisits his decades-old exchange with Foucault concerning the possibility of a 'history of madness' once again in terms of the question of the possibility or impossibility of access to madness. The occasion of Derrida's return to that book (FD) and to the closure of that friendship, which was both intellectual *and* personal, still concerns itself with the double articulation of the personal and the intellectual and of what could be called the hospitable and the juridical. Derrida reopens the problematic of openness to the alterity of the Other (the ethical relation) in the context of the tension resulting from the requirement to submit one's discourse to the law (of Reason and rational argument). His approach to Foucault's text in 1991 is less hostile, or, rather, more hospitable to Foucault, in that it plays less the role of policeman to Foucault's discourse and is more 'hospitable to madness' as Foucault had attempted to understand madness. This theme will be elaborated in detail in due course, but in order to make an inroad into the later engagement, it has to be recalled how the original dispute between them had been ignited by Derrida's 1963 lecture 'Cogito and the History of Madness' (CHM),[8] and how Foucault had later responded to this in an essay which was published as an appendix to the second edition of *Folie et déraison* (1972), translated as 'My Body, this Paper, this Fire' (BPF).[9] In his lecture Derrida had originally attempted to show that the very project of Foucault's book, explicitly to write a 'history of madness itself', was an impossible undertaking. As Bennington summarises, CHM had disputed not only Foucault's substantive reading of the 'progression of doubt' and the place of madness in Descartes's *Meditations*, but also attacked the privileging of this (or indeed any other) particular text in the overall project of FD on the ground that all 'madness-as-negativity' is inscribed into the very 'structure of Reason in general'.[10] In fact one can summarise the cut and thrust of Derrida's CHM as aiming to show that this is as true of Foucault's own work as it is of Descartes's or, indeed, any possible *oeuvre* – and it was, after all, Foucault himself who had defined madness as 'absence of *oeuvre*'. CHM had challenged the book's entire general account of the distinction between Reason and madness and had sought to do so throughout on the book's own terms.

The attempt to write the history of the division, decision, difference runs the risk of construing it as an event, or a structure subsequent to the unity of an original presence, thereby confirming metaphysics in its fundamental operation.[11]

This charges that FD illustrates, articulates and demonstrates the problem of this distinction; it exemplifies it as well as the impossibility of the very thing it explicitly sets out to do; there can only ever be a history of *Reason's account* of its other. Any 'archaeology of silence' is inevitably an articulation of the voice of Reason. As Derrida had built this critique of Foucault's book around its reading of Descartes, Foucault's detailed response delivered and published some ten years later, for the main part, consists of a further disputation of Descartes's text and is aimed at challenging and refuting Derrida's reading. It points out Derrida's 'many omissions', his lack of attention to detail including, for example, the fact that the Cartesian text significantly plays on 'the gap between two determinations of madness (medical on the one hand, juridical on the other)'.[12] This distinction is an important and decisive one in the project of FD because it directs thought and philosophising 'outward' to institutions, practices, locations – to culture – rather than holding them in the sphere of concepts and ideas. For instance, in the discussion of the relation between dreaming and madness, Foucault's reading of Descartes focuses on how he represents the difference between dreaming and madness *within* his 'meditations' as a *practice of thinking*, such that the disqualification and 'silencing of madness' as their progress becomes observable is a *practical event*.[13] At another point Foucault redirects Derrida to Descartes's original Latin, noting his failure to check its translation into French. For instance in respect, especially, of his reference and emphasis on the word 'extravagant', found in the French translation and referring to a mode of mental life, where the original Latin says only 'the invention of something new'. This error, Foucault suggests, leads Derrida to 'hang his whole demonstration' on a reading which supposes dreaming for Descartes to be a figural, rhetorical radicalisation of madness and a strategy devised purely for the purposes of his argument in the *Meditations*. Foucault then charges Derrida with reinscribing Descartes's remarks on madness within the realm of pure philosophy and ideas. And, what this entire 'way of reading' Derrida embarks upon misses, according to Foucault, is that it is all 'a question of the *modification of the subject* by the exercise of discourse'.[14]

Now, the actual details of this argument about how to read Descartes well, or, indeed how to assign his place in the Foucauldian 'history of madness', or how the significant differences between Foucauldian archaeology and Derridean deconstruction might be read off this dispute, are not of direct concern here. What I want to emphasise is how in BPF Foucault clearly thinks he is turning the tables on Derrida by showing that Derrida's critical approach is caught up in the traditional metaphysics which it is most explicitly writing against, and yet ends up repeating. Foucault draws his response to Derrida to a close with the now infamous characterisation of the nascent Derridean deconstruction as the 'most decisive modern representative' of a tradition of philosophical discourse which 'reduces discursive practices to textual traces'.[15] In other words, he says it is precisely this traditional 'textual reductionism' which actually performs the silencing of 'madness' in the history of thought. Amongst the many historical forms of this silencing, one of them, says Foucault, as he gets up close and personal, is Derrida's 'well-determined little pedagogy'.[16] His 'last word' on the matter, in the final paragraph of BPF, is intended to drive his point home like a *coup de grâce*. It barely tolerates summary, nonetheless reflecting on it is important for understanding Derrida's 'ethical return' to the theme of the alterity of madness some thirty years later. This last word takes the form of an illustration of sorts, a little dramatisation: Foucault reminds Derrida of one of the objections put to Descartes by his contemporary, Father Bourdin.[17] Bourdin wrote that he understood Descartes to be saying that it is impossible to doubt what is true/certain, even if one were asleep or mad. Foucault cites Descartes's rejection of this account of his own thesis as a misunderstanding resulting from Bourdin's evident inability to see what is stated clearly in the *Meditations*, namely, that whether or not one is dreaming or mad is not of any consequence for the certainty or truth of a thing, nor indeed for the dreaming or mad Subject, for whom it is simply not an issue: only someone who was unable to distinguish between dreaming/madness on the one hand and wakefulness/reason on the other would make this mistake. These 'last words' of Foucault effectively dramatise and caricature the Derridean repetition of the Cartesian privileging of Reason and the *exclusion* of madness. Derrida's alleged unconcern with the modality of the *experience of madness* is presented as the sign of intellectual complicity with its epochal silencing.

Some twenty or so years later, when Derrida is invited to contribute to a conference commemorating the thirtieth anniversary of the publication of FD, he begins (TDJF) with some brief remarks reflecting on how their dispute in relation to this 'great book' of Foucault had once 'cast a shadow over' their friendship for a decade, and that the departure from and return to the book 'today', mirror in various ways the departure from and return to friendship. Derrida emphasises he does not want 'now' (as he had been invited to do for the occasion) to return to that old dispute: 'In the end, the debate is archived, and those who might be interested can analyze it . . . right up to the last word, and especially the *last word*.'[18] Let us just linger a little longer here and ponder this reference to the last word. The last word can be taken as a reference to the final, Bourdin paragraph I have just referred to.[19] Although Descartes's *Meditations* gets a whipping by Foucault for its historical role in silencing madness, this does not stop Foucault from likening his own relationship to Derrida to that of Descartes to Bourdin – their dispute is complicated further by it being a master–pupil situation. And as an illustration of Foucault's view of Derrida, it is peculiarly double-edged and ambivalent. On the one hand, we are shown by Foucault how Descartes, in response to Bourdin's hostility, aggressively slaps him down and simultaneously excludes madness: Bourdin's inability to discern the true meaning of Descartes is effectively likened by Descartes to *madness itself*. On the other hand, Foucault's 'very last words' in BPF are actually left to Descartes: '"But only as the wise can distinguish what is clearly conceived from what only seems and appears to be so, I am not surprised that this fellow can't tell the difference between them."'[20] Here we see Foucault masking himself as Descartes and saying to Derrida: 'Look, it's your master telling you off, but can you even tell it is him?' This provocation itself is intended to give rise to an unsettling experience of uncertainty (in Derrida, its target); it produces an event of the very kind Foucault charges Derrida's 'textualism' with forgetting: it is a performative slap in the face; a 'here, *feel* that; that's what *maddening*, really is'. Foucault thus closes his piercing response by showing how he too can play the part, act in the name of, a certain Descartes, if he wishes to do so.

These last words of Foucault on the matter, however, remain ambiguous, unfixed in their meaning and open to several interpretations, and this 'ending' of the dispute consequently leaves it open, too. They can as easily be read as ultimately confirming Derrida's critique as they can be taken as a successful expression of Foucault's position: firstly, by virtue of their linguistic expression, they will always remain open to interpretation, and by anyone. And secondly, because Derrida's argument about the impossibility of a history of 'madness itself', which rings like a refrain in CHM, is made to resonate by appealing to Foucault's own account of the epistemo-historiographical exclusions of madness, whilst remaining unshaken and unsilenced itself. Foucault's observations on how philosophical 'cleverness' can tend to be disinterested or forgetful of events and actualities; of states of mind, historical conditions, incarcerations and other institutionalisations of the Subject, on the other hand, are not invalidated as such by the impossibility of fixing meaning in language. There is in fact a discernible proximity between the two of them, and for them, between poets and philosophers whose writings are directly concerned with the limits and borders of expression.[21]

CHEZ FREUD: HOTEL OR HOSPITAL?

On his return to FD some thirty years after his initial assessment of it, Derrida chooses to approach the book from another point of view, or 'border': namely, from the point of view of its relation to Freud and psychoanalysis. His rereading will now focus on the place of psychoanalysis in it, or more importantly, consider it as a work belonging to the 'age of psychoanalysis'.[22] Derrida goes into a confessional, psychoanalytic mode:

> Though I have decided not to return to what was debated close to thirty years ago, it would nevertheless be absurd, obsessional to the point of pathological, to say nothing of impossible, to give in to a sort of fetishistic denial and to think that I can protect myself from any contact with the place or meaning of this discussion.[23]

In the 'age of psychoanalysis' FD has to be read on the basis *of* psychoanalysis, and even, to a degree, on the basis of a psychoanalytic understanding of Derrida's own relationship to it. Rereading the book, and unavoidably recalling everything that had ensued previously, in terms of the questions brought to it and the critique as it unfolded, it is now clearer to him that his relationship to the book and to Foucault's thinking of madness is as much to do with what went *unsaid* about Freud and psychoanalysis in it, as it is about what was *said* about the role of the 'Cartesian moment':

> In my title 'the history of madness' must be in quotation marks since the title designates the history of the book, *The History* (*historia rerum gestarum*) of Madness—as a book—in the age of psychoanalysis and not the history (*res gestae*) of madness, of madness itself in the age of psychoanalysis, even though, as we shall see, Foucault regularly attempts to objectify psychoanalysis and reduce it to that of which he speaks rather than to that out of which he speaks.[24]

Derrida goes back to the book, not to the old dispute, but nonetheless 'revisiting' the old dispute, this time to restate the impossibility of the book's speaking from outside of its own age. This approach is more *hospitable* to Foucault's project: it implicitly acknowledges, for example, the Foucauldian sense of the *episteme* and its articulation of the border between identifiable, historically, conceptually and linguistically determined epistemic totalities. Foucault's particular objectifications of psychoanalysis are made central to Derrida's attempt to evaluate Foucault's own declared intention to 'do justice to Freud'.[25] Against this background, his questioning concerns the nature of the *indebtedness* of FD to psychoanalysis: 'Does the project owe psychoanalysis anything? What? Or would it on the contrary define the very thing from which the project had to detach itself, in a critical fashion, in order to take shape?'[26] How is one to understand, moreover, why having done a certain 'justice' to Freud by crediting him thus, 'Freud went back to madness at the level of its language, reconstituted one of the essential elements of an experience reduced to silence by positivism . . . [and] restored, in medical thought the possibility of a dialogue with unreason'?[27] Foucault, nonetheless, later concludes that psychoanalysis should be inscribed in the same tradition as the likes of Tuke and Pinel, namely, the tradition of the pathologisation and medicalisation of madness. Derrida then summarises this 'negative' characterisation of psychoanalysis, describing how for Foucault: 'Freud would free the patient interned in the asylum only to reconstitute him "in his essential character" at the heart of the analytic situation.'[28] This second negative characterisation of Freud and psychoanalysis in Foucault is not only a matter of the psychoanalytic delimitation of madness as a disease susceptible to a therapy, but equally that of the authority of the analyst/doctor, 'when it confers all powers on the doctor's speech'.[29] Derrida goes on to show how Foucault identifies a tradition running through Tuke and Pinel and then on to nineteenth- and twentieth-century psychiatry converging on Freud. The figure of Freud, more often than not, almost always is included in the account of how, 'since the end of the 18c., the liberation of the mad has been replaced by an objectification of the concept of their freedom'.[30] In TDJF, Derrida returns to Foucault's book on madness, not in order to challenge its reading of Freud and psychoanalysis as such – no more so (nor less) than in his first approach to it had challenged Foucault's reading of Descartes as such. What he does, rather, is attempt to draw out and consider the manner in which in Foucault's text, Freud is already and evidently so, a duplicitous figure, doubly and ambivalently inscribed within the project of FD itself; inscribed in terms of what Derrida thinks of as indebtedness. So, Derrida's reading once again unsettles the project's attempt to write a history of 'madness itself' – there is in all this a characteristic 'compulsion to repeat' the same critique that was offered before; to do the same, but differently. The Foucauldian problematic of the history of madness is now approached on the basis of the psychoanalysis inscribed within it.

FREUD AS THE DOORKEEPER OF AN
AMBIVALENT INSTITUTION

The scene for this new meeting of the two 'old friends' is now set: it is
to be staged, so to speak, before the door (and doorkeeper) of psychoanalysis, namely, 'Freud'. Before the door, let us call it 'Freud's Place'/
Chez Freud. Why not? This dispute is now continued around Freud's
place in the Foucauldian *oeuvre* and the claim of its indebtedness to
Freud. The debt is incurred, first of all, and unavoidably, by belonging
to the 'age' of psychoanalysis. The twist, however, is that the thinking
of the 'age' as such has to be given its most insightful articulation by
Foucault, in his account of the *episteme* (and its associated concepts,
such as the 'historical a priori' and 'archaeology'). And though the
modern *episteme* is not purely or exclusively psychoanalytic, it is
nonetheless partly structured by the set of all psychoanalytic 'statements' (to use the technical terminology of Foucault's *Archaeology of
Knowledge*). Derrida's critique thus far, however, which emphasises
the epochal imbrication of psychoanalysis within Foucauldian archaeology and proposes a Foucauldian understanding of this imbrication,
has a principally strategic function in relation to a further aim beyond
that. Derrida's new aim in rereading FD is to restore to Freud, within
the context of that work, the status of 'liminality': the kind of liminality which Foucault super-valorises and associates explicitly in FD,
for instance, with certain 'mad' poets, artists and philosophers (for
example, Nietzsche, Artaud, Van Gogh, Nerval, Hölderlin)[31] and
even with certain artworks (*Las Meninas*) or fictional characters (Don
Quixote). All of these figures Foucault either substantially or symbolically invokes as transgressors, escapees, drifters or outcasts; inhabitants
of the border zones between *epistemes*. They all have a messianic, or
futural, aspect to them: they appear within the waning *episteme* as
unexpected, unanticipated strangers whose arrival heralds the coming
episteme; figures who are not at home within their own *episteme*.

Foucault consistently expresses a kind of empathetic hospitality to
such figures and Derrida uses Foucault's text to re-establish the place
of Freud amongst them; the Freud who speaks 'on the side', as it were,
of madness, and to whom the Foucauldian hospitality to madness may
consistently, on the basis of his argument, be extended. However, in
doing so, Derrida is at odds to discern the singularity of both Freud's
liminality and Foucault's relation to psychoanalysis:

> The Freudian place is not only the technico-historical apparatus ... Freud
> himself will in fact take on the ambiguous figure of a doorman or door-
> keeper (*huisser*) ... Freud as the doorman of today, the holder of the keys,

of those that open as well as those that close the door, that is, the *huis*: the double figure of the door and the doorkeeper . . . he closes one epoch and opens another . . . this double possibility is not alien to an institution, to what is called the analytic situation as a scene behind closed doors (*huis clos*).[32]

Derrida's invocation and appeal to the double figure of psychoanalysis/Freud as the door/doorkeeper here alludes to another of his discussions of 'Freud's place' undertaken in relation to Kafka's parable 'Before the Law'.[33] In that text Derrida explored the idea of access to a possible origin of the distinction between fact and fiction, only, of course, to show that such an original 'law' determining the identity of either of them is 'neither presentable nor relatable'.[34] The example to which Derrida applies the notion of aporia derived from Kafka's parable of the man who seeks access to the law in 'Before the Law', is on that occasion Freud's early attempts – through a combination of self-analysis and the incorporation of aspects of Fliessian nasal reflexology – to account for the origin of sexual repression. Freud's essentially fictional rendition of the organic, evolutionary transition to the upright position, concerning the distancing of the nose from the anal–genital sexual stench,[35] provides the example of his desire to write the history of the *law itself*, but also, as with Foucault's attempt to write the history of *madness itself*, the impossibility of any such project. And continuing with the same theme in a later essay, Derrida reiterates how the law is ultimately without legal foundation; that every law is premised on a performative act of violence which institutes the law, but also, and this is the most important aspect here, that the lawfulness of the law only depends 'on who is before it (and so prior to it), on who produces it, founds it, authorizes it in an *absolute performative* whose presence always escapes him'.[36] In TDJF, figuratively speaking, Derrida's critique takes Foucault to the threshold of the 'door' to psychoanalysis. From this perspective, he reposes the question around which their earlier dispute had revolved concerning the (im) possibility of access to madness. Casting Freud now as 'the doorkeeper of the age' in TDJF, Derrida principally does two things. Firstly, he sketches out a similarity between Freud and Foucault: they are both equally 'outsiders' to madness – they are not madmen). Secondly, he shows how, depending on how one reads Freud, he can be cast either, as Foucault on balance tended to, as an agent of the law (policing the threshold between Reason/madness) or, alternatively, as Derrida does in this essay (in order to do him 'justice'), as the author of a body of work which is in fact 'hospitable to madness' – this hospitality being marked by the *openness of psychoanalysis to the unknowable* prior to any of the psychoanalytic institutionalisations of madness that might be identified.

Without any hope of a direct response or dialogue with his now dead friend, Derrida raises the question of the place of madness in Freudian psychoanalysis in the context of FD with a view to the sense of madness Foucault would have been sympathetic to, or, in various ways, took it upon himself to speak on behalf of. In doing so he aims, as per his title, 'to do justice to Freud' with respect to madness, by way of a hospitable reading of Foucault. Seen alternatively, from another point in the triangulation of Foucault, Freud and madness, this involves acknowledging Freud's own form of hospitality to madness whilst doing justice to the Foucauldian text (which is found, in part at least – thanks to this reading of it – to actually recognise this hospitality as such). In this way, Derrida performatively exploits and reiterates the aporetic nature of the distinction between the ethical *and* juridical dimensions of hospitality, by thinking of *the conjunction of hospitality and madness* in terms of openness to madness. This is what provides the sense of 'hospitality to madness' to which both Freud and Foucault could subscribe, and it preserves the connection between the problem of justice and question of hospitality as such. Positioning Freud thus as the doorkeeper of an institution (psychoanalysis) which is hospitable to madness, serves to establish the claim that psychoanalysis 'keeps' madness as an unknowable alterity and that this is 'in keeping' with Foucauldian hospitality to madness. All of the evidence for this is found by Derrida to be in Foucault's own relationship to Freudian psychoanalysis: for instance, in his acknowledgement that both 'Freud and Nietzsche like two accomplices of the same age' lifted the 'interdiction against language' and instituted 'the return to a proximity with madness'; and in his recognition of the need to 'do justice to Freud' for the way in which psychoanalysis goes beyond the psychology of madness 'as soon as it takes language into account'.[37] However, no matter how many instances might be cited of Foucault's ambivalent approaches to psychoanalysis as an open or closed door giving or blocking access to madness itself, what Derrida wants to highlight, too, is how Foucault repeatedly found it to be impassable. In other words, at this threshold, Foucault is a little like Kafka's man from the country who seeks access to the law.

> Since the gate stands open, as usual, and the doorkeeper steps to one side, the man stoops to peer through the gateway into the interior. Observing that the doorkeeper laughs and says: 'If you are drawn to it, just try to go in despite my veto.'[38]

Whenever he approaches that door, Foucault repeatedly recoils from what he discerns, or what he thinks he discerns, beyond the doorkeeper, to be a psychoanalytic hospital, a place where madness is 'hospitalised' yet again. In other words, Foucault is more often, even mostly, inclined to see psychoanalysis as a carceral institution. However, it only appears so 'from the outside' and if one forgets that

> the Freud who breaks with psychology, with evolutionism and biologism, the tragic Freud, really, who shows himself hospitable to madness (and I risk this word) because he is foreign to the space of the hospital, the tragic Freud who deserves hospitality in the great lineage of mad geniuses, is the Freud who talks it out with death.[39]

This, he says, is 'especially' true of the Freud of *Beyond the Pleasure Principle*, in view of which Foucault would surely recognise the kinship with thinkers of what he called 'originary finitude'. But rather than open up a dialogue on death at this point, Derrida is more directly concerned with the matter of psychoanalysis as an institution of hospitality – be this imagined as, say, that of a hospital or a hotel – which would always be a place of suspect, highly conditional, hospitality. Talking it out not so much here with death itself then, but with the dead friend Foucault, Derrida makes this concession to his thinking: there are always good reasons to be suspicious of the hospitality offered by institutions – be such institutions malign, benign or even apparently welcoming.

In *Of Hospitality* Derrida explicitly addresses the difficult and ambiguous connection between hospitality, hospitals, hotels, the police and what is internal to the psychoanalytic *situation* (namely, to the analyst–analysand relationship). He refers to 'the situation (a classic and common one, too) of a hotel manager working with the police' – the hotel manager as the betrayer of his 'guests' and thus of hospitality itself.[40] That this collusion, betrayal and complicity with the law 'can happen in hotels but also in night shelters or hospitals' is indicative, says Derrida, of the 'absolute porosity' of doors and borders. More generally, he suggests, the impossibility of using 'devices' of any kind to keep secrets – be these computerised records (credit cards, passports, registers, and so forth) (see Chapter 6) or the device, strange as it may seem to call it this, of the analytic session: 'pervertibility' – the 'effacement of the limit between the private and public, the secret and the phenomenal (the home, which makes hospitality possible) and the violation or impossibility of home'– is 'virtually inevitable'.[41] Whoever checks in with an institution is inevitably exposed to the risk of betrayal by it.

Derrida's post-mortem rendezvous with Foucault then, takes the form of a rereading of FD's account of Freud and psychoanalysis making the question of the institutionalisation of hospitality central to the discussion: what kind of hospitality to madness does psychoanalysis offer? Freud, in the figure of a doorkeeper (*huisser*), is on this occasion made the third party to their lifelong and protracted dispute about the possibility of a history of *madness itself*. This positioning, contrived and elliptical though it is, is comparable to that of Kafka's man from the country, whose access to the law itself is barred by a doorkeeper. It emphasises that any misunderstanding between Derrida and Foucault, of any one and any other one, is a misunderstanding never solely of each other's thinking (with respect to their singular intellectual homes) but of their relation, always and inevitably, to a third party (in this case Freud – just as much as it had once been Descartes). It also illustrates how the 'juridical' requirements of critical thinking had come to cast a shadow over their personal friendship. 'Freud and psychoanalysis' serves as a name for the 'place' common to each of them, and indeed to modern culture as a whole; the culture, or 'age', within which a certain hospitality to madness is *shared* by Freud and Foucault. Bringing these two together, face to face, figuratively speaking, on the threshold of madness, Derrida's reading shows a fidelity to each in their respective roles as 'keepers' of the alterity of madness. Doing justice to Freud thus involves acknowledging the ethical moment of his thinking. Derrida's analysis is hospitable to Foucault in that it shows how Foucault's thought too – despite his early preoccupations with 'madness itself' – also exhibits an openness to madness as a figure of absolute alterity. It finds within both of these discourses an ethical sensibility to what (or who) 'is neither expected nor invited, to whomever arrives as an absolutely foreign visitor, as a new arrival, nonidentifiable and unforeseeable, in short, wholly other'.[42] This is a form of hospitality Derrida defines as *visitation* – the encounter with an unknowable, unanticipatable alterity – and distinguishes from the hospitality of *invitation*. Invitation, which always implies the prior establishment of territorial boundaries, is also always a conditional hospitality. All of this bears directly upon the difference between Derrida's earlier and later reading of FD. Earlier, I suggested TDJF is less hostile and more hospitable to Foucault's thinking. I would now qualify this description by appealing to this thinking of hospitality: the old objections – that Reason can never lay claim to madness itself – are sustained, but instead of simply reiterating the impossibility of objective knowledge of the wholly other, Derrida shows how Foucault, like Freud in his own way, was hospitable to the unknowable alterity of madness. TDJF returns Foucault to his encounter with Freud to think through with him again the aporia of hospitality '*Chez Freud*'.

THE HOSPITALITY OF DOORKEEPERS, UNINVITED GUESTS AND HOSTAGES

Chez Freud: I have placed them all before the door. One can imagine further a sign in the window – 'Open to Madness' or 'Madness Welcome'. Can only the mad check in at such an institution? Can there be welcoming without also exclusion? Is not a doorkeeper's job precisely to exclude as well as allow entry? Do the welcome and access depend on who or what comes here? The two hospitalities of invitation and visitation are in reality abstractions: not so much because they are logically mutually exclusive, but because we live in a world in which gestures of selfless generosity overlap with systemic violent exclusion. It would help to have a single word which forestalls any forgetting of this. Derrida provides one: 'hostipitality'. It is a neologism (and the title of one Derrida's seminars on hospitality) which exploits the undecid-ability of the French term *hôte*, as the one who gives and who receives hospitality.[43] The *hôte*, in its Latin origin *hostis*, means both guest and enemy. The term is able, therefore, to ambivalently express how the possibility of welcome and hospitality includes within it a reference to the hostility and violence implicit to the appropriation of the space of the home as the necessary condition of welcoming the Other. So the condition of possibility of hospitality is also marked by the impossibil-ity of its not having been preceded by a certain violence towards, and exclusion of, the Other and hence remarks how hospitality and hostility are imbricated in one another.

This discussion of 'hospitality' is recalled at this point only for its bearing on the theme at hand, namely, the relationship between hospitality, friendship and fidelity, and with regard to the idiom in which these things can be communicated. In TDJF the difficulties of critical dialogue, and of the personal and intellectual friendship between Derrida and Foucault vis-à-vis Freud and psychoanalysis, are presented, effectively, as issues of translation. In *Adieu* Derrida cites a sentence of Levinas that, I suggest, in the light of the discussion so far, is not in need of translation into the Derridean idiom, and gets to the nub of the matter: 'the essence of language is friendship and hospitality'.[44] Translation is key with respect to everything that has been said here: the translation, for instance, of psychoanalysis into hospitality and the tripartite translation of the Freudian, Foucauldian and Derridean idioms. As soon as we mention the home then we are already assuming a certain familiarity or being-at-home-with. In this case it is possible to anticipate, *chez* Derrida, the eventual impossibility of this translation, and that everything which unfolds will be (and was bound to be) a 'compulsive' repetition of the old objections Derrida made to Foucault; we can anticipate this even before he embarks on a kind of detour *around* a solution by dwelling on the relationship between madness, hospitality and psychoanalysis. There was never any prospect of settling this dispute, *finally*, in the form of cohabitation (a *chez nous* of hospitality *chez* Derrida, madness *chez* Foucault and psychoanalysis *chez* Freud – a dissolution of critical differences). It was always more a case of locating hospitality in relation to critique as such, *as a form of culture*, whilst questioning what it means to be 'hospitable to madness'; a matter of pursuing the chain of displacements (or links) between hospitality/hotel/hospital/hostility/host and so forth, via psychoanalysis and all the way to madness.

In all its fullness this would be a long chain. Just to get the measure of the thing, here are some of the links: (1) the mapping of the guest/host distinction onto the analyst–analysand relation, bearing in mind, as already noted, that the host, in accepting the guest, has already claimed the territory of this welcoming as his or her 'home', and that this is the condition of the possibility of hospitality per se. In other words, the guest-patient is welcomed into the analytic situation, which is under the control of the host-analyst who, for his or her part in the overdetermination of the analytic situation (as the representative of the authority of psychoanalysis as a doctrine or law) is also an enemy (– and which analysand has never felt this at some point only to be told to reflect on it as a 'projection' of him- or herself?). The aim of the analysis is to enable the analysand to be-at-home-with-him- or herself by way of this process; by providing a home-from-home for the patient for the duration of the analysis. (2) There is, therefore, the issue of psychoanalysis as a specific form of 'institutionalised hospitality' as such. (3) We must then consider the possible ways of differentiating between hospitalities – such as those of the home, hotels and hospitals, and any other cultural forms of hospitality. Any critical approach to psychoanalysis (as with any other form of culture) is from the outside, but the measure and definition of it *as* hospitality must also be learned from within, that is, from within the analytic situation, once one has entered into it as an accepted guest. For Foucault, 'psychiatry', as a manifestation of the authority of Reason, legitimates itself by taking 'hostages' – for instance, by sectioning the psychotic. For Derrida, the question of who is taken hostage by whom in all of this remains open, as offering hospitality, welcoming the Other, even into one's home, is necessarily to be taken hostage by the guest for whom one is *responsible*. In Levinas's idiom, this is what it is to be oneself: 'the state of being hostage is always to have one degree of responsibility more, the responsibility for the responsibility of the other'.[45]

(UN)CONDITIONAL HOSPITALITY AND THE APORIAS OF ADMITTANCE

As this chapter has shown, to offer hospitality is, in effect, to be 'before the law'. Psychoanalysis *is* hospitable to madness, but, like any other form of hospitality it is conditional: 'unconditional hospitality is, to be sure, practically impossible to live; one cannot in any case and by definition organize it'.[46] This marks one of Derrida's neo-Kantian moments in his discussion of hospitality: in practice, in the course of our experience; in our encounters with contingency and the singularity of the event and the cultural situations (historical, political, juridical, filial, technocratic, communicative, personal, intellectual, and so forth) which we *live*; in our cultural embeddedness, we are guided by and directed towards an impossible purity and universality. However, 'without at least the thought of this pure and unconditional hospitality, of hospitality itself, we would have no concept of hospitality in general and would not even be able to determine any rules for conditional hospitality'.[47] It may seem extraordinary that Derrida, who once so stridently rebuked Foucault for supposing himself to be writing a history of *madness itself* that he provoked the hostile accusation of articulating a 'vicious little pedagogy', should himself reiterate with extreme insistence now, 'the thought' of 'pure and unconditional hospitality itself'. What we cannot live, we, paradoxically, still have to live with:

> Paradox, aporia: these two hospitalities are at once heterogenous and indissociable. Heterogenous because we can move from one to the other only by means of an absolute leap, a leap beyond knowledge and power, beyond norms and rules. Unconditional hospitality is transcendent with regard to the political, the juridical, perhaps even the ethical. But—and here is the indissociability—I cannot open the door, I cannot expose myself to the coming of the other and offer him or her anything whatsoever without making this hospitality effective, without in some concrete way, giving something determinate.[48]

The 'leap beyond knowledge and power' is the desirous movement of thought itself – and the leap from knowledge/power to desire could be read as a symbol of the trajectory of the Foucauldian *oeuvre* (and perhaps as another moment of homage to Foucault and Derrida's friendship with him). In Foucault, desire points beyond knowledge/power. Derrida acknowledges this and associates it with hospitality: 'without this thought of pure hospitality (a thought that is in its own way also an experience), we would not even have the idea of the other as someone who enters into our lives without having been invited'.[49] However, to welcome the Other (to 'give something determinate' – such as protection, support, rights, and so forth), one must have first appropriated the space as one's own. In other words, there must be governance based on some cultural form of a power/knowledge nexus as such, and with that a certain violence.

Unconditional *hospitality itself* would be madness and would amount to an abnegation of responsibility to the Other. And, rather like the man from the country in Kafka's parable, in his commemorative reflection on a friendship that is at once personal and intellectual, Foucault is once again 'shown the door', but rather than constituting a rejection or refutation of his position, it constitutes an act of hospitality and thus serves as a model of ethical critical practice.

NOTES

1. Derrida, *Of Cosmopolitanism and Forgiveness*, pp. 10–11.
2. Derrida, *Acts of Religion*, p. 361.
3. Derrida, *Adieu to Emmanuel Levinas*, p. 21.
4. Levinas, *Totality and Infinity*, p. 81.
5. Foucault, *Folie et déraison: Histoire de la folie à l'âge classique* (1961). This book was translated into English in abridged form by R. Howard as *Madness and Civilisation: A History of Insanity in the Age of Reason*.
6. This text was originally delivered as a lecture under the title '"*Etre juste avec Freud": l'histoire de la folie à l'âge de la psychanalyse*' in 1991 on the occasion of the thirtieth anniversary of the publication of Foucault's *Folie et déraison*. All references to it here are to the translation, which is included in Derrida's *Resistances of Psychoanalysis*. The text has since been republished in English, in an abridged form, in a collection of Derrida's 'funeral orations' bearing the title *The Work of Mourning*, in each of which, as the book's sleeve notes appropriately observe, Derrida 'bears witness to the singularity of a friendship and to the absolute uniqueness of each relationship'.
7. The theme of the alterity as that which comes to thought 'from beyond death' will be developed further in the final chapter.
8. All references to Derrida's text 'Cogito and the History of Madness', originally presented as a lecture on 3 March 1963, are to the English translation in Derrida, *Writing and Difference*.
9. All references to Foucault's text 'My Body, This Paper, This Fire' are to Geoffrey Bennington's translation in *Oxford Literary Review*.
10. Bennington, 'Cognito Incognito: Foucault's "My Body, This Paper, This Fire"', p. 7.
11. Derrida, *Writing and Difference*, p. 40.
12. Foucault, 'My Body, This Paper, This Fire', p. 17.
13. Ibid. p. 18.
14. Ibid. p. 19.

15. Ibid. p. 27

16. Ibid. p. 27.

17. The second edition of Descartes's *Meditations* (1642) included a 'Seventh Set of Objections' by the Jesuit Fr. Pierre Bourdin, which, as John Cottingham notes, 'were for the most part extremely hostile in tone, and often deliberately malicious', *Descartes Dictionary*, p. 135.

18. Derrida, *Resistances of Psychoanalysis*, p. 71.

19. Foucault, 'My Body, This Paper, This Fire', p. 27.

20. Ibid. p. 27.

21. Especially the figure of Nietzsche, who is the 'mad' poet-philosopher par excellence, but also the role of the artist, in Foucault, as a liminal figure and a creature of the border between *epistemes*, along with 'tragic' figures or 'figures of the tragic'. It is to such a list that Derrida proposes adding the figure of Freud. In TDJF he revives the figure of the 'tragic Freud' to counter Foucault's relegation of Freud to the science of psychology (see below).

22. Derrida, *Resistances of Psychoanalysis*, p. 7.

23. Ibid. pp. 70–2.

24. Ibid. p. 76.

25. Ibid. p. 81, citing Foucault, *Madness and Civilisation*, p. 198.

26. Ibid. p. 76.

27. Ibid. p. 81, citing Foucault, *Madness and Civilisation*, p. 198.

28. Ibid. p. 91.

29. Ibid. p. 91.

30. Ibid. p. 97.

31. See, for example, Foucault, *Madness and Civilisation*, pp. 264–74.

32. Derrida, *Resistances of Psychoanalysis*, pp. 78–9.

33. See Derrida, 'Before the Law'. Kafka's short parable 'Before the Law' appears as a sort of prologue to his novel *The Trial*, though it was published as a separate text during his lifetime. All citations of Kafka's text here are taken from *Wedding Preparations in the Country and Other Stories*.

34. Derrida, 'Before the Law', p. 194.

35. Ibid. p. 193.

36. Derrida, 'Force of Law: "The Mystical Foundation of Authority"', p. 36 (emphasis added).

37. Derrida, *Resistances of Psychoanalysis*, pp. 97–8.

38. Kafka, 'Before the Law', p. 127.

39. Ibid. p. 104.

40. Derrida, *Of Hospitality*, p. 65.

41. Ibid. p. 65.

42. Borradori, 'Autoimmunity: Real and Symbolic Suicides', pp. 128–9.

43. See Derrida, 'Hostipitality'. See also Gil Anidjar's translator's introduction to the text of this seminar.

44. Derrida, *Adieu to Emmanuel Levinas*, p. 207, citing Levinas, *Totality and Infinity*, p. 305.

45. Levinas, *Otherwise than Being, or, Beyond Essence*, p. 117.

46. Derrida, in Borradori, 'Autoimmunity: Real and Symbolic Suicides', p. 129. This remark can be interestingly juxtaposed with the following of Levinas, *Totality and Infinity*, pp. 117–18: 'The unconditionality of being hostage is not the limit case of solidarity, but the condition for all solidarity. Every accusation and persecution, as all interpersonal praise, recompense and punishment presuppose the subjectivity of the ego, substitution and the possibility of putting oneself in the place of the other, which refers to the transference from the "by the other" into a "for the other", and in persecution from the outrage inflicted by the other to the expiation of his fault by me.' I suggest the difference between Derrida and Levinas at this point is one of emphasis. Levinas articulates the relation to an absolute alterity which renders the Subject infinitely responsible, whereas Derrida emphasises the practical impossibility of any such 'transference'. Hence the models of both psychoanalysis (which has laid its own special claim on the word) and hospitality being proposed by Derrida, clearly must 'resist' the tendency to collapse both into either forms of absolution (supposedly producing mental or spiritual health) or forms of violent absorption (such as incarcerations) of the Other by the Same.

47. Derrida, in Borradori, 'Autoimmunity: Real and Symbolic Suicides', p. 129.

48. Ibid. p. 129.

49. Ibid. p. 129.

10. *Death, or the End of the Subject*

. . . At Half-Mast

If a person very close to us is dying, there is something in the months to come that we dimly apprehend – much as we should have liked to share it with him – could only happen through his absence. We greet him at the last in a language that he no longer understands.[1]

EXPLAINING ONESELF WITH DEATH

Death, 'the final chapter'. It seems appropriate to leave death till the end of my small subset of all of the possible ethical subjects this book might have addressed. But, it might just as well have been introduced at the beginning, or indeed be placed at any other point, as death hangs over every ethical subject/Subject as a figure of the inevitable end, of mortality, in other words; as the horizon from which a perspective on the ethical life of the Subject might be gained.

Of course, the contemporary philosophical themes of the 'end of Man', the postmodern critique of anthropocentrism, the 'post-human' and the question 'who or what comes after the Subject?', which set the scene for this book's discussion of ethical subjects, are not simply concerned with the fact of mortality as a natural phenomenon. They are concerned rather with how the identification of 'the human' as the source and measure of both truth and value limits the scope of critical thinking to the sphere of what has been referred to throughout this book as 'the Same'. Humanism encloses critical thinking in a cycle of 'bad repetition'. As Clov in Samuel Beckett's *Endgame* says: 'All life long the same questions, the same answers.'[2] In Levinas's philosophy, the reduction of what is Other to the Same by way of its representation and thematisation has a profoundly ethical significance and, in its broadest gesture gives expression to what exceeds, or is surplus to, this reduction of the alterity of the Other by philosophy. As explained in Chapter 1, and has been articulated in subsequent chapters in a number of contexts, the challenge to humanism posed by rethinking the Subject otherwise than by way of its identification with 'the human' can be claimed to be an ethical matter. In this final chapter I shall address the manner in which this challenge encompasses – both includes and points to – the philosophical question of the life/death dichotomy and the Subject for whom or for which death 'matters'. It points, I suggest, beyond either purely natural or purely cultural understandings of the life/death dichotomy. As the ethical, it is safe to say, is always in some sense 'lived', thinking the ethical must always be the contemplation in view of and from within the finitude of that thinking *as a moment of a* life. And, as will become clear soon, I approach the subject of death here from the perspective a singular and unique death – the ultimate, perhaps only, perspective it can be approached from.

In the opening pages of the 'Exordium' to his book *Spectres of Marx*, Derrida addresses the supposedly 'ultimate' – in the sense of both 'first and last' or 'finally' (one might therefore say 'only' or 'primary') – question of philosophy as the question of 'learning how to live'. He immediately problematises its efficacy, though, by exposing its internal incoherence around the life/death distinction, and the very idea that it might be taught or learned:

> Someone, you or me, comes forward and says: I would like to learn to live finally.
>   Finally but why?
>   *To learn to live*: a strange watchword. Who would learn? From whom? To teach to live, but to whom? Will we ever know? Will we ever know how to live and first of all what 'to learn to live' means? And why 'finally'?[3]

As a 'magisterial locution . . . one that goes most often from father to son, master to disciple, or master to slave', this injunction, he says, will always imply a certain violence. But, alternatively, to suppose that one might learn it *'from oneself and by oneself'*, he asks rhetorically, 'is that not impossible for the living being?'[4]

> To live, by definition, is not something one learns. Not from oneself, it is not taught by life. Only from the other and by death. In any case from the other at the edge of life. At the internal border or the external border, it is a hetero-didactics between life and death. And yet nothing is more necessary than this wisdom. It is ethics itself: to learn to live – alone, from oneself, by oneself? This is, therefore, a strange commitment, both impossible and necessary . . . It has no sense and cannot be *just* unless it comes to terms with death.[5]

This can be condensed further, I suggest to this: to (learn to) live 'from the other and by death', 'heterodidactically', and thus 'to come to terms with death', this is 'ethics itself'. This complex formulation, at least in its own way, expresses the incoherence of the injunction as a *philosophical* demand: with regard to the questions of 'how to live' and 'who or what would either teach or learn such a thing?' And yet it nonetheless 'positively' calls upon us to think of this impossibility as 'ethics itself'. The four pages of this Exordium, I suggest, can be read as a striking condensation of the ethics of deconstruction and an articulation of its ethos, from which the Derridean *oeuvre* never wavers or deviates, even if it is only latterly within it that it is more explicitly claimed that deconstructive thinking had always been en route to 'ethics itself'. This thinking of 'ethics itself' in terms of *the impossible yet necessary commitment to coming to terms with death as the condition of justice*, implies that all philosophising takes place within, or is framed by, the non-philosophical experience of the life/death relationship *as something lived*.

In a final interview, one might say from 'the edge' of his own life/death, in 2004, prompted by his questionner to return to these pages some eleven years after they were written, now from his present *position*, namely, close to his death (and knowing it), he reconfirms this thesis and remaps his 'personal experience' of life onto this general ethos of his philosophical *oeuvre*:

> I never *learned-to-live*. In fact not at all! Learning to live should mean learning to die, learning to take into account, so as to accept absolute mortality (that is without salvation, resurrection or redemption – neither for oneself nor for the other). That's been the old philosophical injunction since Plato: to philosophize is to learn to die. I believe in this truth without being able to resign myself to it.[6]

This declaration of his inability to 'resign himself' to the Greek philosophical injunction, *so long as he lives*, recalls the entire project of deconstruction as the refusal of the totalising force of the *logos*, including, especially, its logic of contradiction. One can no more come to terms *with* one's own death than one can learn *from* life how to live. One can only come, and inevitably so, to the end of one's term (of life) *by dying*.

All of this brings to mind Derrida's many strategic deployments of an 'aporetics of undecidability', via tropes such as the trace, cinders, pharmakon, hymen, parergon, supplement, hostipitality, and so forth, and the role these undecidables play in relation to the many themes his *oeuvre* addresses. In the Exordium it takes just a few sentences to undo philosophy's faulty thinking of the life/death dichotomy. And in the final interview just cited, when recalling those pages, he notes in particular the paralogics of *survival* beyond death in the form of writing:

The trace I leave signifies to me at once my death, either to come or already come upon me, and the hope that this trace survives me. This is not a striving for immortality; it's something structural. I leave a piece of paper behind, I go away, I die: it is impossible to escape this structure, it is the unchanging form of my life. Each time I let something go, each time some trace leaves me, 'proceeds' from me. Unable to be reappropriated, I live my death in writing.[7]

In the context of a final interview with the 'dying writer', there is an obvious interest in the question of literary legacy and its future, but it is necessarily posed as if he or she were already were dead.[8] But Jacques Derrida (still alive, at this point) is still philosophically engaged and he addresses himself one more time to the question of the logic of the structure of the trace as a live issue (he mentions, for instance the uncertainty arising from the changing techno-cultural context of textual storage and retrieval and its bearing on the question of legacy and recall – a theme explored at length in Chapters 6 and 7 here). And what Derrida offers there is not simply a purely self-referential, auto-biographical detail. It is equally a philosophical appendix and a refrain concerning a general thesis presented elsewhere in relation to numerous subject matters and thematic contexts of his writings. To say 'I live my death in writing' represents a form of theoretical and practical commitment to life/death as a subject and to the rethinking of the Subject as only being possible from 'the edge' of the life/death dichotomy.

It is not only those who are 'writers' or 'philosophers' in the conventional sense of what writing and philosophising involves, for whom life is only possible from this 'edge': everyone lives his or her death in the form, as idiomatic English says, of 'making a mark' in life. All lives/deaths have a writerly character in the Derridean sense of writing as inscription (*écriture*). Derrida's philosophy of writing and textuality has always pointed beyond the literal understanding of writing/textuality to a general theory of the trace or 'mark' as both a form of survival beyond death and as the form of life which is understood (as it is in the above citation) as 'living one's death' in every instant of life *by* making marks. All such marks are the external signs of someone's passing, and hence his or her death. This is the meaning of the idea that life can only be lived *as* death, or, perhaps slightly less morbid to say, in the approach to actual death. Any 'writer', at least in this sense, cannot but write autobiographically because, at least for him or her, it is a moment of his or her life, here-and-now, 'spent' engaged in writing as a real-life-activity; the present work and the author's relation to it being no exception to this rule: this text, like any text, in its entirety, not only when addressing the theme of death, is produced at the 'edge' of life/death. This chapter is written from the perspective of this edge in several senses, as will become clear shortly.

SPECTRALITY, DEATH AND MOURNING

In lieu of the first person and the face-to-face address, one is necessarily left with a corpus – a corpse in other words – as the remainder or trace of living thought. This text comes in-between you (the reader) and me (Dave Boothroyd); it is a product of our irreducible heterogeneity, and I refer to its nature as such an interstitial event, as belonging from the outset to the order of what is discussed below through an engagement with the Derridean theme of spectrality. The main body of this text, though revisited and reworked, is in fact already a bit of ghost to me, as its 'main body', I will confess, was written many years ago and under very particular circumstances, which were, at the time, let me say, 'material' to its production. For reasons that will become clear, it would be an act of infidelity to not acknowledge this or to erase the trace of it entirely – if that were indeed possible. What remains to come in this chapter was summoned initially into the region of spectral events, in response to two invitations to appear at conferences. What was to be the first of these was on 'Death and Its Concepts' at the University of Leeds, and the second was mysteriously titled 'Phantom f(x)', an event hosted by Nicholas Royle at Stirling University, for which no particular theme or title, other than 'the spectral', was specified; a theme to be entirely, freely interpreted by the invitees. The theme of the spectral appealed to me at the time as I was already exploring death in the work of Heidegger, Levinas and Derrida and was intrigued by what I had recently read in the Exordium to *Spectres of Marx* , especially Derrida's bringing the spectral into conjunction with 'ethics itself'. Shortly after I accepted both invitations and commitments to appear in person, events of a different nature – 'personal circumstances', to be precise – inter-vened in a way that was eventually to make my *appearance in person* at either conference impossible. Caring for a terminally sick father with, at that time, an uncertain prognosis necessitated my immediate withdrawal from (but, effectively into) 'death and its concepts'. But before long the second deadline (at Stirling) it seemed in all likelihood, would arrive quite some time after his anticipated death, so I accepted the second invitation. As time passed, events overtook my thinking in more senses than one. My decision to appear/not to appear at 'Phantom f(x)' had to be postponed and was eventually only finalised at the last minute, as my father's dying took longer than I had originally been given to think could possibly be the case. It gradually became clear that the deadline of the date set for my appearance, with a text, and my father's deadline for his disappearance from life were uncannily accelerating towards a point of convergence. As a consequence, the scene of my vigil in those last days of his life became the *situation* of this text's original writing.

My father's dying was never intended to figure in my writing about death 'philosophically' as it were, though of course these material circumstances of my thinking and reading about life/death could not but be affected by the intensity of my living in the experience of his dying. It raised new issues for me; not least whether it would be right to continue to write about the topic, for fear of contamination between my philosophical relation to death and – I still do not yet know what to call it – his 'staring death in the face' and, indeed, my staring at death in his face. One cannot but write the present, the situation, the moment into a text – even if one heavily disguises it, or engages in strategies of denial, and, in any case, I was already committed to the idea that every text is autobiographical, at least in the sense described above. The present cannot, strictly speaking, be written into a text at all though; the present is inevitably killed, or written off by writing. I felt strongly I would be engaging in an act of betrayal, without being sure what that betrayal consisted in. On the one hand, I (and the family) were doing all we could to keep him alive; on the other hand, writing about death (which could not help but be about his dying too, even if I 'said' nothing directly about it) would be a form of killing him off. I would be doing this not so much by writing about *his* 'death' – it had not happened yet anyway; but, despite any disguise, I would still be drawing on what constituted *my* situation, which at the time was overwhelmingly defined by it. I tell all this 'in advance' of what is about to come here; of what inevitably came later, because time really is out of joint here, and now doubly so. This 'time out of joint' is, of course, an allusion to a reference to Hamlet in Derrida's Exordium: '"Enter the ghost, exit the ghost, re-enter the ghost"'[9] – any 'writing' is already a manifestation of the spectral.

Writing is a spectral technology; writing is a Hamlet machine. Before Derrida names the spectral in his work it was 'already there' linking in various ways the entire discourse of presence/absence in deconstruction with what is latterly (though this temporality rings a little false in view of it) declared to be 'ethics itself' viewed as a sort of phantom itself and only approachable from the edge of life/death.

If it – learning to live – remains to be done, it can happen only between life and death. Neither in life nor in death alone. What happens between two, and between all the 'twos' one likes, such as between life and death, can only maintain itself with some ghost, can only talk with or about some ghost [*s'entretenir de quelque fantôme*].[10]

I am doing it right now (writing). I am doing it with *his* ghost *again*. But there are others, some of whom will appear later here – this is turning into a seance! And, 'if I am getting ready to speak at length about ghosts, which is to say about certain *others* who are not present, not presently living, either to us, in us, or outside us, it is in the name of *justice*'.[11]

MOURNING AS 'DOING JUSTICE TO . . .' A SINGULARITY

When Derrida declares that he shares with Levinas the premise of the infinitude of responsibility; that to 'give up on the infinitude of responsibility' would mean 'there is no responsibility' and that 'if responsibility were not infinite . . . then I would not be able to engage myself in an infinite debt with regard to each singularity',[12] he is not so much simply affirming the Levinasian account of the infinite within the finite as recalling the aporia of the 'impossibility' of the universalisation of the unique. In other words, the infinitude of responsibility cannot be true as a *general* thesis unless the instance of a particular responsibility can be truly considered to be uniquely 'mine'. What any given situation demands of *me*, ethically speaking, is that I *decide* what to do, independently of any supposed enshrinement of the universal in a moral code, and yet, in the instant of that decision, I must realise the universal in my radically singular action:

> just as no one can die in my place, no one can make a decision, what we call 'decision', in my place. But as soon as one speaks, as soon as one enters the medium of language, one loses that very singularity.[13]

The singularity of the decision, which is the ethical par excellence in Derrida, in the Exordium is referred to as 'ethics itself' and it is said there to be 'given' by my mortality, in other words, by my finitude. But my mortality only becomes thinkable as such, when it is learned heterodidactically. The relation to the Other and to death (hetero-) logically precedes it. Hence 'ethics itself' is, thereby, brought back to its origin, which is, from the perspective of the Subject as a oneself, to be already in mourning for the singular, particular other as *a* mortal. In 'Memories for Paul de Man', one of Derrida's many texts on mourning (most of which are acts of mourning, or 'in mourning', of his friends),[14] this relationship to the absolutely singular other is linked to the proper name. As Nass and Brault summarise this:

We can prepare for the death of the friend, anticipate it, repeat or reiterate it before it takes place, because in 'calling or naming someone while he is alive, we know that his name can survive him and *already survives him*'; we know that 'the name begins during his life to get along without him, speaking and bearing his death every time it is pronounced . . .'. Mourning thus already begins with the name.[15]

Earlier, in Chapter 2, we saw how for Levinas the ipseity of the Subject is accomplished, it comes into being, as responsibility; 'subjectivity awakens from the egological'[16] to find itself responsible and already indebted. In this conjunction of an ethico-existential philosophical discourse of the Subject with the everyday simplicity and straightforwardness of the non-theoretical, Levinas aims at *unsaying* the theoretical in the direction of the ethical life of the Subject as something empirical. The Subject thus presented is not held to be *posited* by thought, it is rather understood, as taking up a *position*, a singular 'my place'. This thinking of the Subject as position rather than as the posited expresses the uniqueness of the place in which only 'I' can die. One can sacrifice one's life for the Other, or vice versa, but no one can die the Other's death for them. This position/place/space is, strictly speaking, unsayable and unthematisable as such because it is the spatialisation itself of a unique space. The quiddity of the Subject as such 'absolute position', as Levinas thinks this, is revealed and evident in the impossible coincidence of the Same and the Other; and any representation of it is necessarily a betrayal:

> *Everything* shows itself at the price of this betrayal, even the unsayable. In this betrayal the indiscretion with regard to the unsayable, which is probably the task of philosophy, becomes possible . . . a secret diachrony commands this ambiguous or enigmatic way of speaking, and because in general signification signifies beyond synchrony, beyond essence.[17]

This equation of the 'beyond synchrony' and 'beyond essence' remarks the impossible *temporal* coincidence of the lived as a saying (or 'pure signifyingness') and its representation in the said (or 'signification'). In a manner of speaking, such representation always kills it off. According to Levinas, there is, therefore, something intrinsically murderous in the philosophical representation of the Other; it is the 'scandal' of philosophy no less: 'every death is murder'.[18] The excessive nature of responsibility for the Other survives this force of totalisation.[19] It can only come through, come to mind, by way of thinking the relation between the life/death dichotomy. This is no more a philosophical and theoretical undertaking than it is something *lived out* in ordinary experience and in everyday life – just doing it does not have to wait for philosophy to claim its privilege in this respect, nor for it to split thinking/life into two distinct realms. And whatever meaning might be ascribed to 'ethics itself', as Derrida calls this 'thinking from the edge of life and death', it is no more literally than it is a figuratively a 'matter of life and death'; it is no more a matter of 'real life and death' than it is a subject matter for philosophy. (Its urgency stems precisely from the fact that ideas are materially expressed in the world.)

It is in this way that *everything* – any thought whatever – is ultimately to be referred *back* to the ethical; in a movement both Levinas and Derrida identify with 'ethics itself'. What Derrida adds to this specifically, is that 'thinking' per se is always also a modality of life and 'live thinking' is the condition of philosophy taking place: each thought; each word uttered or written, is a performative rendering in some medium or other of the recorded mark (in speech, text, in language itself) *and* the moment of a life. This conjunction of thought/life thus becomes recallable only on the basis of the mediality of its expression in 'writing' – which is the Derridean archetype for 'spectral technologies' in general. This thinking of writing as the interzone, or 'edge of life/death', between life and its manifestation in the written; and therefore of the written as, in a sense, the death of the 'living Subject', begs the question of death as an issue both of and for philosophy. It is a theoretical issue for philosophy and for 'thought' as a moment of life itself.

WRITING ON THE EDGE

The 'lived scene of writing' of this text was that of my attending to my father in his dying days. It was written to be presented in person and, it seemed to me, with a certain necessity, would also be a bearing witness to an experience that at the time was still in the future. I was bound in some sense to incorporate the death of a particular other into a 'future thinking' I felt confident would come to me, to use a phrase of Derrida, during 'the "not yet" that bends us toward death'.[20] The time of the text and the temporality of writing in general, I aimed to show – and wanted to demonstrate in a 'singular' fashion and 'performatively' – is always determined by the death of the particular other. This is not so much an idea based on my own experience at the scene of this writing, or to do with the nature of what was, literally, my subjective experience, but to do with the nature of 'writing', understood, after Derrida, as an encounter with the 'edge' of life/death, and hence, in a way yet to be further explained, an example of 'ethics itself'. And therein lay the rub: the onus of any demonstration is that it operate at the level of the text (rather than with respect to what is ordinarily regarded as being outside the text), namely, life and death themselves. (The instability of all of these distinctions structuring reflection, life/death, the literal/the figural, the conceptual/the empirical, the philosophical/'ethics itself', and so forth, imposes itself without its needing to be made a theme of this text or any other.) These reflections on the *theme* of 'spectrality', linking death, ghosts, the border, repetition and 'the father', proceed, and quite obviously so, by way of readings of several texts by Derrida – texts that are the occasion, among other things, of his revisiting yet other texts on death, by Levinas and Heidegger. So, it is quite reasonable to claim that it was also 'just a coincidence' for me to have been so entrenched in the quotidian aspects of death, ghosts and the thought of 'the father' (which, let us recall the citation from the Exordium above, is the first term of the first formulation of what Derrida calls the 'magisterial locution' from whom or which one might 'learn to live') at the same time as thinking through these themes in the various philosophical *alma pater* texts I cite. For this reason, I have chosen not to erase that original text *entirely*; the text which, as I shall explain in a moment, finally made its own spectral appearance (in my absence) at the conference at Stirling University, much as it is doing here now.

A spectral technology, video, allowed me to be in two places at once and to instantiate a 'phantom effect' while raising the question of the relationship between the spectral and appearance as such. However, just as significant as the fact that the spectral might be staged in this manner, is that on this occasion it had been necessitated by the attendance (elsewhere) to the death of a particular other: my thesis, like any other thesis, was in some sense a structural repetition of events. It is, emphatically, quite independently of those 'personal circumstances' in the strictest sense, of what was happening to me (and to my father) at that time, that the following is presented yet again *here and now* and on the ground that it is a way of approaching the theme of spectrality.

PERFORMING SPECTRALITY [WHITE NOISE, TITLE, TALKING-HEAD]

It will have been my aim to be in keeping with the spirit of 'Phantom f(x)', which invites the unexpected, the defiance of expertise and risk-taking and, therefore, as always in these situations, the exposure of oneself to the possibility of death: of dying, as comedians say, here on stage, in the very act of acting something out, staging a kind of performance – one for which, I must apologise, I am not in a position, today, to answer for. An invitation to participate in an event always comes from the future and anticipates that between the asking and the appearance, death will not intervene. My spectral appearance here today on video (or in print) has not been compromised by my own death as such, and my 'absence' does not bear that excuse. However, that is not to say that this text, and perhaps every text, is not overshadowed by death and the ways of thinking about death that are available to us.

It would be pointless to become ensnared in a discussion of what the spectral *is* as such; better to try to get to grips with its multivalent effects: implicit or explicit, centre-stage or in the wings, it belongs to the play of presence/absence in all of Derrida's writing:

> A specter is both visible and invisible, both phenomenal and nonphenomenal: a trace that marks the present with its absence in advance. The spectral logic is *de facto* a deconstructive logic. It is in the element of haunting that deconstruction finds the place most hospitable to it, at the heart of the living present, in the quickest heartbeat of the philosophical. Like the work of mourning, in a sense, which produces spectrality, and like *all* work produces spectrality.[21]

Derrida claims spectrality is a function of writing/textuality per se: as a theme it unsurprisingly emerged on the scene as if out of a blind spot; it is always there but peripheral, a kind of real but unnoticed thing, transparent, as one might expect of all things spectral. True to the concept of the ghost, it surprises and returns in the same moment: 'reapparition of the specter is apparition *for the first time*'.[22]

What is the proper medium for the discourse of the spectral and of ghosts if not that of deconstruction, the writing in which the ghost qua ghost comes through (*advient*) and can be heard, *in absentia*; as 'voices off'; heard as if by means of an act of ventriloquism; by means of the animation of the one by the other, rather like an occult 'possession', in which one acts out an other? When we speak, we make sense to ourselves, but in voices that are never wholly our own and whose words bear the trace of an alterity. What kind of an audience are 'we' gathered here to address the spectral? And what is it that we are attending to, right now even? In the decision of this matter, we have an inkling that everything is at stake: in the sense that all meaning, authority, legitimacy and ways of thought and truth are shaken by the prospect of '*being able to say anything*'.[23] We decide between, for instance, mysticism and reason, religion and science, literature and philosophy, and so forth, and we do so always within a normative cultural context already shaped by past decisions which privilege one mode of discourse over another. This applies to the spectral discourse of deconstruction, too, and its decision for the relational, the interstitial, the aporetic *in lieu of* (any single) position; with its resistances to decision itself and its deferral of meaning and finality: 'it is impossible to over-emphasise the importance of what is being decided, so authoritatively and so decisively, at the very moment when what is in question is to decide on what must remain undecided'.[24] This (in)decision is enacted, for example, in Derrida's analysis of the expression '*tout autre est tout autre*' (every other one is wholly other): in the play of words 'which seems to contain the very possibility of a secret that hides and reveals itself at the same time within a single sentence . . . and within a single language' thereby 'linking alterity to singularity'.[25] To think 'with' the spectral, one might say, is to reflexively take into account that theorising and all 'making-sense-of . . .' proceeds always in-the-wake-of-the-other (including, for instance, in the senses of mourning or remembrance).

My own thoughts on the theme of spectrality (for which I claim no originality) as moments of life, come to me on reading, above all, texts by Derrida and Levinas, and they pursue a train of thought concerning the 'alterity of death' as the conjunction of 'writing' and ethical subjectivity. They seek to explore the link between what Derrida calls 'ethics itself' and writing as 'writing from the edge of life/death'.

[I interrupt myself: I have to confess a troubled stomach, adrenalised by this occasion of my own spectral projection towards an event in the near future (the promise to appear among you, which has been commuted to this 'appearance on TV'). Perhaps it is that, but perhaps it is also in psychosomatic sympathy with another, in some other place today, dying, and with stomach pains of another order. What do I want to contribute in public to a discussion of 'phantom effects' and 'the spectral', in the proximity, and privacy, of attending to a dying father? I am beginning already to wonder: who or what is writing this 'script'?]

The spectral may be current as a theme (at least since the publication of *Spectres of Marx*) but it structures the inheritance, or heritage, of Western philosophy on which I was raised, and I have little power over the spectral voices echoing here, in titles, subheadings and loaded, borrowed terms and discourses. Is the risk I accept in the form of an invitation to appear (to which this is my *final* response) the risk of a mess (namely, that I will perform a subjective televised rant) – this death of all deaths being upon me; a mess, moreover, that will have been all of my own making and from which I am even planning in advance to be absent; in lieu of myself, staging my own disappearance into my text? [*No one else has told me I must speak to this theme, right now. But whenever else would it be more appropriate to do so?*] I am wondering already, haunted all along by the question: what are the limits of my responsibility in *all of this*? Both with respect to a 'phantom event' such as this one, involving the elaboration and presentation of a thesis, fulfilling a promise (and a desire to learn or communicate something) with respect to the responsibility for the other human being in general, but only ever lived out, in reality, singularly in everyday life itself – and above all, right now, for me, in relation to my father. Why must the everyday be philosophised about at all, and what is this 'privileging of death', both philosophically and in its crossing over into life itself?

INTIMATE INTERRUPTIONS AND THE PRIVILEGING OF DEATH

During my father's terminal illness, he seems to be concerned most directly not with the imminent 'nothingness' approaching, but rather with his own 'not making a mess'; with the increasing ambiguity of responsibility for the body over which he is losing control. I intend no pathos in mentioning here (once again) the circumstances of the production of this text: I am not 'present' today, not facing you *in person*, because of my attendance to him *in person*. To what end I weave in this intimacy here, will become clearer as I proceed: I wish to speak of the conjunction between philosophy and the ethical as non-philosophy; of the difference between a life made thinkable on the basis of philosophy and a relation to death which opens the 'possibility of impossibility' or the beyond death, expressed, for example, by the Derridean idea of the spectral, whose ethical significance is the theoretical issue here. To move towards that I shall now consider directly the manner in which the spectral deconstructs the 'privilege of death'.

The privileging of death (in philosophy) is at issue here in more ways than one, and it is a privileging that is challenged, as well as confirmed, in just what imposes itself on thought, in the form of the spectral. Derrida's reading and writing about death, for example in his engagements with texts by Heidegger, Levinas, Freud, Kierkegaard and others – in such texts as *Aporias*, *The Gift of Death* and *Archive Fever* – employs the characteristic deconstructive strategy of setting different voices against each other, 'speaking in the name of' those texts under scrutiny; combining a fidelity to ideas with the exposure of the text to its own limits. In his wanderings in the neighbourhood of death, his discourse of the spectral, the *arrivant*, the *revenant*, the *advient*, the *fantôme*, the ghost, hauntology, and so forth, interrupt the foreclosure of any discussion of death, responsibility, alterity, singularity and the universal. He repeatedly challenges, on the basis of the spectral, the seeking of death in the form of the *finality* of an interpretation. Death approached in terms of spectrality interrupts death such that death as 'meaning something' never takes place. Derrida's readings of death in texts of these others do not lay it to rest. In *Spectres of Marx*, as noted already, he suggests one can only ever 'explain oneself with death' (*s'expliquer avec la mort*) – which his translator reminds us is an expression close to the German *auseinandersetzen*, or perhaps the English 'to have it out with someone'.[26] The key two thinkers Derrida has the privileging of death out with that I shall concentrate on here are Heidegger and Levinas, and I shall turn now to how his reading between the two 'spectralises' death further, 'beyond death', as it were. As briefly as possible, here are the parameters.

HEIDEGGER

Heidegger thinks death as *Dasein*'s very mode of being-ahead-of itself (*sich-vorweg-sein*) and as that which gives rise to the very possibility of thinking at all as a thinking which is mine or the very event of 'mineness' (*Jemeinigkeit*). Dasein is privileged as the possibility of possibility in general, because in the ontological difference between Being (*Sein*) and There-Being (*Da-Sein*) it projects (itself) into the future in anticipation of death, which is first and foremost 'mine'. In Heidegger, the possibility of possibility in general is thinkable as such on the basis of the possibility of impossibility; or, in other words, death is the ground for all possibility: to be *Dasein* is to be able to die. For example, the possibility of this text and the 'performance' presented as a symbol of 'me', of 'my thinking' (no matter how derivative it might finally be judged to be!) becomes what it is in the time, between now and an anticipated time limit – namely, the time of my death. The possibility of (any) presentation, as such, arises in the temporal *ecstasis* of *Dasein* as a projected being-towards-death (*Sein-zum-Tode*). In other words: the being-there of anything as a possibility is tied to my possibility of impossibility – the only certain possibility, which is my death.[27]

LEVINAS

Despite acknowledging the philosophical significance and radicality of Heidegger's attempt to think time in relation to death, which displaces the thinking of time in any number of anthropocentric determinations – for example, as eternity in religion or as atomic decay in physics – and despite his acknowledgement of the necessity of this philosophical passage through Heidegger,[28] Levinas incessantly attempts to articulate the ethical shortcomings of the Heideggerian philosophy of existence which claims its origin in the fundamental anxiety (*Angst*) over *my own* death. Against this, he proposes a reversal that amounts to thinking death from the perspective of time.[29] In Levinas, the 'first death' (the thematically privileged death) is the death of the Other.[30] This could be summarised in the following proposition: time comes to me; it becomes mine, starting from the Other. This does not throw me back on the contingency of my longevity in comparison to the lives of the Others, reasoning that I, therefore, naturally always still have time *for* the Other. For with this, the thinking of time would simply collapse back into a form of chronological calculation. It is rather to propose that the being of the 'I' in its singular existence is given to it in its *attending to* the death of the Other, whose death articulates its very existence as a kind of waiting-on, attendance, witness to, or survival of the death of the Other. Responsibility, for example, manifests itself in the fundamental form of my being-for-the-other – an event in which, Levinas would say, I am a hostage to (my) responsibility, which is something I have not freely taken on but which obliges me.[31]

DERRIDA

Derrida's reading of these thinkers (and others) on death is, of course, subtle, complex and, throughout, in the sense indicated above, *unde-cided* and averse to finality. However, I think that it is useful here to summarise it by saying that, notwithstanding everything which Derrida can say on the basis of, or in the name of, Heidegger and Levinas, and often speaking against one in the name of the other, in several of his writings he summons both on the charge that they each fail to take account of the spectrality implicit to death.[32] On the one hand, in the case of Heidegger, this is a consequence of the refusal of any ontological significance for the everyday experience of the death of a loved one; the death of the unique other. Derrida makes this point in the name of Levinas. Indeed, the everydayness of death is set up by Heidegger as that which must be overcome in the existential analysis which aims to relegate all hitherto unexamined thanato-anthropocentrisms to the sub-philosophical; to the ontic.[33] On the other hand, in view of Levinas's insistence on how my relation to the other person enacts the relation to the 'wholly other' (*Autrui/tout autre*) beyond the finitude marked by my death, and for which, or for whom, my responsibility, Levinas says, is infinite, and 'to the point of including myself' in the Other's death,[34] Derrida chooses to remind us how this difficult thesis is simplified by Levinas in a very telling fashion in the proposition: 'I am responsible for the other in so far as he is "mortal"'.[35] With respect to this, Derrida will then say, in the name of Heidegger, that Levinas's thinking is itself susceptible to the Heideggerian account of inauthenticity.[36]

So, on the one hand, we have Heidegger's analytic of *Dasein*, which lays open for analysis the historical contingency of mortal life conceived as subjective individuality and the inauthentic everyday thinking of death that goes along with it. In view of this we have, on the other hand, an argument that Levinas's attempts to account for how my infinite responsibility comes to me always in the form of my *personal* responsibility for the other individual fall foul of the thinking of the ontological difference by remaining in the order of the ontic, thereby confirming the Heideggerian account of the co-originality of being-with-(the Other) (*Mitsein/Miteinandersein*) and being-towards-death. Derrida argues, moreover, that this is a co-originality which 'does not contradict, but, on the contrary, presupposes a mineness of dying or of being-toward-death, a mineness (even if) not that of the ego or of "sameness"'.[37]

This entire analysis unfolds, then, between the certain possibility of my death and the haunting, spectralising possibility of the impossibility of the death of the Other. This impossibility is 'experienced' in the postponement of the death of the Other. Levinas's most explicit and succinct contra-Heideggerian thesis is perhaps this: '*death is not annihilation but the question that is necessary for [the] relationship to infinity to be produced*'.[38] Derrida's analysis of death, in *Aporias*, wanders in this way between Heidegger and Levinas on death; it retraces a path cut by Heidegger and signposted 'existential analysis of being-towards-death as the fundamental mode of *Dasein*', and it brings it into conjunction with Levinas's warning that this leads not to a clearing (*Lichtung*) for thought, but, ultimately, to the death camp and the trauma of death as murder – which is not simply 'annihilation' but also 'survival' or 'witnessing'.[39] It is such living-on (the possibility of impossibility) beyond death which spectralises or haunts death as the end or finality (the impossibility of possibility).

In a return to the theme of the 'economy of violence', in *Archive Fever*, Derrida comments:

> As soon as there is one, there is murder, wounding, traumatism. *L'un se garde de L'autre*. The one guards against/keeps some of the other. It protects itself from the other, but in the movement of this jealous violence, it comprises in itself, thus guarding it, the self-otherness or self-difference (the difference from within oneself) which makes it one. The One 'differing or deferring from itself'. The One as the Other. At once, at the same time, but in a same time that is out of joint, the One forgets to remember itself to itself, it keeps and erases the archive of the injustice that it is.[40]

The key shortcoming of Heidegger's analysis of death is its failure to attend to the possibility of murder as 'impossibility', and it consequently fails also to attend to what Levinas calls the 'culpability' of the survivor – which might be termed the 'ethical proof' of that impossibility:

> The death of the Other who dies affects me in my very identity as a responsible 'me' (*moi*); it affects me in my nonsubstantial identity, which is not the simple coherence of various acts of identification, but is made up of an ineffable responsibility. My being affected by the death of the Other is precisely that, my relation with his death. It is, in my relation, my deference to someone who no longer responds, already a culpability – the culpability of the survivor.[41]

Responsibility thus triumphs over death in the forms of survival, witness, and so on. It 'opens' the possibility of murder and yet is not 'a new possibility' for the Subject 'offered after the end of every possibility', but is already given, for instance, as Levinas says elsewhere, by the resurrection 'in the son in whom the rupture of death is *embodied*'.[42] Responsibility as the name of 'ethics itself', in Levinas, can be thought of as having the *structure*, metaphorically perhaps, of filiality, but the death of the Other is also literally instantiated and 'embodied' in the survivor – who may well be 'the son'.

DEATH AS APORIA

Although it may be Derrida's most explicit teaching that the aporetic does not belong exclusively to any particular context, or genre of writing about aporia qua aporia, in *Aporias*, death is, nonetheless presented as aporia par excellence: death not only instantiates aporia but is presented as the condition of the aporetic in general. And when Derrida raises the question of aporia per se, I suggest, we can substitute 'the aporia' by 'death'. Just to demonstrate this, in the following citation I make this substitution:

> [W]hat takes place, what comes to pass with death? Is it possible to undergo or to experience death, death as such? Is it then a question of death as such? Of a scandal arising to suspend a certain viability? Does one then pass through this death as such? Or is one immobilized before the threshold, to the point of having to turn around and seek another way without a method or an outlet . . .?[43]

Deconstructive aporetic thinking is already a thinking of death, for death is the name of our mortality itself, and the necessary condition of 'live' philosophising. (And this chapter in its own way exemplifies how thinking death is embedded in everyday life: 'I' am, after all, in the process here of 'explaining myself' with respect to the theme of death *and* with respect to my father's dying, at once, and from the perspective of their bordering on one another.)

But it occurs to me that this would be just as much the case, no matter the theme, because any text is 'parasited', harbouring and haunted by the dead and by their undead ghosts, those textual manifestations who whisper in *my* thinking through the life/death dichotomy here; in *my* attempt to 'explain myself'. They are ghosts I do not claim to know well or fully comprehend, but with whom I am so intimate that they drop in and out of my most personal vigil at the bedside, in my attendance to the death of a singular other, making this scene of writing a kind of atheological convocation: a trinity of father, son and ghosts. And with this thought, I skid once again towards the thought of the end (his end/ my ending – 'how long have I got?'). Some possible last words come to mind: a fantasy, perhaps the voice of yet another phantom; an imagined dialogue at the scene of the death, which is now so close:

> Dying father to son: 'Be a man.'
> Son to dying father: 'Be a Ghost.'

Death is not visible, not even to the dying, who must back into death, rather like Walter Benjamin's 'angel of history' flying backwards into the future, still looking through the eyes (even though his are almost always closed now), in any case through vision, back into life and to the possibility which still remains, namely, to be, just a little bit more, even in a state of almost total ruination and suffering; in the 'death agony' which is the 'the impossibility of ceasing'.[44] Hence, the ontological imperative, or injunction, 'be!', understands what it is 'to live' only in terms of being. But are we not, in every instant of such life referred *back* to the possibility of impossibility, that is, to death? To be for any mortal is to be dying – tick tock goes the clock. The 'be' in the plea to the Other to 'be a ghost', to continue, however, is from the first at odds with the spectral nature of its object and despite its *still being a part of life*. Any ontological imperative is already haunted by impossibility, and, therefore, any border between 'continuance' and 'end', as Derrida conceives of this, is founded not on ontology but a 'hauntology'.[45] The fundamental orientation of hauntology points beyond the life of anyone in particular; and yet it is only thinkable on the basis of the death of a singular other. So, whatever else this ghostly presentation at 'Phantom f(x)' (the live event) is or was, it will have been at the same time (or in another time) – at the same time out of joint – an *instance* of coming to terms with death. This could never be a wholly private nor wholly public matter, for it was bound in advance, in one way or another, to be *mediated* – by culture, technology, literature, philosophy, religion, conferences, publication or any other form whatever of 'writing', and thus in its own way suspended between life and death.

WRITING/DEATH

Just to begin to move towards some sort of closure, or ending, let us recall where this chapter began: Derrida's Exordium argues that this *s'expliquer avec la mort* is inseparable from the desire to 'learn to live', and specifically, it cannot be *just* otherwise. Learning to live has an epicurean ring to it; indeed for Epicurus the secret of how to live also lay in thinking the life/death conjuncture, of which he famously says: 'If you are it is not; if it is you are not.'[46] A suitable epithet on his tomb-stone might have been: 'Here lies Epicurus, only his epithet, "if you are it is not; if it is you are not" survives him.' 'Writing' is the generic term in Derrida for all spectral technologies and the spectral character of technicity as such,[47] (and words carved on a tombstone – as already noted in Chapter 7 – are an example of a spectral mnemo-technology). Levinas, writing in 1947, appeared to be attuned to the spectral, when he wrote this of Epicurus's epithetic remark:

> [I]t misunderstands the entire paradox of death, for it effaces our relation-ship with death, which is a unique relationship with the future. But at least the adage insists on the eternal futurity of death. The fact that it deserts every present is not due to our evasion of death and to an unpardonable diversion at the supreme hour but to the fact that death is *ungraspable*, that it marks the end of the subject's virility and heroism.[48]

Unable to grasp death, literally unable to conceptualise it, all writing about it takes the structural form of such an abyssal 'epithet within the epithet': Derrida's remark about learning how to live/die, heterodidacti-cally, in a way reinforces this Levinasian line of thought by speaking from this edge of life/death.[49] The spectre returns, not from nothing-ness, not from the oblivion of non-existence, but from the border of life/death.

To just resummarise these philosophical differences: the privileged death for Heidegger is mine; the privileged, or 'first' death, for Levinas is the death of the other mortal. For Derrida, however, there is *no* primary death in either of these senses, and his entire discourse of mourning serves to undermine the traditional privileging of death altogether, by appealing to the structural logic of the 'one goes before the other' and of the 'beyond life' as 'survival' (of the death of the Other). Death is to be thought; can only be *thought* in conjunction with 'writing' and as attunement to the 'spectral'. The spectral incessantly interrupts philoso-phy's antithetical thinking of the life/death dichotomy: 'What happens between two, between all the "two's" one likes, such as between life and death, can only maintain itself with some ghost, can only talk with or about some ghost.'[50]

This thinking of the in-between of life/death in terms of spectrality can, I suggest, be read now as a kind of formula for sublating the theory/praxis or philosophy/everyday life divide from the perspective of the ethical. And in *Spectres of Marx* Derrida's 'spectropoetics' raises anew the spectre of a certain communist philosophy and the prospect of a rereading of Marxism that could be properly claim it to be an *ethico*-political project rather than a purely political one, and, controversially Derrida suggests deconstruction be viewed as such a radicalisation of Marxism.[51] Whilst this bigger theme goes beyond the scope of this chapter, the Exordium's meditation on the phrase 'learning to live finally' – which Derrida tells us came to him *after* the book was finished – provides, in the form of a kind of ethical *mise en scene*, the sense of how such a radicalisation must proceed from the rethinking of the life/death border, and can be 'learned', heterodidactically, from the experience of the death of the Other. And as we have seen in this chapter, though barely mentioned in *Spectres of Marx* by name, the ghost of Levinas plays a key role in this.

It may be objected that the entire discourse of the spectral and its thought of the 'alterity of death' is but an imprecise, unphilosophical figure that substitutes for what could be more straightforwardly expressed in terms of an intellectual and cultural inheritance and the concrete socio-cultural situation of the Subject. Traditional culture and society, in other words, defined by such things as religion, the family, the state, history, economy, the arts and media, and so forth, together constitute the materiality determining and defining the parameters of the experience of death. Alternatively, it may be objected that it amounts to a new claim to universality, one which incorporates heterology into its concept such that the disturbances provoked in the One/the Same/the Subject by death, and manifested by all manner of 'ghostly' phenomena, such as conscience, guilt, hallucinations, evil spirits, the uncanny, or simply in the form of the natural 'animal' fear for oneself and one's loved ones in the face of death, can be explained scientifically. But either of these conclusions would render the Subject's experience of death *merely* a 'personal' affair, ruling out in advance the futural prospect of *justice*, as they would make of the relation to the ghost a matter of calculation, and the relation to the Other in death (and to death in general) a matter of settling accounts. The ghost, as a figure of the alterity of death, would effectively be subject to intellectual exorcism and death would be reduced to a purely natural phenomenon; fully and totally accounted for, biologically, psychologically, sociologically, medically, and so forth, and life itself would be assigned a purely economic value within a wider, essentially political project. Derrida's account of life/death approached via the spectral reveals firstly, the impossibility of delivering such finality. Secondly, it argues that it is 'from' life lived 'heterodidactically and in relation to the death of the other' that the thought of the ethical returns, as he puts it, to haunt the political. This no more privileges the personal experience of attending to the death of another than it does the 'writerly' encounter with 'ghosts'; it insists rather on the conjunction of the 'two' as 'ethics itself'.

POSTSCRIPT: THE COUNTERSIGNATURE OF FIDELITY

I shall sign-off finally not with a signature but with a reflection on the countersignature and the idea of fidelity associated with it, and on how death signals, perhaps, end of fidelity.

[Despite the feebleness of his grasp on life as well as of his own hand, my father was upset, just now, that in the midst of the daily family affairs I am trying to sort out on his behalf I had, in order to save him the trouble, forged his signature. (I can now write his signature more convincingly than he can.) Was he upset because the gesture was one of writing-him-off? I suspect it was because it signalled I had not yet learned the one thing he had wanted to teach me, and never more so than in death: do not so casually disregard the law. Fidelity to the law/ the father is not trumped by death.]

How should I respond to this 'live situation' of attending to the death of a particular other and at the same time speak to you on the theme of spectrality and its relationship to death? What I have tried show here is how ethical subjectivity, whatever else it is, is a matter of life/ death; and I have sought to illustrate the sense of its being learned, as Derrida says, heterodidactically. And, on the basis of a certain fidelity to his notion of 'hauntology', I have done so in the company of various 'ghosts'. I have tried to show how thinking death involves fidelity to the spirit of various philosophical theses on death *and* fidelity to the quotidian origin of all concepts and tropes through which the life/death dichotomy can be approached and theorised; fidelity to various *alma pater(s)* and to my dead father for their respective 'gifts of death'. The question as to whom or what this fidelity is ultimately owed or paid in relation to death, however, remains open; and, if we go along with Derrida, all one can do is go on living and surviving *by* 'writing', the only (or *final*) form of which is life-lived-in-relation-to-death. For this to stand a chance of being an instantiation of 'ethics itself'; of being just, it has to be true to the ungraspable beyond of life/death which can only be written of 'this side' of death, the only place the absolute alterity, or the Infinite, as Levinas understands this, comes (to pass).

NOTES

1. Benjamin, *One-Way Street*, p. 54.
2. Beckett, *Endgame*, p. 13.
3. Derrida, *Spectres of Marx*, p. xvii.
4. Ibid. p. xvii–xviii.
5. Ibid. p. xvii–xviii.
6. Derrida, *Learning to Live Finally*, p. 24.
7. Derrida, *Learning to Live Finally*, p. 32.
8. See also Derrida, 'As if I Were Dead'.
9. Derrida, *Spectres of Marx*, p. xx.
10. Ibid. p. xviii.
11. Ibid. p. xix. The previous chapter provided an example of this in its examination of how doing justice to Freud in the company of the ghost of Foucault was at the same time to do justice to Foucault's *Folie et déraison*, too. It was a writerly act of mourning.
12. Derrida, 'Remarks on Deconstruction and Pragmatism', p. 86.
13. Derrida, *Gift of Death*, p. 59.
14. See, for example, Derrida, *Work of Mourning*.
15. Michael Nass and Pascale-Anne Brault, Editors' Introduction to Derrida, *Work of Mourning*, p. 13, citing Derrida, *Memories for Paul de Man*, p. 49.
16. Levinas, 'Philosophy as Awakening', p. 213.
17. Levinas, *Otherwise than Being, or, Beyond Essence*, p. 7.
18. Levinas, *God, Death and Time*, p. 72.
19. See the discussion of the Levinasian thinking of responsibility as surplus to signification in Chapter 2.
20. Derrida, *Aporias*, p. 69.
21. Derrida, 'Spectographies', p. 121.
22. Derrida, *Spectres of Marx*, p. 4. Below I shall return to this idea of familiarity, the unsurprising surprise, or, predictability, in so far as this is implicated in the systematic representation of a body of thought. An example of this is the representation of Derrida's thought by Geoff Bennington in *Derridabase*: on one level it sets out to entomb 'Derrida' in a systematic 'philosophical biography', but at the same time it is also part of a project which poses a challenge to Derrida; it calls upon him to surprise, yet again, in defiance of the death this representation imposes upon him by its very nature. (See Derrida's commentary on this demand in the parallel text in the same volume, *Circumfession*, p. 16.)
23. Derrida, '"This Strange Institution Called Literature"', p. 39.
24. 'It is impossible to over-emphasise the importance of what is being

decided, so authoritatively and so decisively, at the very moment when what is in question is to decide on what must remain undecided', Derrida, *Aporias*, p. 54.

25. Derrida, *Gift of Death*, p. 87. See discussion of 'the secret' in Chapter 6.

26. Derrida, *Spectres of Marx*, p. 177 fn.2.

27. See Derrida, *Aporias*, pp. 23ff. His commentary there centres on Heidegger, *Being and Time*, Section 50.

28. See Levinas's lecture 'An Obligatory Passage: Heidegger'.

29. See Levinas, *Time and the Other*. See also Chanter, 'Traumatic Response: Levinas's Legacy'.

30. Levinas, *God, Death and Time*, p. 43.

31. In *Aporias*, p. 60, Derrida explicitly discusses the connection between the Levinasian trope of responsibility as being 'hostage' to the ethical demand of the Other and the 'ghost'. They are members of the same series: 'this is the series constituted by hostage, host, guest, ghost, holy ghost and *Geist*'.

32. Derrida, *Gift of Death*, pp. 47ff.

33. Derrida, *Aporias*, p. 60.

34. Levinas, *God, Death and Time*, p. 43.

35. Derrida, *Aporias*, p. 39, citing Levinas, *God, Death and Time*, p. 43.

36. Ibid. pp. 68–78.

37. Ibid. p. 39.

38. Levinas, *God, Death and Time*, p. 19 (emphasis added).

39. See Chapter 4.

40. Derrida, *Archive Fever*, p. 78.

41. Levinas, *God, Death and Time*, p. 12.

42. Levinas, *Totality and Infinity*, p. 56 (emphasis added). The text continues (p. 57): 'Death – suffocation in the impossibility of the possible – opens the passage toward descent. Fecundity is yet a personal relation, though it be not given to the 'I' as a possibility.' Space does not permit a digression at this point into Levinas's account of this rupture of (the time of) the Subject in the form of the 'fecundity' of the child. And in view of the discussion in Chapter 3 of Irigaray's reading of Levinas on this theme, at the very least one would want to consider the possible 'sexing' of the role of fecundity in one's thinking of the birth/death relation in terms of maternity.

43. Derrida, *Aporias*, p. 33.

44. Levinas, *Totality and Infinity*, p. 56.

45. Derrida, *Spectres of Marx*, p. 10.

46. Epicurus, 'Letter to Menoeceus'.

47. Chapters 6, 7 and 9 here variously illustrated how this characterisation of the technics of communication is at work in mediated communications; in relation to secrecy, memory and censorship.

48. Levinas, *Time and the Other*, p. 71. See also *God, Death and Time*, p. 19.

49. And, in *Aporias*, p. 42, Derrida reiterates, stressing that 'this edge would itself be the place of the first problematic of closure, of a domain of questioning or of absolutely preliminary research'.

50. Derrida, *Spectres of Marx*, p. xviii. A point of distinction between Derrida and Levinas here would be the scope of this 'all the "two's" one likes'. For instance, in *The Animal that Therefore I Am* Derrida considers how this formula perhaps ought to be considered inclusive of the animal and perhaps even the environment. See pp. 106–12.
51. See Derrida, *Spectres of Marx*, pp. 92–3.

Bibliography

Agamben, G. (2000), *Means Without Ends: Notes on Politics*, Minneapolis: University of Minnesota Press.

Alliez, E. and J.-C. Bonne (2007), 'Matisse with Dewey and Deleuze', *pli* 18, 1–19.

Ansell-Pearson, K. (2005), *How to Read Nietzsche*, London: Granta.

Badiou, A. (1999), *Manifesto for Philosophy*, trans. N. Madarasz, New York: SUNY Press.

Badiou, A. (2002), *Ethics: An Essay on the Understanding of Evil*, trans. P. Hallward, London: Verso.

Bataille, G. (1985), *Visions of Excess*, trans. A. Stoekl, Minnesota: University of Minnesota Press.

Bataille, G. (1989), *Tears of Eros*, trans. P. Connor, New York: City Lights.

Baudrillard, J. (2001), 'The Masses – The Implosion of the Social in the Media', in M. Poster (ed.), *Baudrillard: Selected Writings*, London: Polity Press, pp. 210–22.

Beardsworth, R. (1996), *Derrida and the Political*, London: Routledge.

Beckett, S. (1982), *Endgame*, London: Faber and Faber.

Benjamin, W. (2000), *One Way Street and Other Writings*, trans. E. Jephcott and K. Shorter, London: Verso.

Bennington, G. (1979), 'Cognito Incognito: Foucault's "My Body, This Paper, This Fire"', *Oxford Literary Review*, 4:1, 5–8.

Bennington, G. (1993), 'Derridabase', in G. Bennington and J. Derrida, *Jacques Derrida*, Chicago: Chicago University Press.

Bennington, G. and J. Derrida (1993), *Jacques Derrida*, Chicago: Chicago University Press.

Bergson, H. (1991), *Matter and Memory*, trans. N. Margaret Paul and W. Scott Palmer, New York: Zone Books.

Bernasconi, R. (1995), 'One-way Traffic: The Ontology of Decolonization and its Ethics', in G. A. Johnson and M. B. Smith (eds) (1990), *Ontology and Alterity in Merleau-Ponty*, Evanston: Northwestern University Press, pp. 14–26.

Bernasconi, R. (2005), 'Hegel and Levinas: The Possibility of Reconciliation and Forgiveness', in C. E. Katz (ed.), *Emmanuel Levinas: Critical Assessments of Leading Philosophers*, Vol. II, London: Routledge, pp. 49–68.

Birchall, C. (2006), *Knowledge Goes Pop*, Oxford: Berg.

Blanchot, M. (1982), *The Space of Literature*, Nebraska: University of Nebraska Press.

Blondel, E. (1991), *Nietzsche, The Body and Culture: Philosophy as a Philological Genealogy*, Stanford: Stanford University Press.

Boldt-Irons, L. A. (1995), 'Sacrifice and Violence in Bataille's Erotic Fiction', in C. B. Gill (ed.), *Bataille: Writing the Sacred*, London: Routledge, pp. 105–16.

Boltanski, L. (1999), *Distant Suffering: Politics, Morality and the Media*, Cambridge: Cambridge University Press.

Borradori, G. (2003), 'Autoimmunity: Real and Symbolic Suicides: A Dialogue with Jacques Derrida', trans. P.-A. Brault and M. Nass, in G. Borradori, *Philosophy in a Time of Terror: Dialogues with Jürgen Habermas and Jacques Derrida*, Chicago University Press, Chicago, pp. 85–136.

Boyd, D. (2008), 'Facebook's Privacy Trainwreck', *Convergence: The International Journal of Research into New Media Technologies*, 14:1, 13–20.

Boyle, J. (2007), 'When Does Ignorance Become Racism?', BBC News, 17 January 2007 <news.bbc.co.uk/1/hi/uk/6275363.stm> (last accessed 1 September 2012)

Brannigan, J., R. Robbins and J. Wolfreys (eds) (1996), *Applying: to Derrida*, Basingstoke: Palgrave Macmillan.

Brunton, F. (2011), 'WikiLeaks and the Assange Papers', *Radical Philosophy*, 166, 8–20.

Butler, J. (1993), *Bodies that Matter*, London: Routledge.

Butler, J. (1997), *Excitable Speech*, London: Routledge.

Cadava, E., P. Connor and J.-L. Nancy (eds) (1991), *Who Comes After the Subject?*, London: Routledge.

Caygill, H. (2002), *Levinas and the Political*, London: Routledge.

Chanter, T. (1995), *Ethics of Eros*, London: Routledge.

Chanter, T. (2005), 'Traumatic Response: Levinas's Legacy', in C. Katz with L. Trout (eds), *Emmanuel Levinas: Critical Assessments of Leading Philosophers*, Vol. IV: *Beyond Levinas*, New York: Routledge, pp. 400–13.

Chanter, T. (2007), 'Hands that Give and Hands that Take: The Politics of the Other in Levinas', in M. Diamantides (ed.), *Levinas, Law and Politics*, London: Routledge, pp. 71–80.

Chossudovsky, M. (2010), 'Who is Behind Wikileaks?', Centre for Global Research (13 December) <http://www.globalresearch.ca/index.php?context=va&aid=22389> (last accessed 11 January 2011).

Chouliaraki, L. (2006), *The Spectatorship of Suffering*, London: Sage.

Clark, T. (2000), 'Deconstruction and Technology', in N. Royle (ed.), *Deconstructions: A User's Guide*, Basingstoke: Palgrave, pp. 238–57.

Cohen, R. A. (2001), *Ethics, Exegesis and Philosophy*, Cambridge: Cambridge University Press.

Cottingham, J. (1993), *A Descartes Dictionary*, London: Blackwell.

Cottingham, J., R. Soothoff, D. Murdoch and A. Kenny (eds) (1991),

The Philosophical Writings of Descartes: Volume 3 The Correspondence, Cambridge: Cambridge University Press.

Critchley, S. (2007a), 'Five Problems in Levinas's View of Politics and a Sketch of a Solution to Them', in M. Diamantides (ed.), *Levinas, Law and Politics*, London: Routledge, pp. 93–106.

Critchley, S. (2007b), *Infinitely Demanding: Ethics of Commitment, Politics of Resistance*, London: Verso.

Critchley, S. and P. Dews (eds) (1996), Deconstructive Subjectivities, New York: SUNY Press.

Davies, P. (1995), 'On Resorting to an Ethical Language', in A. Peperzak (ed.), *Ethics as First Philosophy: The Significance of Emmanuel Levinas for Philosophy, Literature and Religion*, London: Routledge, pp. 95–104.

Dean, J. (2001), 'Publicity's Secret', *Political Theory*, 29:5, 624–50.

Dean, J. (2002), *Publicity's Secret: How Technoculture Capitalizes on Democracy*, Ithaca: Cornell University Press.

Dean, J. (2010), *Blog Theory: Feedback and Capture in the Circuits of the Drive*, London: Polity.

Deleuze, G. (1983), *Nietzsche and Philosophy*, trans. H. Tomlinson, New York: Columbia University Press.

Deleuze, G. (1988), *Foucault*, trans. Sean Hand, London: Athlone.

Deleuze, G. (1990), *Logic of Sense*, trans. Mark Lester and Charles Stivale, New York: Columbia University Press.

Deleuze, G. [1953] (1991), *Empiricism and Subjectivity: An Essay on Hume's Theory of Human Nature*, trans. C. V. Boundas, New York: Columbia University Press.

Deleuze, G. (1992), 'Postscript on the Societies of Control', *October*, 59, 3–7.

Deleuze, G. (1994), *Difference and Repetition*, trans. P. Patton, London: Athlone.

Deleuze, G. (1997), *Cinema 1: The Movement Image*, trans. H. Tomlinson and B. Habberjam, London: Athlone.

Deleuze, G. and F. Guattari (1992), *A Thousand Plateaus*, trans. B. Massumi, London: Athlone.

Deleuze, G. and F. Guattari (1994), *What Is Philosophy?*, trans. H. Tomlinson and G. Burchell, New York: Columbia University Press.

Derrida, J. (1973), 'Difference', in *Speech and Phenomena*, trans. D. B. Allinson, Evanston: Northwestern University Press, pp. 129–60.

Derrida, J. (1974), *Of Grammatology*, trans. G. C. Spivak, Baltimore: Johns Hopkins University Press.

Derrida, J. (1978a), 'Cogito and the History of Madness', in *Writing and Difference*, trans. A. Bass, London: Routledge, pp. 31–63.

Derrida, J. (1978b), 'Violence and Metaphysics', in *Writing and Difference*, trans. A. Bass, London: Routledge, pp. 79–153.

Derrida, J. (1978c), *Writing and Difference*, trans. A. Bass, London: Routledge.

Derrida, J. (1982a), 'The Ends of Man', in *Margins of Philosophy*, trans. A. Bass, Chicago: University of Chicago, pp. 109–36.

Derrida, J. (1982b), 'Ousia and Gramme', in *Margins of Philosophy*, trans. A. Bass, Chicago: University of Chicago, pp. 29–67.

Derrida, J. (1982c), *Margins of Philosophy*, trans. A. Bass, Chicago: University of Chicago.

Derrida, J. (1991), 'Eating Well', an interview with J.-L. Nancy, in E. Cadava, P. Connor and J.-L. Nancy (eds), *Who Comes After the Subject?*, London: Routledge.

Derrida, J. (1992a), 'Before the Law', in D. Attridge (ed.), *Acts of Literature*, London: Routledge, pp. 181–220.

Derrida, J. (1992b), 'Force of Law: "The Mystical Foundation of Authority"', in D. Cornell and M. Rosenfeld (eds), *Deconstruction and the Possibility of Justice*, New York: Routledge, pp. 3–67.

Derrida, J. (1992c), 'Passions: "An Oblique Offering"', in D. Wood (ed.), *Derrida: A Critical Reader*, Oxford: Blackwell, pp. 5–35.

Derrida, J. (1992d), '"This Strange Institution Called Literature": An Interview with Jacques Derrida', in D. Attridge (ed.), *Acts of Literature*, London: Routledge, pp. 33–75.

Derrida, J. (1993a), *Aporias: Dying – Awaiting (One Another at) the 'Limits of Truth'*, trans. D. Dutoit, Stanford: Stanford University Press.

Derrida, J. (1993b) 'Circumfession', in G. Bennington and J. Derrida (1993), *Jacques Derrida*, Chicago: Chicago University Press.

Derrida, J. (1994), *Spectres of Marx*, London: Routledge.

Derrida, J. (1995), *The Gift of Death*, trans. D. Wills, Chicago: University of Chicago Press.

Derrida, J. (1996a), *Archive Fever: A Freudian Impression*, trans. E. Prenowitz, Chicago: University of Chicago Press.

Derrida, J. (1996b), 'As if I Were Dead: An Interview with Jacques Derrida', in J. Brannigan, R. Robbins and J. Wolfreys (eds), *Applying: to Derrida*. Basingstoke: Macmillan, pp. 212–26.

Derrida, J. (1996c), 'Remarks on Deconstruction and Pragmatism', in C. Mouffe (ed.), *Deconstruction and Pragmatism*, London: Routledge, pp. 77–88.

Derrida, J. (1996d), *Resistances of Psychoanalysis*, trans. P. Kamuf, P.-A. Brault and M. Nass, Stanford: Stanford University Press.

Derrida, J. (1998), *Monolingualism of the Other: or, The Prosthesis of Origin*, trans. P. Mensah, Stanford: Stanford University Press.

Derrida, J. (1999a), *Adieu to Emmanuel Levinas*, trans. P.-A. Brault and M. Nass, Stanford: Stanford University Press.

Derrida, J. (1999b), 'Hospitality, Justice, and Responsibility: Dialogue with Jacques Derrida', in R. Kearney and M. Dooley (eds), *Questioning Ethics: Contemporary Debates in Philosophy*, London: Routledge, pp. 65–83.

Derrida, J. (2000), *Of Hospitality*, trans. R. Bowlby, Stanford: Stanford University Press.

Derrida, J. (2001a), *Of Cosmopolitanism and Forgiveness*, trans. M. Dooley and M. Hughes, London: Routledge.

Derrida, J. (2001b) *The Work of Mourning*, ed. P.-A. Brault and M. Nass, Chicago: Chicago University Press.

Derrida, J. (2002a), *Acts of Religion*, ed. Gil Anidjar, Routledge, London.

Derrida, J. (2002b), 'Hostipitality', in *Acts of Religion*, ed. Gil Anidjar, Routledge, London, pp. 355–420.

Derrida, J. (2002c), 'The Right to Philosophy from a Cosmopolitan Point of View', trans. E Rottenberg, in *Negotiations*, Stanford: Stanford University Press, pp. 329–42.

Derrida, J. (2002d), 'Spectographies', in J. Derrida and B. Stiegler, *Echographies of Television*, trans. J. Bajorek, London: Polity, pp.113–34.

Derrida, J. (2002e), 'Typewriter Ribbon', in *Without Alibi*, trans. P. Kamuf, Stanford: Stanford University Press, pp. 71–160 .

Derrida, J. (2002f), *Without Alibi*, trans. P. Kamuf, Stanford: Stanford University Press.

Derrida, J. (2004), *The Eyes of the University*, trans. J. Plug, Stanford: Stanford University Press.

Derrida, J. (2005a), *On Touching – Jean-Luc Nancy*, Stanford: Stanford University Press.

Derrida, J. (2005b), *Paper Machine*, trans. R. Bowlby, Stanford: Stanford University Press.

Derrida, J. (2007a), 'A Certain Impossible Possibility of Saying the Event', *Critical Inquiry*, 33, 441–61.

Derrida, J. (2007b), *Learning to Live Finally: The Final Interview*, trans. P.-A. Brault and M. Nass, New York: Melville House.

Derrida, J. (2008), *The Animal that Therefore I Am*, trans. D. Wills, New York: Fordham University Press.

Derrida, J. and M. Farraris (2001), *A Taste for the Secret*, Cambridge: Polity.

Derrida, J. and B. Stiegler (2002), *Echographies of Television*, trans. J. Bajorek, London: Polity.

Dews, P. (2004), 'States of Grace: The Excess of Demand in Badiou's Ethics of Truths', in P. Hallward (ed.), *Think Again*, London: Continuum, pp. 106–20.

Eagleton, T. (2009), *The Trouble with Strangers*, Chichester: Wiley-Blackwell.

Elam, D. (1994), *Feminism and Deconstruction*, London: Routledge.

Epicurus (2005), 'Letter to Menoeceus', in *Letters and Sayings of Epicurus*, trans. O. Makridis, New York: Barnes and Noble Books, pp. 48–55.

Featherstone, M. (2009), 'Ubiquitous Media: An Introduction', *Theory Culture and Society*, 26:2–3, 1–22.

Foucault, M. (1961), *Folie et déraison: Histoire de la folie à l'âge classique*, Paris: Plon.

Foucault, M. (1965), *Madness and Civilisation: A History of Insanity in the Age of Reason*, abridged and trans. R. Howard, New York: Random House.

Foucault, M. (1979), 'My Body, This Paper, This Fire', trans. G. Bennington, *Oxford Literary Review*, 4:1, 9–28.

Foucault, M. (1986), *The Order of Things*, London: Routledge.

Foucault, M. (1988), 'What Is an Author?', in D. Lodge (ed.), *Modern Criticism and Theory*, London: Longman, pp. 196–210.

Foucault, M. (1989), *The Archaeology of Knowledge*, London: Routledge.

Freud, S. (1974), *Beyond the Pleasure Principle*, Standard Edition, vol. XVIII, London: Hogarth Press.

Gallop, J. (1990), *Thinking Through the Body*, New York: Columbia University Press.

Garber, M., B. Hanssen and R. L. Walkowitz (eds) (2000), *The Turn to Ethics*, London: Routledge.

Geertz, C. (1973), *The Interpretation of Cultures*, New York: Fontana Press.

Gilbert, J. (2007), 'Public Secrets', *Cultural Studies*, 21:1, 22–41.

Gill, C. B. (ed.) (1995), *Bataille: Writing the Sacred*, London: Routledge.

Gregg, M. and G. J. Seigworth (eds) (2010), *The Affect Theory Reader*, Durham, NC and London: Duke University Press.

Grosz, E. (1995), *Space, Time and Perversion*, London: Routledge.

Hand, S. (ed.) (1989), *The Levinas Reader*, Oxford: Blackwell.

Hansen, M. B. N. (2004a), *New Philosophy for New Media*, Cambridge, MA: MIT Press.

Hansen, M. B. N. (2004b), 'Realtime Synthesis and the *Différance* of the Body: Technocultural Studies in the Wake of Deconstruction', in G. Hall, D. Boothroyd and J. Zylinska (eds), 'Deconstruction is/in Cultural Studies', *Culture Machine*, 6 <http://www.culturemachine.net/index.php/cm/article/viewArticle/9/8> (last accessed 30 October 2012).

Hansen, M. B. N. (2006), *Bodies in Code: Interfaces with Digital Media*, London: Routledge.

Hegel, G. W. F (1979), *Phenomenology of Spirit*, trans. A. V. Miller, Oxford: Oxford University Press.

Heidegger, M. (1962), *Being and Time*, trans. J. McQuarrie and E. Robinson, New York: Harper Row.

Heidegger, M. (1975), *Early Greek Thinking*, London: HarperCollins.

Hillis Miller, J. (2009), *For Derrida*, Fordham University Press.

Hogben, G. (ed.) (2007), 'Security Issues and Recommendations for Online Social Networks', ENISA Position Paper No.1, 14 November 2007 <http://www.enisa.europa.eu/act/res/other-areas/social-networks/security-issues-and-recommendations-for-online-social-networks> (last accessed 16 April 2012).

Hughes, R. (2007), 'Riven: Badiou's Ethical Subject and the Event of Art as Trauma', *Postmodern Culture*, 17:3.

Ince, K. (1996), 'Questions to Luce Irigaray', *Hypatia*, 11:2, 122–40.

Irigaray, L. (1977), 'Women's Exile', trans. C. Venn, *Ideology and Consciousness*, 1, 62–76.

Irigaray, L. (1985a), 'Any Theory of the "Subject" Has Always Been Appropriated by the Masculine', in *Speculum of the Other Woman*, trans. G. C. Gill, Ithaca: Cornell University Press, pp. 133–46.

Irigaray, L. (1985b), *This Sex Which Is Not One*, trans. C. Porter, New York: Cornell University Press.

Irigaray, L. (1985c), *Speculum of the Other Woman*, trans. G. C. Gill, Ithaca: Cornell University Press.

Irigaray, L. (1985d), 'When Our Lips Speak Together', in *This Sex Which Is Not One*, trans. C. Porter, New York: Cornell University Press, pp. 205–18.

Irigaray, L. (1991), *Marine Lover of Friedrich Nietzsche*, trans. G. C. Gill, New York: Columbia University Press.

Irigaray, L. (1991), 'Questions to Emmanuel Levinas: On the Divinity of Love', in M. Whitford (ed.), *The Irigaray Reader*, Oxford: Blackwell, pp. 178–89.

Irigaray, L. (1992), *Elemental Passions*, trans. J. Collie and J. Still, London: Routledge.

Irigaray, L. (1993a), *An Ethics of Sexual Difference*, trans. C. Burke and G. C. Gill, London: Athlone.

Irigaray, L. (1993b), 'The Fecundity of the Caress', in *An Ethics of Sexual Difference*, trans. C. Burke and G. C. Gill, London: Athlone, pp. 185–217.

Irigaray, L. (1993c), *Je, Tu, Nous: Toward a Culture of Difference*, trans. A. Martin, London: Routledge.

Irigaray, L. (1993d), *Sexes and Genealogies*, trans. G. C. Gill, New York: Columbia University Press.

Irigaray, L. (1996), *I Love to You*, trans. A. Martin, London: Routledge.

Jardine, A. (1985), *Gynesis: Configurations of Woman and Modernity*, Ithaca: Cornell University Press.

Johnson, G. A. and M. B. Smith (eds) (1995), *Ontology and Alterity in Merleau-Ponty*, Evanston: Northwestern University Press.

Kafka, F. (1978), 'Before the Law', in *Wedding Preparations in the Country and Other Stories*, Harmondsworth: Penguin Books, pp. 127–9.

Lasswell, H. D. [1927] (1972), *Propaganda Technique in the World War*, New York: Garland.

Levinas, E. (1969), *Totality and Infinity*, trans. A. Lingis, Pittsburgh: Duquesne University Press.

Levinas, E. (1973), *The Theory of Intuition in Husserl's Phenomenology*, trans. A. Orianne, Chicago: Northwestern University Press.

Levinas, E. (1978), *Existence and Existents*, trans. A. Lingis, The Hague: Martinus Nijhoff.

Levinas, E. (1979), 'The Contemporary Criticism of the Idea of Value and the Prospects for Humanism', in E. A. Mariaz (ed.), *Value and Values in Evolution*, New York: Gordon and Breach, pp. 179–87.

Levinas, E. (1981), *Otherwise than Being, or, Beyond Essence*, trans. A. Lingis, The Hague: Martinus Nijhoff.

Levinas, E. (1986) 'The Trace of the Other', trans. A. Lingis, in M. C. Taylor (ed.), *Deconstruction in Context*, Chicago: University of Chicago Press, pp. 345–59.

Levinas, E. (1987), *Time and the Other*, trans. R. A. Cohen, Pittsburgh: Duquesne University Press.

Levinas, E. (1988), 'Useless Suffering', trans. R. A. Cohen, in D. Wood and R. Bernasconi (eds), *The Provocation of Levinas: Rethinking the Other*, London: Routledge, pp. 156–67.

Levinas, E. (1989), 'Substitution', in S. Hand (ed.), *The Levinas Reader*, Oxford: Blackwell, pp. 89–125.

Levinas, E. (1990), *Difficult Freedom: Essays on Judaism*, trans. S. Hand, Baltimore: Johns Hopkins University Press.

Levinas, E. (1991), 'Philosophy as Awakening', in E. Cadava, P. Connor and J.-L. Nancy (eds), *Who Comes After the Subject?*, London: Routledge, p. 206.

Levinas, E. (1996a), 'Transcendence and Height', in A. Peperzak, S. Critchley and R. Bernasconi (eds), *Emmanuel Levinas: Basic Writings*, Bloomington: Indiana University Press, pp. 11–31.

Levinas, E. (1996b), 'God and Philosophy', in A. Peperzak, S. Critchley and R. Bernasconi (eds), *Emmanuel Levinas: Basic Writings*, Bloomington: Indiana University Press, pp. 129–48.

Levinas, E. (2000a), 'An Obligatory Passage: Heidegger', in *God, Death and Time*, trans. B. Bergo, Stanford: Stanford University Press, pp. 22–7.

Levinas, E. (2000b), *God, Death and Time*, trans. B. Bergo, Stanford: Stanford University Press.

Levinas, E. (2006), *The Humanism of the Other*, trans. N. Poller, Chicago: University of Illinois Press.

Llewelyn, J. (1995), *Emmanuel Levinas: The Genealogy of Ethics*, London: Routledge.

Marks, J. (1998), *Gilles Deleuze: Vitalism and Multiplicity*, London: Pluto Press.

McLuhan, M. (1964), *Understanding Media*, Routledge: London.

Merleau-Ponty, M. (1962), *Phenomenology of Perception*, trans. C. Smith, London: Routledge.

Moufe, C. (ed.) (1996), *Deconstruction and Pragmatism*, London: Routledge.

Nancy, J.-L. (1993), *The Birth to Presence*, trans. B. Holmes, Stanford: Stanford University Press.

Nancy, J.-L. (2000), *Being Singular Plural*, trans. R. D. Richardson and A. E. O'Byrne, Stanford: Stanford University Press.

Nietzsche, F. (1968), *The Will to Power*, trans. W. Kaufmann and R. J. Hollingdale, New York: Vintage Books.

Nietzsche, F. (1969), *Thus Spoke Zarathustra*, trans. R. J. Hollingdale, London: Penguin Books.

Nietzsche, F. (1974), *The Gay Science*, trans. W. Kaufmann, New York: Vintage Books.

Nietzsche, F. (1975), *Beyond Good and Evil*, trans. R. J. Hollingdale, London: Penguin Books.

Nietzsche, F. (1994), *On the Genealogy of Morality*, trans. C. Diethe, Cambridge: Cambridge University Press.

Nietzsche, F. (1997), *Daybreak: Thoughts on the Prejudices of Morality*, trans. R. J. Hollingdale, Cambridge: Cambridge University Press.

Parr, A. (ed.) (2005), *The Deleuze Dictionary*, Edinburgh: Edinburgh University Press.

Peperzak, A. (ed.) (1995), *Ethics as First Philosophy: The Significance of Emmanuel Levinas for Philosophy, Literature and Religion*, London: Routledge.

Peperzak, A., S. Critchley and R. Bernasconi (eds) (1996), *Emmanuel Levinas: Basic Writings*, Bloomington: Indiana University Press.

Pepys, S. (2010), *The Diary of Samuel Pepys: Vol. 1 1660*, ed. R. C. Latham and W. Mathews, Middlesex: The Echo Library.

Poster, M. (ed.) (2001), *Baudrillard: Selected Writings*, London: Polity Press.

Rancière, J. (2006), 'The Ethical Turn of Aesthetics and Politics', *Critical Horizons*, 7, 1–20.

Rousseau, J. J. (2003), *Emile*, trans. W. H. Payne, New York: Prometheus Books.

Royle, N. (ed.) (2000), *Deconstructions: A User's Guide*, Basingstoke: Palgrave.

Simondon, G. (1989), *Du mode de l'existence des objets techniques*, Paris: Aubier.

Sproule, J. M. (1989), 'Progressive Propaganda Critics and the Magic Bullet Myth', *Critical Studies in Mass Communication*, 6:3, 225–46.

Stiegler, B. (1998), *Technics and Time, 1: The Fault of Epemetheus*, Stanford: Stanford University Press.

Sunstein, C. R. and Vermeule, A. (2008), 'Conspiracy Theories, 15 January. Harvard Public Law Working Paper No. 08-03; University of Chicago, Public Law Working Paper No. 199; University of Chicago Law and Economics, Olin Working Paper No. 387 <http://papers.ssrn.com/sol3/papers.cfm?abstract_id=1084585##> (last accessed 27 January 2011).

Swedish Media Council (n.d.), 'Film Classification' <http://www.statensmedierad.se/Om-Statens-medierad/In-English/Film-Classification/> (last accessed 10 August 2012).

Tester, K. (2001), *Compassion, Morality and the Media*, Maidenhead: Open University Press.

Vasseleu, C. (1998), *The Textures of Light: Vision and Touch in Irigaray, Levinas and Merleau-Ponty*, London: Routledge.

Vismann, C. (2008), *Files: Law and Media Technology*, trans. G. Winthrop-Young, Stanford: Stanford University Press.

White, A. (1990), *Within Nietzsche's Labyrinth*, London: Routledge.

Whitford, M. (ed.) (1991), *The Irigaray Reader*, Oxford: Blackwell.

Whitford, M. (1991), *Luce Irigaray: Philosophy in the Feminine*, London: Routledge.

Williams, R. R. (1997), *Hegel's Ethics of Recognition*, Berkeley: University of California Press.

Wilson, S. (1995), 'Feting the Wound', in C. B. Gill (ed.), *Bataille: Writing the Sacred*, London: Routledge, pp. 172–92.

Zita, N. (1992), 'Male Lesbians and the Postmodernist Body', *Hypatia*, 7:4, 106–27.

Zylinska, J. (2005), *The Ethics of Cultural Studies*, London: Continuum.

Index